INTO THE BLUE

INTO THE BLUE

Wing Commander
Norman Macmillan
OBE, MC, AFC

GRUB STREET • LONDON

NOTE FROM PUBLISHER

The style of the original publication has been retained.

Published by
Grub Street
4 Rainham Close
London SW11 6SS

First published 1929 by Gerald Duckworth & Co. Ltd.
Revised edition © Norman Macmillan 1969
This edition first published 2015
© Grub Street 2015

A CIP data record for this title is available from the British Library.

ISBN-13: 9781910690017

Printed and bound in the Czech Republic by Finidr

To the Mothers, Wives and Sweethearts
of all flying men, for everything they do for us

CONTENTS

AUTHOR'S NOTE

Parts of *Into the Blue* were written at the time, or shortly after the time, of the incidents portrayed, and some of these writings were published then. The book was first published by Gerald Duckworth & Co. Ltd in 1929 and reprinted by them. In that edition Chapter XII appeared substantially as in *Chamber's Journal*; some other chapters, or parts of them, in *The Bailie*. My acknowledgments and thanks are due to the editors of these journals. Extracts from the book have appeared in several anthologies and elsewhere and many writers have quoted from it. It gained a place among WW1 air classics.

The title, *Into the Blue*, was suggested by my wife.

Extracts from official Royal Air Force records were reproduced by permission of the Air Ministry. I wish to express my thanks also to Captain Joseph Morris, BA, AFRAeS, then the Head of the Air Ministry Historical Branch, for historical aid he gave me and for reading the manuscript.

The original type formes and plates, unfortunately, were destroyed by fire when Paternoster Row was burned down in the WW2 bombing of London. Existing copies of the Duckworth imprint have since been much sought as 'a collector's piece'.

I readily acknowledge further informative help from many sources since the first edition appeared. In particular I am grateful to Mr L. A. Jackets, Head of the Ministry of Defence Historical Branch (RAF), and his indefatigable Staff; Marshal of the Royal Air Force Sir Arthur T. Harris, Bart., GCB, OBE, AFC; Wing Commander W. R. Read, MC, DFC, AFC**; Group Captain G. H. Cock, MC; the late Group Captain J. Cottle, MBE, DFC; Air Commodore R. J. Brownell, CBE, MC, MM; Dr J. P. Huins, OBE, AFC*, LRCP, MRCS, Wing Commander; Captain Frank T. Courtney; Captain T. F. Williams, MC; the late Captain E. D. Clarke, CBE, MC; the late Major J. A. Crook MC; Captain G. H. Bush; Captain C. S. Emery, OBE; Lieutenant E. A. L. F. Smith; Mr H. W. Grimmitt, CBE; Mr B. Wetherall; Mr E. T. Ward; Mr J. W. Loughlin; the late Mr H. H. Russell.

While this edition retains the original narrative, I have taken the opportunity to make corrections arising from subsequent knowledge, and have revised the syntax and rearranged the text, replacing statistics that obtruded in the first edition by narrative, and giving many names previously withheld, including those of now identified opponents. But my story makes no pretence to be a full squadron history. Rather it is a picture of a pilot in the making in the winter of 1916–17 and of his service and surroundings in a squadron in action in WW1, flying both two-seaters and scouts. It ends with his work and experiences as a wartime flying instructor.

Since I now see events from the pinnacle of 50 added years, an elevation in time affording a wider aspect, as of vision from a mountain-top, when I have thought it to be right to make comments on what then occurred within my personal experience I have done so.

N.M.

Part One

PUPIL

Chapter I

THE VISIONARIES

British military flyers have always been volunteers. Before WW1 a candidate for the Royal Flying Corps had to prove his aptitude by first obtaining a Royal Aero Club pilot's certificate at his own expense at a civilian flying school. War changed this. Then volunteers were first interviewed by an RFC officer. His questions followed the pattern of the time.

'Why do you want to transfer to (or join) the Royal Flying Corps?'

'Because I want to fly.'

'Can you ride?' (This question sprang from a belief that the hands of a horseman made a natural pilot, and by analogy with cavalry reconnaissance the RFC was seen as 'The Cavalry of the Clouds'.)

'I have ridden.'

'Have you sailed a boat?'

'Yes.'

'Do you know anything about internal-combustion engines?'

'I know the Otto cycle and two-stroke principles.'

'Have you driven motor cars or motor cycles?'

'Yes.'

'Do you know anything about flying?'

'I have read *Flight, Aeronautics, The Aero* and *The Aeroplane* since Blériot flew the Channel. And I know something of Lanchester's books,' averred one enthusiast.

The interviewing officer smiled.

He knew that most aspirant pilots knew very little about flying.

What they did know was only sufficient to whet their appetites.

It was best so.

Otherwise, in the then state of knowledge, they might have been obsessed with theories and ideas which, in those days, from errors of assumption, might have proved disastrous to a novice in the art of flying. 'You'll do,' he said.

Candidates from the infantry could not be accused of seeking greater personal safety by transferring to the RFC. They might be incurring even greater risk, but at least they had a chance of living a cleaner life than the men in the muddy, verminous trenches.

Their medical examination was perfunctory. Colour vision was tested from a bunch of different coloured wool threads held by the examiner. From them the candidate picked those the colour of which the examiner mentioned. I suppose it defeated any with vision less than tri-colour.

In 1916 the probationer's next move was to a course at one of the two new Schools of Military Aeronautics (Reading or Oxford) to study rudimentary theory under a capable staff.

There pupils became acquainted with the mysteries of rigging wood, wire and fabric aeroplanes and the mechanism of internal-combustion engines, learned to read maps and understand compasses, struggled with Morse and that instrument of torture to sensitive souls, the buzzer. With these and many other subjects – theory of flight, electricity, magnetism, meteorology, clock codes, magnetos, carburation, lubrication (of engines) – they lived their days and dreamed their nights for a month.

On 12 October 1916 I reported at No. 2 School of Military Aeronautics at Oxford. The War Office had taken over some of the colleges. I was allotted to Lincoln. I recall the narrow, winding steps I traversed when climbing to and descending from my small cell-like room, with its mullioned window overlooking the quadrangle. It gives me quiet nostalgic pleasure to remember that my shoe leather wore yet another imperceptible fraction deeper the rounded hollows in those ancient stones.

One room was locked. It was said that an officer sleeping there during an earlier course awoke one night and saw an Indian's head at the foot of his bed. Next he felt as if fingers were contracting on his throat. He fought against this thought, or fact, whichever it was; but the experience unnerved him and he could not continue the course.

The Army had no psychiatrists to handle such matters then and the military authorities would not admit that apparitions were on their roster. The room was allotted to another officer who knew nothing of the story. When he suffered the same infelicific fright in the night the room was locked and kept out of use. The legend we heard was of an Indian being chased up to that room and done to death in it at the time of the Black Hole of Calcutta. The tale may have been a myth. The locked door was not.

A high wall divided Lincoln and Brasenose colleges. These adjacent colleges had once maintained a jealous rivalry. Sixteenth and seventeenth-century Town and Gown often fought, using any weapons to hand, with scant respect for the dignity or value of human life. Townsmen, hunting a

Brasenose undergraduate through the streets, intent on exacting a sacrifice to all that they in their folly believed to be their honour, drove their hounded man, panting, to the gate of Lincoln. He beat upon its nail-studded, oaken door. The visor trap opened. The fugitive demanded sanctuary from the man of the peering face.

'Where are you from?' demanded the guardian of the door.

'Brasenose.'

'No Brasenose man enters Lincoln.'

The visor trap shut. The door remained barred.

The mad, unthinking mob caught up with their prey there and battered him to death. Lincoln Collegers have ever since paid yearly penance to the Brasenose Collegers in ale spiked with ivy; the anniversary of the murder became the one day in the calendar when the gate in the high dividing wall was unlocked – for the penance to be paid.

At Lincoln I was awakened every morning by the pealing of many bells, for these were not silent during the First World War as they were in the Second. Each morning, after breakfast, we paraded in the quadrangle and marched through the streets to our instructional centre in wartime wooden buildings at the periphery of Port Meadow, on Sundays to a church parade which was then a compulsory feature of Army life (and, I think, better so).

Horatio Barber, the designer of the pre-war Valkyrie canard monoplane, with which he had run a flying school at Hendon, was now a captain in the RFC and one of our technical instructors. He was capable, but austere. Another instructor with an ebullient nature I afterwards met when he was a salesman for a prominent gin distillery. The others left little mark on one's memory.

Our instruction ranged over past and obsolescing equipment of the RFC. It did not forecast developments; probably these were kept secret even from the instructors. The result was a suitable grounding for the previous year, not for the year ahead, which was the one that mattered to us.

After the final examinations a party of officers (of whom I was one) was sent to Coventry on a special course from 26 November to 12 December 1916. There we were comfortably billeted in the King's Head, an old coaching hostelry destroyed in the 1939–45 war. I think the purpose of the course was to keep us occupied until there were vacancies for us at the flying training schools, but it brought us right up to date in knowledge of current equipment.

An RFC Crossley tender came for us daily and drove us to Coventry and Birmingham factories. These we toured with expert factory engineers as guides. The Siddeley Deasy Motor Car Company was making air-cooled V-aero-engines, but I saw a small batch of BHP water-cooled aero-engines under early conversion to the Siddeley Puma straight six, an engine that looked a tremendous advance on the others. The shops were a noisy symphony of clattering machine tools, driven from overhead shafting by ballata belting, and the percussive sounds of small drop hammers. Swarf from lathes fell to the floor like glittering snow. A first-aid post stood ready to deal with accidents. Engines were tested without silencers in a row of rough-built, open-ended sheds along one side of the factory ground.

The firm also made shell cases and parts for shell fuses. We saw one young woman with deft fingers operating a fuse ring stamping tool so fast that she could earn £27 a week on piece work, money worth about £100 today. Most of us had already fought with the PBI in France. It hit us starkly that tommies in the trenches were paid seven bob and flight commanders leading formations into battle over enemy territory about £7 a week. But we had not been sent to Coventry to make pay-packet comparisons. We were there to see the effort behind the fighting troops and more especially the build-up of material for the RFC. Yet we could see no reason why workers in safe jobs were paid so much more than men who daily risked their lives to keep those workers safe; and we realised that the firm's profits must have risen in proportion. Here was a pattern of inequity that needed scrutiny.

We saw Standard Motors making Sopwith Pup single-seater fighters and during their assembly a transfer of the maker's Union Jack trade mark was stuck on the interplane struts. Here there were more women workers than men. At Daimler's we examined aero engines and engines for tanks, both during manufacture and under test. Near the factory was a tank-testing ground. We watched them there and rode in one and found it a battering, unwieldy monster of rude metal that ripped one's clothes and abraded one's skin when its elephantine motions heaved one about its interior as it fell into and laboured out of the artificial ditches and shell-holes of the proving ground. Those were early tanks, without differential track steering; trailing, articulated, steel twin wheels served them as rudders; part ship, part land vehicle thinking had inspired their elementary design. After this experience I never wondered that the 1916 tanks did not achieve more for us in France than they did.

One evening when we returned to the hotel one of our party found a letter awaiting him. He came down from his room looking utterly miserable and drank more than his customary one glass before dinner. He told us his fiancée had written, breaking off their engagement. He seemed inconsolable, but there was little we could do to comfort him, for we knew nothing of the girl or the circumstances.

We always had our after-dinner coffee in the bar room, where a coal fire burned in an open grate about which we pulled our chairs. Usually we turned in at about 10 o'clock. But this evening an open Silver Ghost drove through the *porte-cochère* and parked in the courtyard. Its occupants, a tall man and two girls, entered the bar room, where sandwiches were served to them because the dining room had closed for the night. The man, a civilian, was uncommunicative. He stood at one end of the bar, eating and drinking numerous whiskies, without saying a word to anyone. But the girls seemed delighted to find so many officers. They chattered freely and had drinks with us. Both were dressed in black, had dark hair and eyes, were comely, trim, attractive and vivacious, spoke well and seemed of good family. They might have been sisters; we did not know. The elder was rather buxom; the younger, of full, rounded figure, was the prettier.

When I went up to my room, its other occupant, a fellow Scot, was sitting up in the farther bed, reading; in the Service fashion we were all billeted two to a room; whether this custom is for economy or morals I have never been able to decide. He was a teetotaller and always retired early. He looked up from his book and said there had been a din ever since that man and these two young women had arrived. He turned to his book again as I unbuttoned my tunic and loosened my tie.

At that moment the door opened. The younger girl came in, fully dressed, looked quickly about the room, then walked over to me and raised her arms as if to put them about my neck. But I took a step back, away from her. She must have picked up my forename in the bar room, for she looked straight up into my eyes and said in a perfectly conversational voice: 'Come and sleep with me, Norman. My man's drunk and useless and I want a man tonight.' I had never known a girl make such a blunt carnal invitation before and was too surprised to answer. I suppose I looked at her with an expression of distaste.

My brother Scot looked at us and saw that I wanted nothing to do with her. He reached up for the bell-push that hung on a cord from the ceiling between the bed-heads. 'If you don't get out of this room quick, you Jezebel,' he said, 'I'll ring for the hotel manager.'

She turned and left without a word and we never saw her again. But she found the man whose engagement had just been broken off and he slept with her. At breakfast he looked more morose than the night before and it was obvious that he now regretted not only his lost fiancée but the lapse that had lost him forever his own irrecoverable virginity.

When our visit to Coventry ended we returned to Oxford and were posted to various reserve squadrons (the term then given to flying training units) and many of my temporary companions I never saw again.

Picture the pilot-to-be in a railway compartment on his way to the real thing, the actual flying at a flying school. He knew so much theoretically, but practice was the only thing that could really count. He did not even know if he possessed the flying temperament. He had not had to pass any aptitude tests. He might not be able to balance his machine.

His ignorance of his new profession struck him as overwhelming. Mentally he framed unanswerable questions.

What was the sensation of flying?

How extraordinary it must be to sit up aloft in a frail structure of wood, wire and fabric, with the wind whistling about his head and shoulders.

Would his nerves stand it?

Would it inspire terror or delight?

Would he be able to endure the effects of altitude, a factor his medical examination had ignored?

Would he – but there were a thousand questions in the new adventure, questions with which his imagination grappled defeated. Gazing out of the windows at the passing hedgebound fields, he wondered which would be suitable for the landing of an aeroplane. He had to admit he did not know. He was in square one.

He knew that the elementary training aeroplanes of the RFC at that time were Maurice Farman biplanes of French origin and 1913 and 1914 design. He knew what they looked like from pictures. The later one had all its stabilising and elevator and rudder surfaces at the tail and was nicknamed the Shorthorn. The earlier model had an additional forward elevator on projecting booms, which earned it the sobriquet of Longhorn.

He had heard that these affectionate and appropriate names arose from a chance remark of Major J. F. A. (later Air Marshal Sir John) Higgins who, seeing a line up of Maurice Farmans on an airfield, exclaimed: '*Voilà les vaches mécaniques!*' and from mechanical cows the herd was subdivided into Longhorns and Shorthorns.

He had heard, too, how much easier the Longhorn was to fly because its forward elevator gave its pilot a head-up display. The Shorthorn denied its pilot any such visual aid to balance and this was said to make it more difficult to manage. He had also heard that previous pupils had flown the Longhorn before passing on to the Shorthorn as an advanced type, but he did not know if this was still the drill.

He knew enough to understand the primitiveness of Maurice Farman's design. The leading edges of the Shorthorn's wings were the front spars; these carried the front struts, just as in the Wrights' gliding and motorised biplanes of 1901–3. A complicated array of external wiring was used to brace the lightly built structure and to interconnect the pilots' controls with the movable air surfaces; pilots called this wiring system 'the birdcage'.

But of two inherent faults in Shorthorn design, about which no one had told him anything, he was blissfully ignorant.

The centre wing cell had four pairs of struts. The body (nacelle) which carried the main load, of crew, engine, propeller, fuel and oil, was attached to and fitted between the innermost two pairs of struts. To assist the cell's spars to take that concentrated weight on their central part (especially during bad landings) these spars were arched, like a bridge, across the whole span of the cell. But this upward curvature was a weakness when side (compression) loads were applied to these spars. Thus Shorthorn strength for one load was gained by loss of it for another and at that time a less well apprehended one; this may have been at the root of some Shorthorn wing breakages in flight.

A cambered, lifting tailplane was the second design fault. It carried part of the Shorthorn's weight in flight, but it provided less fore-and-aft stability than a non-lifting stabiliser and lift from it could automatically increase the steepness of a dive and retard recovery to level flight – another possible cause of accidents.

The Shorthorn was docile enough when flying level. But then its fastest speed was only about 60 miles an hour. Its latent dangers emerged in abnormal flight. Most contemporary flying instructors' knowledge of aerodynamics was insufficient for them to be able to analyse Shorthorn design defects and advise pupils against possible consequences of ignorance. Their own safety routine was to fly sedately and eschew stunts. So it is probable that some, perhaps most, of the unfortunately too numerous fatal accidents during Shorthorn flying training were contributed to by ignorance of its inherent design defects.

From Ludgershall railway station RFC transport conveyed me across the bleak wintry landscape of Salisbury Plain to Netheravon airfield, where I entered No. 24 Reserve Squadron, commanded by Major Frank Walker Smith. I found that all my flying while there was to be on Shorthorns.

I was lucky in my instructors – Lieutenants Ryan, Spencer and Aird; all did the best they could do at that time. Before I went for my first preliminary joyride on 16 December 1916 Spencer showed me how to pass through the birdcage and climb the footholds properly, since a foot put in a wrong place could damage the frail structure. I wore the clumsy leather crash helmet that was obligatory for all pupils. Goggles could not be worn with it and we flew without them.

The nacelle was half-way up the interplane struts. A shallow side panel hinged down to simplify the gymnastic feat of entering it. When seated I lifted the panel and secured it with ordinary door bolts. I was in the nose, well ahead of the wings. Spencer sat behind, perched between the upper and lower wings' front edges.

Wooden bearers, running aft from the nacelle's structure, supported part of the engine between the wings and part behind them where the pusher propeller could revolve. An ack emma (signalese for air mechanic) stood within the booms and wires behind the propeller. It was his unenviable task to help to start the engine from his encaged position.

Before doing anything he first assured himself by question and answer that the pilot's ignition was switched off and the gasoline turned on. Then he primed the engine from the carburetter. He did this by manually rotating the two-blade wood propeller as if he were himself a starter motor. It was hard work. When he thought he had done enough he paused and called to the pilot: 'Contact, sir.'

After the pilot had responded by switching on his ignition and then announcing 'Contact', the ack emma hopefully and lustily heaved the propeller a quarter-turn round, while the pilot twirled a hand starter magneto to boost the spark at the plugs. Usually the Renault rattled into life after one or two heaves and the ack emma could emerge from his cage.

This air-cooled V8's pistons had ample clearances. One could always hear them slapping against the cylinder walls, loudest when the engine was cold. With no device to compensate for cylinder expansion and contraction, its valves and tappets chattered incessantly. Its propeller revolved on an extension of the camshaft at half engine speed and the reduction gear was noisy. Since the Renault could not be enclosed and had only a scoop to direct the air flow on to its cylinders, there was nothing to deaden the medley of sounds it made.

The fuel tank, between the rear seat and the engine, was in a nasty place should a crash occur. The hot engine could break away from its mounting, rupture the gasoline tank, ignite its contents, and the burning mass might fall on the aircrew. The commander of at least one pusher squadron ordered his aircrews not to use safety belts, believing that in a crash they would be thrown clear of wherever the engine might fall.

Fortunately for their peace of mind, few, if any, pilots or pupils thought about the several features of the Shorthorn that lowered its safety level below par. Enough that they were flying! For what more should they ask?

Wartime flying-training schools never sang the pre-war RFC lament for victims of pusher crashes:

Take the cylinders out of my kidneys,
The connecting rods out of my brain, my brain,
From the small of my back take the crankcase,
And assemble the engine again.

Spencer waggled the flying controls. He did not watch the movable air surfaces to see that each moved in the appropriate direction. Nor did anyone ever tell me to do so. Instructors merely ensured that the controls were not slack, sticking, or stuck.

A dual set was fitted in my place. I put my hands lightly on it to follow its movements, but kept my feet clear of the rudder pedals.

A gentle wind blew from the east. We could take straight off without taxiing. Spencer opened the throttle. My seat vibrated in tune with the thrumming Renault. A7004 slowly moved off. She travelled faster and faster, bounding a little on the uneven ground of the grass airfield. The bounding had a nice, cushiony effect. The grass rushed past underneath, became a blur ... We were in the air.

There had been no sense of acceleration and now speed seemed to disappear. There was only a steady upward glide and the endless vibrations from the engine.

Suddenly I felt the machine bump, literally bump, on something – a different centre of air pressure. Spencer righted the momentary unevenness. The red liquid in the air-speed indicator tube showed 55–60 miles an hour. The nose dipped slightly; at the same time the starboard wings tilted downward. I felt like leaning over to the other side to balance her. Before I really knew what had happened she was on an even keel again and facing another direction. We had merely turned. It was delightful and not too cold.

In the old Maurice Farman there was no sensation of speed once she had left the ground. She simply floated along. It was strange, just at first, to look sideways and see the wings resting on nothing that was visible. It was uncanny, weird! But, remembering my aerodynamics, I settled down to enjoy the perfect view of the countryside below. There were woods, farms, sheep, haystacks, and there, almost underneath the nose, was a winding river, the Avon.

Bump! The whole machine lifted bodily upward in the vertical plane and hesitated. It seemed to have taken her forward motion away. Spencer dipped her nose and she went on. The difference in the air currents above the river caused the bump where we were flying at 500 feet. She banked again to turn and, looking down to earth between the wings, I imagined what a glorious slide one could have down them back to earth. This first flight made fantasy come true to me.

The engine's humming ceased and the nose went down at the same moment. The engine 'phut-phutted' – just ticking over. I looked down hurriedly to see where we were going to land and saw we were gliding straight toward the airfield, which I had forgotten existed. In another minute we touched lightly, uncertainly; then, gathering confidence, the wheels clung to Mother Earth. The Shorthorn bumped over the uneven surface and slowly stopped rolling. The Renault sang again and we taxied to the hangars. I had had my first flight.

Spencer turned to me.

'Well, what d'you think of it?'

'I enjoyed it immensely, but I thought there would have been more sensation in it.'

'Yes, there would be on a fast machine. But it's a great game, isn't it?'

'Yes! It is a game, and a good one, too.'

Therein lay the spirit of the RFC. Its flying members were more devotees of sport than warriors. They were hunters of big game, and some of them were, by nature, killers.

Three days later, Spencer took me up again, this time to 1,200 feet (the greatest height I reached in a Shorthorn) to practise letting out and winding in the wireless aerial that was housed on a hand-operated drum

at the side of the nacelle. A bob-weight at the end of the copper wire held
it taut against the air flow. It seemed to me to be a tedious and unnecessary
chore, its sole advantage that it gave me a little more experience of being
airborne.

That afternoon I had my first dual instruction. The method was very
crude. There were no speaking tubes. If the instructor wanted to say
something he had to throttle the engine and shout. As soon as he throttled
the Renault he had to push the nose down, because the Shorthorn's speed
range was only about 20 miles an hour and her built-in drag was so great
that she quickly slowed to a stall if the nose were not pushed down. Most
instructors pushed the nose down before throttling the engine, to avoid
the slightest risk of a stall. Pupils were not shown a stall and its effect.
If they found this out later when flying solo they did so by their own
incompetence or at their own choice and risk. My instructors' methods
were to fly with their hands and feet on their controls and mine on mine
while I followed the movements they made to climb, fly level, glide, correct
bumps, and turn, and later land and take off. When they guessed I had
obtained reasonable imitative proficiency they gave me more freedom of
control and in the end almost complete control but with their own hands
and feet ready for prompt action if their pupil boobed. During this latter
period an instructor's hand would press on my right shoulder as a sign that
I was to turn to the right. A left hand on my left shoulder meant turn to
the left. A push or pull on my crash helmet meant nose down or up. If the
synchronisation of the controls was not as good as it ought to have been
I would feel them being moved against me with a force I had been told
in advance not to resist. Then I was to watch to see what correction was
needed to put my wrong right.

There was no speech pattern in flight, no standard form of verbal
instruction on the tarmac. Instructors varied greatly in natural teaching
ability and also in their degree of confidence (or timidity) in allowing
pupils to handle the controls. Instructing then was neither a science nor an
art and for the pupil it was largely a matter of luck. The most apt pupil was
the one having the best imitative faculty. The faster he could thus engender
confidence in his instructor's mind the sooner he was given more freedom
with the controls and so his progression towards solo flight became more
rapid. But by flying solo sooner he had less airborne experience and was
liable to fall victim to his own copyist's skill by finding himself in a situation
he had never had a chance to witness; and then, with his all too little

theoretical or practical knowledge, he might be unable to sort things out alone in time to reach a safe conclusion. The glib pupil did not have always the best subsequent accident-free record.

In mid-winter, with such aircraft as we had, flying was impossible on many days, but instructional flying continued every day weather permitted. After my first dual-instruction flight three days passed before I was again airborne; then, after more dual instruction, I was allowed for the first time to take complete control to taxi in after the instructor had landed.

We fledglings spent much time on the tarmac awaiting our turns to fly and there we eagerly discussed the relative values of Longhorns and Shorthorns, spoke in awed tones of the terrors of the stall and nosedive (neither of which had we ever seen) and looked ardently forward, but with trepidation, to our first solo ascent. Our worst fear was of making a poor show then.

Whether we flew dual or solo we always sat in the front seat of a Shorthorn because the instructor's presence or absence made little difference to its trim, since his seat was near the aircraft's centre of gravity. This was an undeniable advantage to us because we encountered little change when first going solo, other than the beneficial one of an aircraft lightened by the removal of the instructor's weight.

Flying the Shorthorn was our first real aptitude test. Some of us were naturally more apt than others who were deficient in sense of balance, clumsy with hands or feet, or erratic in judging distance from the ground when trying to land. If the duds were rejected they either went back to their previous unit or, if of the right spirit, volunteered to become observers, the two-seater pilot's wonderful companion.

We flew through Christmas Eve and on Boxing Day, but Christmas Day was a holiday for everyone flying.

We watched the first solos of more advanced pupils and saw the majority land safely, but a few came down badly and splintered parts of the undercarriage timbers and a minority crashed with an ominous boom.

On 5 January 1917 my turn came. I had been fortunate in having sympathetic and painstaking instructors. Ryan, who completed my instruction, insisted on keeping me flying dual with him until he felt certain I could make my first solo safely. He took me up for a final 10 minutes to determine that my hands and eyes were 'in', then gave me a Shorthorn I had never flown in –4141– to take up into the air, alone, for the first time. I had then had four hours and a half of dual instruction (as it was known in those days) and a few extra flights as a passenger when an instructor was going up 'to test the air' or an overhauled Shorthorn and when I was required to wind the aerial out and in.

The MFSH (as we usually signalesed the Maurice Farman Shorthorn) had 'spectacles' on top of a vertical control column. Rocking these spectacles operated the ailerons. Fore and aft movement of the column controlled the elevator. Foot pedals actuated the twin rudders. When my hands and feet first rested on these controls free from any instructor's inhibitory muscles on his dual set, a delicious tingle of anticipation ran through my being at the thought that I was going up by myself in this wonderful aeroplane, to take it aloft, to keep it there, and bring it again down to the airfield to land.

In preparation for my first solo I had been shown how to climb and glide and fly level and how to make turns with up to about 40-degree bank and how to correct for such air bumps as we had experienced on comparatively calm days in winter when thermal disturbances were rare, and, perhaps most important, how to land. That was the limit of my pre-solo instruction. If I were to do anything more than the little I had been shown, whether by intention or inadvertence, the consequence of my temerity or ill-fortune would be laid upon me and described as 'pilotage error'. But these thoughts did not disturb my pleasure as I opened the throttle.

The 70 hp Renault behind me rattled all its valves as it turned the propeller faster and faster. The speed of the wood-and-wire-framed structure increased until at length I could ease it off the ground. Up we climbed at a gentle angle. I watched the ground recede and made quick glances at the height indicator and the crude air-speed indicator. Presently I turned in a wide half-circle and flew back across the airfield. I was perfectly happy, for I found I could fly. With so little instrumentation to see to in that elementary aeroplane every moment could be given to the sheer pleasure of flying. For three-quarters of an hour I flew around at 500 feet, always within reasonable reach of the airfield. I was literally unconscious of any thought save the joy of flying, of controlling the live apparatus that bore me along on outstretched wings, until – I looked down at the tarmac. There I saw the khaki-clad figurines of my fellow pupils, of my instructor watching as I passed overhead, and of the ack emmas at the hangar door probably speculating whether I was going to present them with another repair job.

Suddenly I felt acutely alone. I became conscious of a feeling that I wanted to be back amongst them, to sense the friendliness of their company, to chat to them and smoke a cigarette with them and, above all, to know that I could land an aeroplane, that I was its master and it my servant. This feeling was not panic, but something different, a sense of isolation and of incomplete achievement, both clamouring to be overcome. No longer could I enjoy the detachment that the exhilaration of flying had previously obliterated. Now the sense of detachment obliterated the exhilaration of flying. I felt I had to reattach myself to my fellow men, whom I could see, but not speak with, nor be amongst, until I had accomplished the final act of my first solo, by landing. Only my vision of them, where they were, separated me from a loneliness, as of death. To rejoin them would be like a return to the living world.

I turned until I was facing the airfield at what I thought should be the correct distance for beginning the approach. Then I throttled the engine as I pushed the spectacles forward. Unswervingly, 4141 glided steeply through the still air until I eased back the spectacles in accordance with the instructions I had received: '*When you can distinguish separate blades of grass instead of a green plane, land her.*' I did just that and after the Shorthorn ceased rolling I taxied her in and discovered that the two sensations of exhilaration and detachment I had experienced during my first solo had merged into one of extreme pleasure now that it was successfully accomplished and I was back among my fellows. Perhaps these are the psychological phenomena of all first solo flights.

I completed two hours of solo flying in 4141 that day and next morning was off in her again before nine o'clock. I was flying down wind at 500 feet when her engine began to flag. No instructor had ever landed me away from the airfield. Now it was too far away to be reached with my failing engine. I had had drilled into me the maxim: *Never turn with a failing engine* — there was too great a risk of a stall if one did. So I nosed 4141 straight down into the steep glide of the MFSH towards my first forced landing. I saw myself aiming across a steep-sided valley. I should come to earth on its farther rising slope. Its steep gradient and my steep glide were at right angles. It would be all too easy to nose into that hill. Just before 4141 hit I hauled the specs back into my stomach. This hoicked her nose up into the air, parallel to the ground slope. She stall-landed gently on the hill face with no forward movement and immediately began to run backward. I undid my belt and was in the act of jumping overboard when the curved, spring-steel tailskid under each rudder dug into the turf and stopped her. But for them 4141 would have run backward into the valley and been wrecked. I climbed down, thankful for her unique tailskids.

Five minutes later another Shorthorn passed overhead. Its pilot saw
mine and waved to me. I knew by his face-fitting leather flying cap that he
was an instructor and he must have known from my clumsy crash headgear
that I was a 'Hun' – the generic RFC joint term for German airmen and
RFC flying pupils, presumably because of their common frightfulness. He
circled and flew off towards the airfield. About half an hour later a Crossley
tender ran up the spur of the slope to the top of the hill above me. With
its aid we hauled 4141 to the top. The sergeant and a couple of mechanics
adjusted and locked the valve tappets, the looseness of which had caused
my trouble, while my instructor and I discussed various features of the
MFSH. Then the engine was run up and found satisfactory.

It was impossible to take off along the hill-top because of the cross-
wind. There was no other level stretch. The instructor said it was all right to
take off down the hill into wind. I was dubious about it, but took his word.
We turned 4141 round, facing down into the valley. I climbed into my seat,
fastened my belt, waved away the chocks and 4141 began to move. I opened
the throttle quickly and she charged ever faster down the hill, with her tailskids scraping twin furrows on the higher slope behind. When I tried to
pull her off, the tailskids negatived the requisite wing angle and held the
nose down in a dive it was impossible to pull out of. The valley bottom was
narrow and the gradient on its other side, although not as steep, was much
steeper than a Shorthorn could possibly climb in flight.

I never supposed my predicament presented the same harsh aspect to
those who watched from the hill-top. The other fellow's problem never
does. But with no equivalent dual experience to guide me and only two
hours and a half of humdrum solo flying and four solo take-offs behind
me, this fantastic take-off demanded every ounce of sweaty concentration
from me.

I could not stop if I would and as 4141 ran on, I realised that if we left
the ground at all I should have to make an instant turn to avoid hitting
the slope. This was something I had been told never to do, but now, in the
narrow valley, I had to do it or crash.

We were nearly at the bottom of the hill before 4141 came unstuck,
with a mighty swish of surplus speed that fortunately made my hasty and
none too skilful turn comparatively safe, because I could not possibly stall.
Tension relaxed as I flew down the valley, gaining height, and at its end
turned towards the airfield.

Confident in my new-found skill, I decided to spiral down over the centre of the airfield and land off the spiral. This I had never done dual and my brash attempt at showmanship taught me I had a lot yet to learn. As I neared the ground I found I had misjudged the manoeuvre. Wind direction, my height, and the spiral turn were all out of alignment. I dared not open the throttle and go round again because the hangars were to windward and too near to clear if I attempted to take off. So I had to land as best I could. I saw that if I came out of the spiral before touching the ground I should land cross wind (which had risen considerably) – a risky thing to do in a big-winged, light-loaded Shorthorn. The alternative was to touch down into wind while still spiralling and hope that one side of the flimsy undercarriage could take the load without breaking.

I decided to land into wind. Before I could level up, the right undercarriage wheels touched. The unbalanced load was too much for the flimsy structure and I heard something go. When I taxied in I found a slightly cracked rear half main skid and two undercarriage-bracing piano wires broken. I had learned a useful lesson. From that day I knew what no instructor had taught me, probably because most of them flew the same type of aeroplane in almost constant conditions. I knew that the landing of an aeroplane must be divided into two parts: first, the approach; and second, the actual alighting. The approach is the more difficult of the two. It must vary according to wind and obstacles, to size and slope of airfield or pasture, and its angle alter with changes of load and with different aeroplanes. Actual alighting is much the same with any aeroplane and is a normally constant operation.

The damage to 4141 was slight. Within four hours that included lunch I was up in 4141 again and on that day flew for two hours ten minutes. My last flight ended in the dusk and haze of a winter evening and it was not until I was almost in it that I saw a five-foot-deep gully just ahead of where I was touching down. I slammed the throttle forward, eased back the specs, the good old Renault responded and I lifted 4141 over the gully like a well-trained horse in my fourth unexpected test of the day.

Before half past ten next morning I completed the five hours' solo that was required by the programme for elementary flying with five minutes more than that to my name. I had flown the same Shorthorn throughout all my solo flights. No refresher dual was given during them, nor was my flying tested to find out if I had developed any faults while flying solo.

Right down the line from the Directorate of Military Aeronautics at the War Office it was considered good enough if I could fly alone for five hours without breaking my neck or the Shorthorn.

With the RFC penchant for nicknames the MFSH trainer was often called the 'Rumpety'. I never discovered the origin of this Lewis Carrolian kind of word that seems to go well with *mome raths outgribing*. Probably it was an onomatope derived from the sound of a Shorthorn bounding slowly across the airfield and rising lazily into the calm air to the song of piano wires and their orchestral accompaniment of slapping pistons, rattling valves and tappets, and the propeller drumming within its cage – rumpety, rumpety, rumpety, rump. I left Netheravon with an affection for the Rumpety MFSH which has lasted ever since.

Chapter II

CENTRAL FLYING SCHOOL

From Netheravon I was posted five miles north to the Central Flying School at Upavon, home of the pre-war joint flying school of the Navy and Army when their air services were two Wings of one Royal Flying Corps. After the Naval Wing broke away in 1914 and renamed itself the Royal Naval Air Service, the Army Wing became exclusively the Royal Flying Corps. In January 1917, when I went there, CFS was one of several schools where Army pupil pilots were raised from their elementary to the proficiency standard then required of them before they were posted to RFC operational squadrons.

On arrival I reported to the adjutant.

'Posted to "D" Squadron, Macmillan, to fly pushers,' he said.

'If you please, sir, I'd rather go on tractors,' I replied. 'Why?' he asked bluntly.

'Because I'm sure the tractor is the better type mechanically and I don't want to continue flying pushers when I feel they will be obsolete in the future.'

Major Wilfrid R. Freeman, DSO, MC, smiled. He was an understanding type both then, and afterward when he had attained air rank and its responsibilities before and during WW2.

'All right, Macmillan, if you feel that way I'll post you to "B" Squadron, Sopwith 1½-Strutters.'

That brief interview had an irrevocable effect on my future. It changed the men I should serve under and with; the squadrons, operations and war areas wherein I should find myself; even the types of aircraft and engines I should have to fly. Sequentially, I became a pilot of rotary-engined aircraft for the duration of the war, engines that reached their limit of development during it.

But I look back without regret. Who knows what might have happened had I accepted a posting to fly pushers? I admired, but never wished to join, the chaps who flew pushers, and my reason was precisely the one I gave Freeman.

Upavon had two airfields, each with its own line of hangars. One row faced south, the other east. 'B' Squadron was on the south airfield. There I reported to its commander, Captain F. G. Dunn, a short man. I have been told that he was partly responsible for the rejection of the excellent Bristol M.1C Monoplane for use on the Western Front, because he found its landing view bad. I flew this aircraft in 1918 and found the landing view from the pilot's cockpit partly obstructed by the shoulder-high position of the wing, but I had no difficulty in landing. However, his lesser height must have aggravated this feature for Dunn. He, and his second pilot, Captain P. T. Rawlings, DSC, died from injuries when the six-engined Tarrant Tabor triplane bomber prototype they were to test at Farnborough crashed on the take-off for its maiden flight on 26 May 1919, believably because the thrust from two highly mounted engines pushed the nose (where they were sitting) into the ground.

Upavon housed four training squadrons. Major Gordon Bell, a well-known pre-war civilian pilot, commanded the south sector. In uniform he was rather a dandy and would stroll along the apron, inspecting what was going on, clad in off-white breeches with yellow leather strappings, carrying a yellow walking cane, with his Dalmatian dog trotting proudly at his heels. He had a bad stutter and this exaggerated the nonchalance of his mannerisms of speech. An immortal story was told of him. He had crashed into a tree after having been shot down. As he shinned down the tree to the ground, a resplendent staff officer rode up to him and said, 'Have you crashed?'

'N-n-n-n-no,' replied G.B., 'I a-a-a-a-always l-l-l-l-land like that.'

Flying morale at CFS was good, but there was discontent about the food served in the officers' mess, especially as mess bills were higher than at the elementary schools. The pupils' murmurings resulted in a parade being called by the commandant, Colonel A. C. H. MacLean, who told us that perfectly plain food and milk puddings were the best things to fly on and that while he was Commandant this was the food which would be served.

'One point I should like to emphasise,' he concluded, 'is that the foodstuffs served here have been selected by me. Flying requires plenty of good, healthy feeding. It is useless, criminal, to fill your stomachs with trashy rubbish. I won't have it.

'You know our record here. We have not had a fatal or serious crash for several months. And that I attribute to the judicious messing.

'Now, gentlemen, I do not wish to hear any more of this matter.'

Although he did not convert us into liking a milk-pudding diet, his parade ended the grumbling, because we junior officers realised that our commandant, appetent of the well-being of the whole station, was to be respected and admired. Yet, when some serious and fatal crashes occurred not long afterward, it seemed to us that the former run of good luck had been due to more than milk puddings.

Rotary engines were unsilenced and there was then no provision for instructors to speak through their noise. They told us before we entered the cockpits what we were to do during the lesson. In powered flight one simply imitated, monkey-fashion, the instructor's movements of the controls. If a mistake were made he corrected it. Occasionally he shouted advice while gliding with the engine shut off.

My first two flights in 'B' Squadron were made as a passenger on 12 January 1917, in the front seat of an Avro 504A built by Blériot and Spad. I found the carburetter located between my knees; the Gnôme engine had an unpleasant habit of back-firing into its carburetter and whenever it did this I saw little flames flickering between my legs. When my first instructional flight came next day I found I had to sit in the front seat again. Instructors always sat in the rear seat then. We pupils never questioned this at the time; it was current practice and we automatically accepted it.

The interrelationship between physio-psychological disturbance and flying stress had not then (as it has since) been investigated and after acute personal strain during operational flying a posting to teach pupils to fly was supposed to provide an adequate period of rest – a false hypothesis, as all who have ever been flying instructors know.

My first instructor lacked confidence. I later heard that he was suffering from the after effect of having been shot down from 8,000 feet by AA. He never allowed me to have complete control over the Avro. His hands and feet were always on the controls. I asked him to let me have complete control, since I could not otherwise know the true feel of the machine. He was frightfully indignant and said he always did. On my next flight, when he rocked the stick from side to side to indicate that I was to take over, I decided to leave the controls untouched. We flew around for about 15 minutes, making gentle turns, while I sat and watched the controls moving in my cockpit. Finally, the instructor shut off the engine and shouted, 'Very good today'. I suppose he thought my touch was light. 'Now land,' he bellowed.

We glided down. I waited. The stick came back. We bumped. The stick moved fore and aft. We bumped again. As we taxied in after a third bump, the instructor shouted from the rear cockpit, 'That was a bad landing.'

Back on the tarmac I turned to him

'If it was a bad landing, then blame yourself, for you made it. You said I was flying well, yet I never once touched the controls since we left the ground.'

This was a double insult, for he was not a bad pilot, only a nervous one, and his bumpy landing may have been due to his control movements having been made too late, after awaiting mine, which never came.

We saw the flight commander. His face was grave, but immobile. I wondered if I should be sent to the commandant for indiscipline. Instead, Captain McCall took me up and, for the first time, I discovered how light and pleasant the Avro was. Flying her after the Shorthorn was like driving a sports car after a truck. Her universally-mounted mahogany stick was more convenient than spectacles on a one-way column, her rudder-bar neater than pedals for operating her featherweight air-balanced rudder.

One snag was the engine in the nose. Because its fuel was fed to its cylinders through its crankcase, a rotary engine's lubricating oil had to be immiscible with petroleum. For this reason pure castor oil was used. But the revolving engine threw out much oil and oily vapour through its exhaust valves. Dirty oil rippled back along the fuselage and lower wings and made the windshield opaque. One flew in a constant atmosphere of half-burnt castor oil and one's clothing became permanently stained with it.

McCall's tuition soon concentrated on landings. In 50 minutes we made 19. Perhaps wisely for the record, he passed me back to my first instructor before I was sent solo after less than three hours' dual, during much of which I had been little more than a passenger.

We landed some distance away from the airfield, on a natural runway formed by a long, level stretch of short turf. There we both climbed out, because the Avro was not flown solo from the front seat. I now had the honour and glory of occupying the instructor's seat for the first time. This altered my view and sense of feel at the critical moment of first solo and was a bad feature of Avro flying training then.

McCall flew out to watch and, perhaps, to take the lieutenant back if I should crash. On their instructions I made one short straight flight and landing, then went up again to make a circuit and land near them. With much concentration I managed (I thought) reasonably well, but my instructor slated me after I had landed because (he said) I had glided down too slowly. I knew at the time that I was coming down slower than he did and I did so intentionally because I did not want to balloon up by flattening out with surplus speed. I really think, to this day, that it looked too slow to him only because habitually he approached too fast. My touchdown was not criticised. It was all right.

To me it was enough that I was now flying solo and could begin to learn for myself by a process of trial and error. I had never been looped, stalled, rolled, side-slipped, or spun, nor told anything about aerobatics or flying abnormalities. Most pilots then avoided stalling, rarely looped, and considered spinning a prelude to the funeral march played by the Station Band.

The instructor flew me back to the airfield as his front seat passenger. My subsequent 20 hours on Avros at CFS were all flown solo, with no refresher instruction or check for faults. Looking back, I realise how crude even the most advanced instruction there then was and how far it fell below the standard needed to produce efficient operational pilots.

Yet there was a feeling of real morale at CFS. Pupils were keen. For that period, instructors were mostly conscientious and good. But from insufficient theoretical knowledge of flying phenomena and absence of any analysis and practical exposition of control movements and their reactions, no standard system of flying instruction had then been developed or applied. The method of each instructor's tuition was based on his own flying experience and natural aptitude (or lack of it) for teaching and efficiency varied widely.

There were neither Link Trainers nor simulators to teach us to fly on the ground before going into the air. But two or three of us sometimes met in one of our rooms in the wooden huts where we slept, to discuss the manipulation of the controls. One, sitting on the only chair, would put his feet on the fender for rudder-bar and hold a poker in one hand for joystick and simulate a pilot at the controls. In this way we devised combinations of control movements and theorised their probable effects. We thought, if ever we should encounter an unknown problem while flying, it would be best to centralise the controls and trust to the stability of the Avro to do the right thing for us.

On my third solo flight I flew into turbulent air over a deep, tree-bordered gully (known as 'Death Valley' because so many pilots had previously crashed there over the years) and stalled accidentally at 1,000 feet. Before I knew what was happening the stall became a spin, the first I had ever known. The Avro fell, with her nose pointing down at the trees, which appeared to rotate beneath me. I shut off the engine and centred the controls. Some types of aircraft might not have responded, but the stability of the Avro was such that she came out of the spin.

Near the end of my time at CFS I saw my first demonstration of spinning. The pilot was Captain E. L. Foot, who was then visiting training airfields in a Sopwith Pup, to show at each one that spinning was a controllable feature of flying. He came from Gosport airfield where Maj R. R. Smith-Barry had recently been given permission, by Brigadier-General J. M. Salmond, who commanded the RFC Training Brigade in Britain, to experiment with his ideas concerning flying training. Smith-Barry's ideas were to bear fruit later, but I do not recall that we then received from Foot (or anyone else) any information about how spinning was done or recovered from. I certainly never saw a CFS staff pilot spin while I was there, but I do remember the skilful stunting of Gordon Bell on a Sopwith 1½-Strutter and the clever piloting of a Henry Farman by Philip Fullard.

Bell did not live long after the war had ended. Leslie Foot (who became a major) died in the Grosvenor Cup Race of 23 June 1923 when his 140 hp Lucifer-engined Bristol M.1D Monoplane dived and crashed and caught fire near Chertsey. P. F. Fullard scored 39 (some say 46) victories in WW1 with the Nieuport 17 and SE5a scouts of No. 1 Squadron, RFC, and ended his Service career as an air commodore of the RAF; he appeared to me a quiet type who might have reached higher air rank had he been less modest.

We budding pilots put in a lot of work and began to realise the difficulties and dangers of flying, which was then an art and not the science it has since become. Among our number some names are ineradicable from memory, among them Jones-Williams, Rhys-Davids, Hervey (who wore an observer's badge with the MC and Bar below it and had the bad luck to be brought down and taken prisoner soon after he reached France as a pilot in 60 Squadron), Muspratt. They were a wonderful lot to be with.

Drawn from all quarters of the globe, the flying personnel of the RFC, as a whole, were superstitious. The variety of forms of 'ju-ju' they practised was legion. There were those who would not drink unless a preliminary drop from the bottle had first been spilt upon the floor (a ceremony of antiquity to placate the ancient gods); the bottle, when passed, had to go round from left to right (as does the port in the mess), probably the survival of some sun-god ritual. One might not assert anything with assurance without touching wood, lest the contrary should occur or a run of good luck change to evil. Almost every Service camp had an ill-omened hut, tent, or bed. Something always happened to the man who slept there and the older established squadron members would not sleep in the fateful place for a king's ransom.

It was unlucky to go up with another man's mascot on board. Numberless crashes were instanced as proof of this. Most would not willingly sit down 13 at a table and many were loath to fly an aircraft with a number like 3523, the digits of which add up to 13 (although exceptions to this included Barker, VC). One man always turned round three times before climbing into his cockpit. And to show that these foibles were not confined to one race, early Swedish pilots would not be photographed before a flight.

These positive or negative actions were done religiously, as they frequently are by men engaged in dangerous work, when that which we call luck often proves a useful asset.

One pupil had a novel experience. He started with his altimeter set to zero (as we all did) and climbed up through gaps in the clouds. Finding the cloud world a realm of rapture he failed to observe that all the earth below was rapidly disappearing from sight by the fusion of the clouds.

After about an hour and a half he decided to go down. Everywhere below was white cloud. He flew around, looking for an opening. There was none.

He decided he must glide down through the clouds for the first time in his life. He shut off his engine and entered the clouds at 1,500 feet. At 1,000 he was still shut in by opacity. At 500 feet the clouds were still dense.

He watched the altimeter needle winding down ... 400, 300, 200, 100 feet... still no improvement. His nerves began to tingle.

Zero.

He was down to the level of the airfield. He dared not think of what might happen at any second. He dared not try to climb; even if he succeeded in reaching the sunshine, he would merely be once again in a lost world.

Determined to go down whatever might happen, he glided onward, watching the needle move across the altimeter dial. He wiped the mist from his goggles, braced himself to meet anything, expecting at any moment to crash into something.

With the needle on his altimeter showing 500 feet below ground level he glided into thinning mist among the tall masts of shipping on Southampton Water. He opened the throttle. How he missed the masts he did not know. With a full-throated roar from his engine he swung away from the danger, found a good field and landed.

He had set his altimeter to zero at Upavon airfield, 600 feet above sea level, drifted away from its vicinity while flying above the clouds and glided down into the sea fog at the base of the cloud-layer, very fortunate not to have crashed ashore. His was one of the hazards created by lack of ground to air communication. In those days the pilot truly was the captain of his aircraft – and of his soul.

During solo flying we were not supposed to leave the area adjacent to the airfield and we were not given maps. I soon became bored with the unending vision of Salisbury Plain and as I knew that one of the proficiency tests to qualify for the pilot's wings was a cross-country flight, I studied the map pinned on the wall of the flight office and began to make short cross-country flights from memory of the map features. When I had flown just under three and a half hours solo I ventured farther than before, to Andover, Basingstoke and Reading, where I circled at 3,500 feet before setting out for home by following the Bath Road.

On the way back the Gnôme began to lose power. Thinking it might be overheating, I shut off and glided down to 1,000 feet to let the engine cool off. There it picked up its power again. The wind was NE, the air bumpy, and the late January sky began to fill with cloud and mist. I lost sight of the ground features. With no compass and the sun invisible, I had nothing to guide me. When the engine again began to misfire I cut out, glided down, and landed uphill into wind on a ploughed field, without damage.

A small crowd of excited country folk quickly surrounded me. I found I had landed at Colthrop Farm, Thatcham. Mr H. Lay, the farmer, was most kind and helpful. I decided the Avro must be moved to the top corner of the field where it would be under the shelter of hedgerow trees. I made several attempts to start the engine, but the voluntary mechanics were unable to swing the propeller properly and the Gnôme would not run. So, with a rather timid farm-horse, we towed the Avro there and picketed her wings with ropes. Then I wired Upavon for assistance.

When the ack emmas arrived they had to overhaul the engine before it would run properly. Mr Lay kindly invited me to stay at the farm. Next day, fog and snow prevented flying, but on the following day I took off, flew into thick fog at 600 feet and landed again, on a grazing field which I had previously inspected, on the other side of the trees.

By this time Captain A. M. Vaucour had taken over 'B' Squadron from

Dunn. He sent an instructor to fly the Avro back, with orders for me to return ignominiously in the sidecar that brought him to Colthrop Farm. I felt this was a poor reflection on my flying. I had felt rather proud at having landed on and taken off from a ploughed field and at having landed again on a grass one (which made take-off easier for the instructor) all without damage to the Avro. I thought Vaucour might at least have let me fly back as a passenger. I assumed his order was a preliminary punishment and while shivering in the cold sidecar I thought I must expect to be disciplined on my return. But I never heard a word said about my illicit cross-country flight. Probably, under Vaucour, I was lucky to escape with mere 'loss of face' at Colthrop Farm when the winged pilot arrived.

Vaucour wore the MC ribbon and Bar rosette, decorations he had won while flying as an observer with No. 10 Squadron in 1915 and as a pilot of 1½-Strutters with No. 70 Squadron in 1916. Like many good operational pilots he was not a strict disciplinarian of the regimental pattern and he could turn a facile blind eye on minor breaches of unimportant regulations.

More snow fell and frost bound the ground white for some weeks. But I continued to fly almost daily until I was ready to make my official cross-country test by a flight to Gosport airfield and back. Pupils were supposed to pass this test on the operational type of aircraft they were earmarked to fly, in my case the Sopwith 1½-Strutter. But so many 1½-Strutters had been damaged that I was instructed to make the flight on a Gnôme-engined Avro, which meant flying with a much less reliable engine.

I had no trouble in reaching Gosport and started back with my cross-country voucher signed as having landed there. The Gnôme failed and I landed alongside the railway line at West Dean. A signalman gave me a hand to restart after the over-heated engine had cooled down and I hopped on (200 revolutions down) as far as Longford Castle, where I had to land in the park. Here I found a convalescent home for wounded officers, a training school for lady land-girls, and much hospitality.

I rang up the squadron and reported where I was. The instructor asked what the place and landing room were like. I described the convalescent home. He didn't seem very interested. Then I mentioned the school for land-girls and he said he'd fly over at once. He brought a corporal fitter with him, who ran over my engine and reported it OK after making a few adjustments. I ran it up and said it was still not right, but the instructor disagreed and ordered me to proceed.

Ten miles farther on I had to land on top of the highest hill of a desolate neighbourhood, whence I had to walk two miles to the nearest village. Again I telephoned 'B' Squadron. While the village policeman guarded the Avro during the night, I, in the squalid precincts of the village inn, regretted having had to leave the luxury of Longford Castle and its jolly company.

Next morning a tender came from Upavon. Fitters again looked over and adjusted the engine. It was still running badly when I left late in the afternoon, but I was glad to get away from that inhospitable spot. No sooner had I reached the air above Upavon airfield than a loud bang from within my engine announced both my return and the final disruption of an internal inlet valve in a piston head (a unique feature of the Gnôme), the impending failure of which had been throughout the hidden cause of all my trouble, one which no amount of external inspection and adjustment could have discovered and rectified. I switched off my engine and landed near the squadron hangar.

Lieutenant-Colonel Walter Lawrence was the first of the eight flying fatalities at CFS while I was there. Wednesday, 28 January 1917, was fine and clear, but the north wind was considered too strong for pupils to fly. With others I visited the hangars of the east airfield to see several types of aircraft our squadron did not have and which we had not been able to look over before. While we were there the colonel arrived and a Vickers Bullet was brought out for him. It was a single-seater with a round fuselage and stubby biplane wings with no stagger. To us it seemed a nasty, vicious little thing, with a cruel look, which its Clergêt engine did not soften. But Lawrence was an experienced pilot. He had obtained the Royal Aero Club's 113th pilot's certificate on 1 August 1911. As an Essex Regiment (TA) captain seconded to the RFC he had gone to France in August 1914 as a supernumerary flight commander attached to No. 2 Squadron of the British Expeditionary Force. Now he was second-in-command at CFS.

We saw him almost soar off the ground and expected to gain knowledge by watching him perform in the gusty half-gale. After a brief flight up wind he came hurtling back, flying parallel to the hangars of the east airfield. When he reached the last one he made a steep right-hand turn into wind at about 100 feet up, evidently with the intention of landing. But he stalled in the turn. The Bullet dived and hit the ground before he could recover. He was killed almost at our feet.

The official verdict was that he overbanked too near the ground. I theorised about his crash and decided that he stalled because he made a geometric half-circle in relation to the ground, instead of the terrestrially elongated curve that would have described a true half-circle in relation to the air flow. I concluded that when near the ground and turning one must fly by the air flow and never by geometric ground patterns.

On the evening of the day I returned from Gosport I made my debut on the Sopwith Two-Seater (its official designation). It seemed to me to be a large and powerful aeroplane, but today it would look both small and flimsy. Designed late in 1915, it was the first British operational aeroplane having a machine-gun firing through its propeller's disc. (But those at CFS were unarmed.) Its structure was the contemporaneous combination of wood, wire and fabric, its engine a 110 hp Clergêt rotary driving a fixed-pitch wood propeller with brass overlay protecting its tips.

Wing mounting was the novel feature of this aircraft. The upper wings were longer than the lower, but the overall span of both coincided in the assembled aircraft by the attachment of the lower wings to a wide centre section and the upper ones to a narrow rib. Port and starboard wings each had one pair of interplane struts; these were correctly located for the shorter wing spars, not for the longer. To neutralise this asymmetry (and strengthen the upper wing) flattened steel tubes (rather shorter than the interplane struts) ran out and up at 35 degrees from the top of the fuselage sides, one to each upper wing spar. This wing arrangement offered less drag than that of conventional biplanes with two pairs of interplane struts on each side, and from it the Sopwith Two-Seater derived its familiar name of '1½-Strutter', a descriptive (if not quite accurate) term that signified an efficient design – the brainchild of that brilliant trio, Tom Sopwith, Fred Sigrist, and Harry Hawker.

1½-Strutters had no dual control. Pupils were supposed to be able to fly them straight off after having flown Avros solo for 20 hours. But no check of a pupil's Avro flying skill was made before he was sent up alone in a 1½-Strutter. Lieutenant Kempsley took me up from the east airfield in the observer's seat of Ruston, Proctor-built Sopwith 7810. The fuel tank was between us and there was no means of communication. He did no stunts. The 20-minute trip gave me some idea of the angles of take-off and approach and little more.

He landed and climbed out and I climbed into the front seat under the centre section, a position I had not occupied since my dual instruction on Avros had ended five weeks before. Unlike the Avro, the Sopwith had an adjustable tailplane, the angle of which the pilot could alter by turning a hand-wheel on the right side of his cockpit, thus permitting solo flight from the front seat without ballast in the rear. The wheel had to be correctly set before take-off. It was also another detail to remember when coming down to land, for the wheel had to be wound back to reset the tailplane for the correct gliding speed. Other than this, there was little difference in cockpit drills between the Avro and the Sop.

The sun had already set when I took off for my first solo. This restricted me to a 15-minute flight. I found the aircraft smooth and stable, but heavier on controls than the Avro. In the half-dusk I came in rather low and fast and at the last moment saw a grey heap of road metal piled alongside the public highway (running through Upavon air station) that formed the south boundary of the east airfield. There was no time to take avoiding action. My wheels hit near the top of the pile and sent stones flying, without damaging the propeller or undercarriage. I had enough speed to plough through them without stalling or tipping up on my nose and I landed smoothly beyond them.

This 1½-Strutter first solo qualified me for four days' leave and two days' extension for travel to Scotland – really farewell leave in anticipation of an early operational posting.

Second Lieutenant Sutherland, a tall, brawny Australian pupil who had become rather a friend of mine, was flying 1½-Strutters just ahead of me and in the evening after my first Sop solo he told me he had been practising dives and zooms on them. That very day he had climbed to 3,000 feet, shut off his engine and dived for 2,000 feet. Then he pulled out of the dive into a climb and opened his engine full out. His best zoom so far was 800 feet and he wanted to push that up to 1,000. I asked him not to do it and told him I was certain it was too much to ask of a 1½-Strutter, but all I could get from him was a promise to stop once he had succeeded in zooming 1,000 feet. What force is it that impels some men onward to their doom?

Next day his tail came off and he was killed instantly.

The court of inquiry found that excessive strain during a steep dive had caused the machine to collapse. I do not believe the members of the court knew what I knew of Sutherland's ambition, else they would have defined the cause as excessive strain during a too rapid pull-out of a dive. The 1½-Strutter's tailplane was not stressed for the load that Sutherland applied to it and so this too courageous Australian lost his life trying to do more than the aeroplane he was flying was ever built to accomplish. He died, exactly one month to the day, after Lieutenant-Colonel Lawrence. I did not see him crash because I had already gone on leave – and I was glad not to have witnessed his terrible end.

Six more fatal flying accidents occurred at CFS in February 1917, three when DH2s stalled on turns, two through a collision between a BE2e and a Martinsyde 'Elephant', and a quite fantastic one on an FE8 after a bad landing. The bump sheared the pin that kept the undercarriage wheels on the axle. As the FE8 bounced off the ground the pilot opened up his engine to make another circuit and come in again. In the air the wheel caps came off and flew back into the propeller. The prop burst and cut a tail boom. The FE8 went out of control and crashed. With these four pusher scout deaths while I was there I was glad I had asked for tractors. Both DH2 and FE8 were already out of date, but were still in use in France pending later replacement when better types of fighters came along.

After my return from leave I flew five hours' solo (on Vickers-built 1½-Strutters A1089 and A1090) and my flying training was then complete. I had been taught nothing but straightforward flying and had never flown in formation. I had had to learn how to make steeply banked turns empirically. I had flown solo in strong winds, mist, clouds at 200 feet, had practised S-turns, vertical banks, spirals, stalls, made an inquisitive speed test that showed 97 miles an hour on the 'clock', and flown another unofficial cross-country flight to practise picking up landmarks on the ground from memory of the map.

On the evening of my last 1½-Strutter flight I was given a scout to fly, Sopwith Pup A659, built by the Standard Motor Car Company. It brought my dream of flying to reality. I have never since flown in a sweeter aeroplane than the Sopwith Pup. The nearest I have known was the Douglas DC2. I never knew why I was given a Pup to fly. Perhaps if I had thrown it about the sky I might have been transferred to scouts and have found myself in a Pup squadron. But it was late in the evening, night was near, and I was just too thrilled to be up in a single-seater to think about those who watched me from below. I tried no stunts – just enjoyed the smooth delight of graceful flying to my heart's content until the swiftly fading light ended 25 minutes of sheer joy.

Before I left Upavon another crash occurred almost at my feet. Captain T. Davidson had come to 'B' Squadron. He took an Avro 504 up for test after an overhaul. When about 80 feet up he moved stick and rudder to turn. One biplane wing went down and the Avro began to sideslip dangerously. Davidson pushed the stick hard over to correct, but the dropped wings banked still more and the Avro fell and smashed about 10 feet from us. The breaking up of the Avro absorbed much of the impact and Davidson was lucky to emerge from the smashed cockpit with only facial cuts. Examination revealed that riggers had crossed the aileron wires and reversed the stick control. Davidson's 'correction' had therefore made his sideslip worse. He was not high enough to have time to discover what was wrong. Even if he had found out it would still have been very difficult to reverse all practice and instinct in the operation of the ailerons in order to be able to fly properly.

Seeing that accident made an indelible mark in my mind that I should always try my controls on the ground before every flight, not only for freedom of movement, but also for correct responses. Someone had blundered in not doing this before passing the Avro out ready for flight test and the fact that this could occur taught me that it was my duty before every flight to make my own inspection of every detail that lay within my power to check. No lecturer had told us to do this. But Davidson's crash was a more potent lesson to me than any lecturer's words would have been. I never forgot it, to my own, and others', subsequent benefit.

During my pupilage at CFS there was much to be done in addition to flying. There were Morse schools, gunnery schools, artillery observation classes, lectures on many subjects, parades and inspections, some pleasant, some irksome, but all forming part of the training system laid down for the RFC by the Directorate of Military Aeronautics at the War Office. There was little free time, but one of our number who went on leave brought his father's six-cylinder Sunbeam tourer back with him and sometimes we could drive down to Salisbury, have a meal at the Haunch of Venison and see a local theatrical show. The 17-mile drive along the Avon valley with the wind blowing in our hair was a most pleasant relaxation from the relative isolation of a military camp on Salisbury Plain.

Although it was no longer necessary for RFC pilots to obtain the Royal Aero Club pilot's certificate, the grant of the brevet to wear RFC (or RNAS) wings was acceptable by the club for the issue of its pilot's certificate to those who wished to have it; the original procedure had gone into reverse. The RAeC was the body controlling the sport of flying within the United Kingdom, but the only sport of flying during the war was in (or for) the

Services. Many RFC pilots did not trouble to apply for the RAeC certificate at the time because at the same moment we were involved in final stages of training and these entailed movements usually followed by abrupt posting to a war zone. We talked about it, but few did more. Many thought there was little point in paying over the guinea fee while the war continued, for the certificate conferred nothing during hostilities and if one were killed it was a guinea thrown away. I qualified on 28 March 1917, but did not take my RAeC certificate until about two years later; it was post-dated, but its number was of 1919 vintage and almost double what it would have been had I applied for it when I received my wings.

From Upavon I was sent to Turnberry Aerial Gunnery School, on the Ayrshire coast of Scotland. For six days we stripped and fired machine-guns and made notes about them. The full course included flying and shooting in the air, but pilot shortages in France cut my course short and before it was completed, without having flown at Turnberry, I was ordered to report at Training Headquarters, RFC, Mason's Yard, off Regent Street, London. I reported there next day, was told I was posted to No. 45 Squadron, in the Field, and given travel documents to St Omer. The railway transport officer at Victoria Station told me when the train would leave. Dumping my kit at the station luggage office I had my last meal in London, alone, pondering what might lie ahead. I knew that I knew a little about flying, but nothing at all about aerial warfare or how it was conducted. The training system had improved since the war began, but it had a long way yet to go before it could produce adequately trained operational pilots. At least I was not going to a strange place. I knew St Omer and Flanders from my Army days. I had no doubt of my ability to find my way from the air. I had made sure of that by my own actions during training. But I was ignorant of formation flying and a whole host of things; even the concept of what lay ahead had not been revealed during the instruction I had received. Too many of the instructors had seemed not to know because their knowledge was out of date. Those who did know, having just returned from the Front, were concerned with other things than giving their time to teach the 'Hun' pupils. They would learn soon enough when they got there. The methods of teaching pupils to fly were bad and this was the reason why there were so many accidents, so many needlessly killed during training. The great military machine went grinding on its way. It required a man of genius to revolutionise flying training. That man existed and within a year the result of his work would be felt throughout the flying training schools and after the war throughout the world, but he would reap as reward only the knowledge of work well done and of lives saved. Even the name of his system would be changed so that its origin would be obliterated and the individual would be almost forgotten. But I did not know all this then. This knowledge was to follow later.

Part Two

FRANCE

Chapter III

STRUTTERS AND NIEUPS

A London taxicab driver named Chamberlain, for the duration of the war transformed into an RFC transport driver, met me at St Omer. Nearing nightfall on bleak, windy 31 March 1917 his 20 hp Crossley tender rumbled off the *pavé* and stopped on 45 Squadron's location at the north-east corner of St Marie Cappel airfield, about 20 miles from Ypres. There I was received, as was every new man on joining an operational squadron, with interest and kindliness, but without enthusiasm.

I was aware of the sudden transmogrification that debased me from the comparative pinnacle of a finished soloist with 'wings up' at a flying school in England to the abysmal status of the most newly joined pilot in a fighter-reconnaissance squadron in France. Only the catalyst of time could establish my place among my new companions and sift, from indifferent others, friends.

Squadron HQ posted me to 'C' Flight as my martial home. Captain L. W. McArthur, my flight commander, said briefly that tomorrow he would see what my flying was like. I assumed that the white-purple-white ribbon I saw on his tunic had been won with the RFC. Not until long afterward did I discover that he had gained the decoration as an infantry officer with the Honourable Artillery Company, which he had joined in 1913 as a private, been promoted to sergeant in that Territorial Force regiment, then commissioned. He went to France with the 1st Battalion in September 1914 and was wounded on 15 February 1915. On 16 June 1915, when our troops were forced back from the German third trench-line at Hooge, Second Lieutenant McArthur rallied some of the retiring troops and with them reoccupied the vacated trench and held it under heavy fire until, later, retirements on his flanks forced him to withdraw; he was severely wounded in this action and for it he was awarded the MC. He was now 26 years old.

The squadron's aircraft were housed in sheds. Our sleeping quarters were Nissen huts. The mess was built of wood. Its smallness, in size and the number of its inmates, made for closer companionship than had been possible at Upavon's larger mess. Pilots with experience of flying over enemy-held territory spoke to me casually, but with strangely grave wisdom for young faces, of what I might expect and of what I should do there. Then the life of the mess closed around me and absorbed me in its midst. As I looked about I could not distinguish pilots and observers who had been with the squadron for a long time from those but slightly senior to myself in joining it.

Neither radio broadcasting nor television existed. The only available form of recorded entertainment was the clockwork gramophone and its fast-speed discs. When the mood was upon them, members of the mess preferred to make their own entertainment. Selby, an observer, was an excellent impromptu pianist. There was a violinist of some talent. Solomon, the only Jewish pilot who flew with 45 Squadron in WW1, was a skilful exponent of the one-string fiddle – the jamboogoo, we called it. These three musicians were a wonderful uplift to the spirit. When they ran through the melodious score of the currently popular *Chu Chin Chow*, one thought of Oscar Asche and Lily Brayton, Ali Baba and the Forty Thieves, and forgot the war. When they played the popular songs of the day they were accompanied by a rousing chorus of masculine voices of varied melodic charm. Some notes from the jamboogoo pained one's ears; then someone (perhaps Solomon himself) would stuff a rag into its horn to mute the fervour of its vibrating string.

Next day McArthur took me up in the observer's seat of his 1½-Strutter to show me over the surrounding countryside. As I felt her lift under me I was conscious of a thrill of admiration for the man who controlled her and gave her life. He was a good-looking Irishman of stout courage, even temper, good humour and great kindliness, a fine type. I could see the back of his leather-helmeted head four feet in front of me and the reflection of his face in the tiny round mirror that enabled the pilot to see what the observer was doing. (This mirror, carried by all 45 Squadron Strutters, was mounted at the apex of the front pair of steel tube supports for the upper wings' attachment rib.)

45 Squadron's Strutters also had speaking tubes, a length of rubber tubing rove through the fuselage past the fuel tank between the cockpits. Mouthpieces and ear-boxes for them were made of tin in the squadron workshops, but I had not yet had time to have a box fitted to my flying helmet. McArthur turned his head and smiled to me as he pointed out the sausage balloons hanging in the sky; Bailleul; and the road between Bailleul and Cassel, a useful guide for pilots returning in bad visibility. We

flew parallel to the trench-lines and I recognised places I had known when I was with the infantry. How different was this airborne aspect of those grim ditches of discomfort!

St Marie Cappel airfield lay on the flat farm land of the plain of Flanders, where even small hills assumed the importance of mountains. On one 175-metre hill, three kilometres north-east of the airfield, was the little Flemish town of Cassel, which had once prided French's and Foch's HQs. Just south of the hill, at Oxelaere, was HQ 2nd Brigade, RFC, commanded by Brigadier-General Tom Ince Webb-Bowen, who had come up from captain since the war began; 45 Squadron was in the 11th (Army) Wing of his brigade. Three kilometres eastward from Cassel rose the 150-metre, forested, Mont des Recollets. These two prominent hills provided St Marie Cappel pilots with natural beacons on which they could home visually.

The aerodrome was a square field bounded by two roads, three ditches, a row of trees, a hedge partly obscuring camouflaged hangars, a farm and its poplar-lined paddock. A narrow and rough-surfaced overshoot projected from the south-east of the square. Some obstruction had to be avoided on every approach.

The raw two-seater pilot had an advantage over the scout pilot in that, at the end of his passenger flights to show him the surrounding countryside and 'the lines,' he could gain some idea of the judgment required to make a safe landing on his new airfield. This was particularly helpful to 1½-Strutter pilots, for these aircraft floated far on ground effect, thus making it all too easy for anyone flying them to overshoot a smallish airfield.

Sopwith's test pilot, Harry Hawker, must have known this, because the 1½-Strutter was fitted with so-called air brakes and it may have been the first aeroplane in the world to be so equipped. But these were rudimentary devices. The surface areas behind the rear spar of the lower wings' centre section did not droop, like flaps, but rose to the vertical when the pilot turned a handwheel on the left of his cockpit. These wing segments were too far aft and too far inboard to be really effective as lift spoilers. Although they functioned as air brakes to some extent, they simultaneously caused severe turbulence over the tail and the effect of this so adversely affected fore and aft stability and control that pilots seldom used them twice. Once was enough!

There were only three ways to reduce a 1½-Strutter's tendency to float: (1) to approach very slowly; to approach at normal speed and either (2) tail swish or (3) sideslip. But one had to be very expert to do any of these on an aircraft with an incredibly flimsy undercarriage that bent or broke all too easily in any landing with the least drift or drop. Even expert pilots, after long flying of 1½-Strutters, damaged their undercarriages from time to time and, in the month before I joined the squadron, the half-axle tubes were strengthened by driving ash broom-handles into them.

McArthur took me up four times at odd moments of my first two days with the squadron; then, like all the other newly arrived pilots, I had to fly and practise until I was considered ready to go into action. This use of the squadron's first line aircraft by newcomers whose names were added to the pilot establishment of the squadron was unpopular with everyone, from the commanding officer down to the fitter and rigger of the aircraft. Cynical squadron observers turned out to watch the practice landings of new pilots with whom they might later have to risk their necks.

I had never damaged an Avro or a 1½-Strutter at Upavon, but when I reached St Marie Cappel I had not flown for a fortnight and to give its obstructions ample clearance I was apt to come in too high. As a result, I had some minor mishaps, nothing much; I broke a few bracing wires (they might have been over-tensioned) and slightly bent one half-axle. Many new pilots did far more damage; even pilots of long experience with the squadron occasionally bent the fragile 1½-Strutters badly.

Told to approach more slowly I came in slow and low, floated over the squadron office (a hut at the airfield's edge), almost singeing the wings of another Strutter parked in front and made a very good landing just beyond. I taxied in with some pride, but Major W. R. Read, MC, the CO, aroused by the sound of my low passage over his roof, was ready to greet me.

'It's bad enough to risk your own machine coming in like that, Macmillan, but it's too much when you endanger other machines standing on the aerodrome as well,' he said.

And for what I proudly thought was a very skilful piece of flying he very nearly sent me back to England for further training. I think McArthur pleaded for me and I remained with 45; but some new pilots of that period were sent back, or transferred to squadrons in France having BE aeroplanes that were easier to fly, but hopelessly inferior as warplanes.

Some practice flying had to take place late in the day, after the main work of the squadron was done, or because of weather. Then the fitter and rigger involved had aerodrome duty when others might be enjoying a spell off. About 40 years later, at a squadron reunion, my former fitter told me that one evening when they had to turn out specially for me I said to them I was very sorry they had had to do so. I had forgotten the incident, but he told me he had never forgotten this because they were not used to being spoken to and treated in that way, and when they were, duration-only types remembered. Since WW1, nothing I have ever heard from any of my then associates has given me more pleasure than Mr Tetlow's words.

Our squadron commander, one or two officers, and a few of the most senior non-commissioned officers were the only pre-war regular soldiers in the squadron. Crime was almost unknown. A general court martial reduced one corporal to second-class air mechanic for being drunk in an estaminet and hitting a young woman over the head with a bottle; but by climbing up to sergeant before the end of the war he proved the truth of the adage that 'you can't keep a good man down'.

Yet 45 did not seem a happy squadron when I joined it. If he flew with his crews a squadron commander became one of them. But at that period RFC HQ prohibited squadron commanders from flying over and beyond the lines. This rule was made during a period of swift expansion, to prevent loss of officers with adequate experience to command squadrons, a type then in short supply. Read did not like this prohibition. Superimposed on his natural tendency to reticence, it kept him even more aloof from his pilots and observers. We did not then know that he was living under great stress from having had to serve for six months under a succession of senior officers possessing temperaments incompatible with his. Continued irritating petty interferences from above and inhibited participation in combatant duties made him unhappy, and possibly this could be sensed by others.

At that time the RFC was fighting a difficult battle with the German Air Service for mastery in the air. The Germans were newly armed with the latest Albatros Scout, a redoubtable fighter which was exacting a heavy toll from our reconnaissance and artillery aeroplanes in the course of their constant work behind the German lines. RFC HQ policy was to keep up a continuous offensive and this must be said of the British war flyers: That whatever the quality of the aeroplanes on which they were mounted they always carried out their orders and in doing so they pushed even their most obsolete aircraft far across the German lines. Losses were often heavy; sometimes a squadron lost a number of pilots and observers equal to the strength of the whole squadron in killed, wounded, and that too often dreaded classification, missing, in less than a month. The infantryman may reply that whole battalions were sometimes almost wiped out in a few minutes. True! and Flying Fellows would be the very last to disallow the PBI in France the honour of having fought the muddiest, most intolerable job in the whole war, the most continuously uncomfortable and dangerous of all the war's worst jobs. Trench warfare, however, was not all attack and counter-attack, for there were periods of comparative quiet, and there were withdrawals for rest in billets behind the lines; but every time the RFC rode out to war in their frail chariots of the sky they flew east across the lines and over enemy territory. Theirs was a continuous offensive. Thus it came about that German airmen mostly fought and fell over their own captured ground and their fate was known at once. But when downed in aerial combat, our men were accounted missing and the wounded and unhurt became prisoners. Out of the 80 aircraft claimed to have been shot down by Manfred von Richthofen, by that tally the greatest German air fighter of WW1, 62 fell behind the German lines and eight between the front-line trenches. Some writers appear to believe that this defensive fighting by the German Air Service was a clever strategy devised by themselves. In fact, it was forced upon them, by first, the policy of RFC HQ, for it was Trenchard's dictum that the practitioner of the offensive imbues within himself a feeling of superiority; and, secondly, by the spirit of the British aircrews who carried out that policy.

Albatros Scouts increased on the Ypres front as German Jagdstaffeln moved up from the Somme. The persistent air fighting there reached a greater pitch of efficiency. Casualties on both sides rose in numbers and frequency. The character of 45 Squadron changed with these unavoidable changes in its personnel, to me at first almost imperceptibly, because I was a stranger myself, then more obviously, and sometimes with heart-breaking abruptness.

Our patrols were divided into offensive, defensive, and line patrols. Offensive patrols usually operated at ten to twelve miles beyond the German trenches; defensive patrols flew about four miles beyond them; line patrols flew above the lines. The north and south limits of their beat and the heights at which they were to be flown were stated in orders. Patrols from the different squadrons of the Army Wing overlapped, so that the front and the aircraft of the 2nd (Corps) Wing were always protected from dawn until dusk. The Corps Wing was responsible for artillery co-operation and infantry contact.

Artillery observation was carried out from about 3,000 feet under the indirect protection of the fighting patrols. Only when the gunners required observation to be carried out many miles behind the German trench-line were the BEs and REs escorted by fighters detailed for the purpose. Ordinarily the artobs aircraft flew round and round in wide circles between our guns and their objectives, which usually lay not more than four or five miles behind the Front line, giving the signal to fire and wirelessing the registration of the shot by clock code. These machines worked singly, the pilot flying his machine, watching the shots and bursts, and tapping out on his wireless key codewords that trembled into the ether from the copper-wire aerial outwound below the fuselage to be picked up at the wireless post beside the guns and translated into alterations of angles in the sights before the next shot spewed from the gun muzzle in search of the object foredoomed to destruction; and all the time the gunner observer searched the dome of sky above, ready for marauding enemy aircraft which, eluding our patrols of fighters, loved nothing better than a headlong dive upon a lone artillery spotter.

From above I have watched the artobs aircraft wheel in circles, like gulls above the Cornish cliffs, and always sensed within me a feeling of thankfulness that fate had spared me their onerous and often thankless duty. Doubtless there was excitement in directing unseeing eyes that looked along the gun-sights, in watching the shell-bursts creep nearer to the target; doubtless there was a tremendous thrill in the final crash and, when the smoke cleared, in the uncovering of the successful accomplishment of the intended destruction (for is there not an inbuilt love of destruction in the heart of man?); yet, after all, the part played was negative; artobs men were pawns on the chessboard of artillery science, not the kings or queens of the air game.

For us there were many minor incidents; rents and rips in fabric and timber; shell- and bullet-holed tanks that let the air pressure escape so that it could no longer force the fuel to the engine, making us return to our own side of the lines as best we could on our emergency gravity tank; of these and many other details one could write, but the major tale must carry on and the lesser things give way before it. Sometimes we had propaganda papers to drop overboard and occasionally we encountered a solitary Hun. These were odd jobs of work, not the big scraps in which our formations fought out long odds against bigger enemy formations. They were quiet times and there were minutes among them filled with beauty. Let me attempt to convey a composite picture of such a flight, not detailing any one in particular, but rather, by encompassing many, taking, for the nonce, the novelist's cloak upon my shoulders.

Overhead the sun shone in a cloudless sky. Its heat parched the wheat in the fields; the scarlet poppies drooped their heads, despairing of life-giving moisture. The sun's rays sparkled from the white chalk ridges that scarred the cornfields like rolling waves breaking into foam upon a sandy shore. No sound disturbed the quiet of the afternoon. All nature was somnolent under the welter of the insufferable heat. The air danced and shimmered over the beautiful white ridges.

But for the stagnant whisper of decay it was a pretty picture. No human was visible in the landscape. But behind and below the sparkling ridges was a subterranean city housing the troglodytes of war. Above them was a country of the dead. Theirs was a tortuous township of the quick. The beauty of the ridges hid the ugliness of war, but the scarlet of the poppies sensed the trailing smear of blood. Small wonder that the poppy came to be the emblem of the British Legion.

Into the sullen silence came a distant droning sound. It came from the blue of the heavens. Its vibrations danced with the shimmering air. There was a compelling fascination in that low-toned drone. From the trenches a hundred thousand men gazed heavenward. Up yonder, silhouetted against the blue of the sky, they saw the aeroplane flying eastward, its white wings, that might have been fashioned of silver gauze, glinting and flashing in the sunlight; it seemed evanescent, ethereal, utterly removed from the sordidness of trench warfare.

Suddenly, from beyond the opposite rise, came a short, loud-mouthed bang. It was followed by others, ever faster in succession, and more insistent. Little dark clouds opened out beside the white-winged wonder in the heavens, some near, some far off. But the shimmering aeroplane continued to pursue its unwavering purpose amid the growing puffs that told their tale of hate and death.

Yonder, said the Men of the Underworld, was Romance, the Glory of War. Yonder was Life, *joie de vivre!* Here, in the trenches, were but Stagnation and Death.

The shining aeroplane flew onward to its accompaniment of the droning engine. The cloud puffs, thinning by expansion, all but disappeared in the blue of the heavens. Swish! patter, patter! The lead and iron that had risen towards the shining wonder overhead fell back with hissing menace among the beings of war's underworld, the Children of the Trenches, with whom dwelt the fallen twin stars of Stagnation and Death. When the entrenched ones gazed at the fleeting vision overhead, they knew nothing of whence it came, of the purpose for which it ignored the hatred of those vengeful, artificial clouds, or of the men who flew with it and gave it life.

They could not picture the aeroplane standing on the edge of the airfield, a thing of beauty, with a bevy of beauticians fluttering round it; riggers vetting the wings with practised eyes, fitters testing the valve clearances with the meticulous care of the mechanical lover, an armourer fitting the observer's Lewis gun on its mounting and placing the drums of ammunition in their boxes.

The pilot and observer walked down the cinder track to the airfield. The pilot glanced at his wrist-watch and spoke to his companion, for service aeroplanes flew to scheduled time. They buttoned their leather coats, strapped their fur-lined flying caps tight under their chins and pulled on great gloves. Their feet and legs were encased in monstrous, sheepskin thigh-boots. Their appearance was grotesque. They looked like the bloated shadows of men that a candle sometimes throws upon a wall. Yet no one appeared to notice these things; they were far too commonplace to arouse any interest and were taken for granted.

The two men climbed into the cockpits, the pilot in front and the observer behind. The latter tested his gun-mounting for freedom of rotation, then glanced around his cockpit to see that everything was stowed with each item in its proper place: Very pistol and flares, ammunition drums, revolver; maps he carried he stowed in their canvas bag. The pilot loaded his Vickers gun, wriggled himself comfortably down into his wicker seat. He tested the air controls and looked quickly over his instruments. Then he glanced up.

A watchful ack emma, awaiting this moment, called out: 'Switch off, petrol on, suck in, sir!'

From the pilot's cockpit came the soughing sound of an air pump, the clicking of levers, then the gruff reply: 'Suck in!'

The mechanic swung the propeller round while excess petrol dribbled out on to the ground from a pipe beneath the engine. He stopped swinging and wiped his oily hands upon his overalls, then scraped his boots on the ground to make sure of his foothold, preparing for his next movements as does the bowler on a cricket field. Striking a somewhat graceful attitude, with his legs and body inclining forward, his arms upraised, his hands resting on the propeller's horizontal blade with their fingers curling over its sharp trailing edge, he tried his balance before calling out: 'Contact, sir!'

During a moment of silence one heard the upward clicking of the main and starter magneto switches.

'Contact !' confirmed the pilot.

The ack emma balanced on one foot, held his other leg wide and swung lustily on to its foot, thus adding his weight to aid his arms in pulling the propeller round, while the pilot twirled the starter magneto's handle. Perhaps the engine fired first pull. If not, the ack emma called: 'Switch off, sir!' then, after receiving the assurance that the magnetos were switched off, he turned the propeller one way and the other, until he felt that he had given the engine's cylinders a better mixture. Then he repeated the original ritual until the engine tremored into life.

For a full minute the pilot ran the engine steadily, with his head inside the cockpit watching the engine revolution indicator and the pulsator glass within which the oil beats of the lubrication pump were visible, the fuel-tank air-pressure dial, listening the while to the rhythm of sound and sensing that of vibration. Satisfied, he moved a lever and turned a tap. The engine roared and the aeroplane quivered with pride of power. But the wooden chocks, one at the front of each wheel, the ack emma at each wing-tip, and the grim-faced individual who laid his torso crosswise over the tail end of the fuselage in the full blast of the slipstream to keep the tail down and so prevent the nose from tipping to save the propeller from breaking by striking the ground, all together checked its impetuous desire for movement.

The roar changed to a gentle hum as the pilot throttled down. A hand waved from side to side above his head gave the mechanics the all-clear signal. The long-suffering one at the tail end crawled from inside the elevator control cables and went off to retrieve his forage cap from the cornfield. The others removed the chocks by a jerk on the rope that wrapped round the front of each to its inner end where it was rove through a hole and knotted within. The pilot fastened his wide single belt, adjusted his goggles comfortably over his eyes.

The hum of the engine rose again as the pilot taxied the aeroplane out. From the rear, as she rolled and swayed over the uneven ground, the 1½-Strutter looked like a huge butterfly. She turned to face the wind. The sound of her engine came across the airfield full-throated. Unchecked, she gathered speed, her tail rose slightly ... more... she rushed along the ground... and rose into the air, her natural element. For a moment she flew close to earth; then, as if growing in confidence, soared upward and onward, climbing as fast as she could. The ack emmas gazed after her fondly. It was their care, their expressions seemed to say, that enabled her to do it.

The pilot circled the airfield twice, the drone of his engine becoming fainter as he gained height. A last sweep round, then he was off, heading east towards the lines.

On the ground the heat was suffocating. The pilot and observer had left the ground with their pores running sweat under their heavy flying kit. But up at 8,000 feet it was cold. Whenever the pilot glanced out from behind the shelter of his cunning little windshield between the traversing arms of the machine-gun, the blast of cold air met his face and penetrated the leather and fur that appeared so invulnerable on the ground. The observer, poor devil, was always in the terrific hurricane that hurtled backward from the propeller. It was his birthright. He had no place for a windscreen, and no time to shelter behind one had he had it. Once across the line, he had to keep a constant look-out for Huns, be ready to use his gun at a second's notice, watch where they were going and expose the photographic plates when they reached the pin-points.

Below them the country was spread out like a map. But there was one small difference. It appeared saucer-shaped. The rim of the horizon rose to meet the sky, and where they met there was a light haze. Overhead the sky was very blue. Occasionally a light, trailing wisp of vapour drifted past, the kind seen from the ground as a fleecy cloudlet, but from the aeroplane scarcely obscuring their downward vision. As it passed about them the aeroplane lifted quickly, and as suddenly fell again. A cloud 'bump' is a peculiar phenomenon, usually accompanied by changes of temperature which alter the air flow about the cloud.

Straight down, the country was beautifully clear; roads, canals, rivers, lakes, and forests stood out distinctly. In between and all around there were little towns and villages that appeared absurdly close together. To the left, fringed by a sparkle of sandy foreshore, the sea hung dull and leaden, apparently slanting upward towards the distant sky. England lay over there, somewhere, hidden in the haze of heat. Almost underneath was a perfect picture, the tiny, circular Flemish town of Bergues; splendidly laid out in clearly defined lines, it looked clean and healthy; and around it, completely encircling it as if in loving embrace, ran a river and a canal and moats. Beauty was in its artistry of outline and its harmony of colour, the silver cincture of the enfolding water separating the blue-grey of the ancient buildings from the greens and browns of the surrounding country. It was like a jewel of great price.

But, ahead, a great smear, like the trailing slime of a giant slug, lay across the land. Dirty brown it looked; not the healthy brown of a pleasant land, but the brown mortification of disease, the blight of death. It was the living weal of war. And even from the air, where earthly tragedy seems so remote, where sordidness is oft-times witched to charming beauty and ugliness hid beneath a veil of smoke, it looked what it was, an open sore.

Towards it the Sopwith floated, rising and falling slowly, rhythmically, to the song of the engine and the accompaniment of the air currents. For an aeroplane when seen from another in the air behaves quite unlike itself as it appears to an observer from the ground. In the air it has a motion like that of a small yacht riding at anchor in an oily swell. From the ground an aeroplane in flight may appear to be a thing of beauty and of wonder. It is thrice so when seen from the air.

The pilot glanced at his altimeter. The pointer read 10,000 feet. His watchful glance took in the meaning of his many indicators; his ear read the music that his engine sang. All had to be well, for they were about to cross the lines; on the farther side a faulty engine might force them to land on enemy territory, unwilling prisoners of war, powerless to evade the almost certain possibility of capture.

The dirty brown smear appeared scarcely behind them, but things seemed to move so slowly from that height that it might have been three or four miles back.

'Woof! ... Woof! Woof! Woof!'

The sound of the bursting Archie shells reached them through the song of the engine; but the pilot kept almost straight on, for Archie was wide of his mark. Again and again the same sound came to their ears, like the unhealthy cough of a missing engine. The pilot smiled quietly to himself.

'Crack-rack-rack-r-r-rack!'

The pilot moved his controls rapidly. The Sopwith heeled up and swerved. Up! Steady, then a swoop to the other side. The pilot's face was fierce below its mask.

'Archie was bloody good that time,' he muttered to himself. He had smelt the reek of the smoke-fumes in his nostrils, heard the whine of metal hissing through the air. He saw a rent in his wings.

Again it came, the hideous, horrible, sudden 'Crack!' that Archie mouthed when he burst close. The wuff of it forced the tail up, the nose went down, and at the same instant the Sopwith swerved and side-slipped. Archie had their height. They could not climb fast enough to change height quickly, so they had to go lower. Down they dived.

'9,000 feet!' warned the altimeter.

The pilot levelled out again. He glanced hurriedly down to earth. There was the place to be photographed. Good! Shells burst high overhead as he flew steadily along above the line they had to take. He lifted the mouthpiece and called down the speaking-tube to the observer: 'How are the photos?'

'Got six still to go,' came the muffled answer in his ear.

He turned the Sopwith in a quiet circle over the remaining places they were required to photograph. Archie had stopped. The pilot looked around him, scanning the sky suspiciously to find the reason. He could see nothing. Then he heard the muffled whisper in his ear again: 'Finished. Turn for home.'

As he banked up on the turn he saw ahead, and just below, the cause of Archie's cessation, an enemy scout coming up under their tail. He had been climbing up, sitting on his tail, in such a position that the observer, intent on his pin-points, could not see him, and also in the blind spot of the pilot. He had very nearly had them sitting, for in another few seconds he would have been close enough to open fire on them unseen. The pilot took it all in instantly, automatically. He stuck the Sopwith's nose down in a dive and simultaneously shouted down the mouthpiece to the observer: 'Hun below!'

With engine off he was diving fast; and as the Hun came into his sights he pressed the gun trigger. The Hun swerved in a graceful Immelmann turn as the bullets went cracking past his ears with the sound as of whips. But the observer was ready for just such a chance. As the Hun turned over, the sharp staccato of the Lewis broke out above the now opened up engine's roar. He could not miss; the range was too close. The tracers flew straight into the Hun's guts. The Hun slipped, dived; then went spinning down in that terrifying, twisting dive. Splinters flew out from his machine. Faster and faster he fell. The observer, still holding on to his silent gun, watched the enemy aeroplane go down, saw a wing fold back that seemed to check its fall. Then it spun round slowly, drifting down like a handful of crumpled paper.

The observer looked around and scanned the sky. There was nothing above. He looked below. For a few seconds he saw nothing. Then he spotted three machines coming up fast. He grabbed the mouthpiece: 'Put your nose down and go like stink. Three Huns coming up.'

The pilot pushed the tailplane incidence wheel forward. The engine roared. The air-speed indicator moved round the dial, 90, 100, 110 miles an hour. He glanced at the altimeter: 7,000 feet. The air-speed indicator read low at that height. He could go no faster without losing too much height.

'Woof-oof-oof-woof!'

The line Archie. There were the trenches. He put his nose down a little steeper now: 115, 120 indicated. He was going too fast for Archie. Archie could never touch him at that pace. The Huns had dropped out of the chase. The photographs were safe. The 'woofs' of the Archie shells became fainter, and died away.

The muffled whisper sounded in his ear again: 'It's all right now, you can flatten out.'

The pilot cut off the supply of fuel to the engine and slowly wound the tail wheel back. The rush of air diminished and the Sopwith glided sedately west towards the airfield at a steady 60 miles an hour.

Late in February 1917 holes were cut in the floors of our observers' cockpits to accept vertical cameras for photographic reconnaissance. Thereafter our longer reconnaissances took us far beyond all fighter patrols. Sometimes our formations met with no resistance, as on 24 March 1917, which was a perfect flying day. Despite (or perhaps because of) a strong east wind that morning, six 1½-Strutters completed a peaceful long reconnaissance over Dixmude-Thourout-Bruges-Ghent-Oudenarde-Roulers. The air-crews saw no Huns in the air and were shelled only over Bruges and, especially, Ghent. Read was pleased with the excellent results gained under McArthur's leadership, whose observer, Senior, took 23 good photographs. Truscott, flying with Newling, made the visual reconnaissance.

Yet these photo-reconnaissances brought many of our casualties. Because our 1½-Strutters had been designated as two-seater fighters and were now designated fighter-reconnaissance aircraft, the staff thought it unnecessary to give us an escort of scouts, in spite of the very low horsepower of our engines, with consequent slow speed and climb. In any event, none of the available scouts could have accompanied us all the way, for the 1½-Strutter's duration of over four hours much exceeded theirs (thus adumbrating the same problem in WW2). We had to have clear skies to take effective photographs and our slow speed in formation made it necessary to fly straight towards our objectives, with our formation tight packed for defence. The Huns often allowed us to go east with no attention save from their AA batteries, but when our work was done, evidenced by our turning westward at our most easterly point, enemy scouts came down upon us out of the sun, in numbers exceeding ours. Losses split up our formations fighting every mile of the way westward towards our lines, carrying information of value to the staff (how great its value really was we never knew) in exposed but undeveloped plates and observers' and pilots' notebooks.

During some of our flights across the lines to photograph and make notes of enemy activities the little single-seater Nieuport Scouts of No. 1 RFC Squadron came voluntarily to our assistance. Down they came on top of the Huns who dogged our track, their single Lewis guns spitting fire and bullets, their young pilots turning and swerving their handy little mounts in smaller circles than the bigger Albatros Scouts, making up in manoeuvrability for some of their inferiority in horse and gun power. More than once they saved us from heavy losses, sometimes at the expense of gaps in their own ranks, but never when they were about did the Nieups of No. 1 RFC fail us.

Our 1½-Strutters always took off singly and manoeuvred into formation at about 1,000 feet above the airfield in clear weather. For this reason, formations could never start before full daylight. Then they usually met opposition. But it was thought (by whom no one now knows) that a lone 1½-Strutter leaving just before dawn might often complete a long reconnaissance without attracting enemy interceptors, and on 29 March 1917 it was decided that a single machine should be sent off early to go it alone whenever weather permitted. Bad weather at last dark prevented any such attempt being made until 4.30 a.m. on 6 April, when Mountford, commanding 'A' Flight, with his observer, Vessey, took off by the aid of flares – tins containing burning rags and paraffin – to reconnoitre Lille, Roubaix and Tournai. Ten minutes later he landed alongside the flares. When his oil trouble (pure castor oil coagulates in cold weather) was corrected, it was too late to restart.

Read organised a formation to go later and nine 1½-Strutters left at 9.5 a.m., under McArthur, two with cameras, six as escort machines. Blake, with Brayshay as observer, flew in reserve for anyone who might have to fall out before crossing the lines. If none did, he would return. But Garratt with Carey went down to No. 8 Naval Squadron at Auchel airfield with a blocked fuel pipe. Blake took his place. Soon after crossing the lines a near miss from an AA shell blew a blade off Findlay's propeller. Despite vibration that almost tore out his engine from its mounting, he reached our side, but turned turtle when forced landing and wrote off his aircraft, without hurting himself or his observer, Moore.

An unidentified type of enemy two-seater closed on the right of the formation of seven 1½-Strutters. Its observer fired broadside at them, without effect. It then drew quickly ahead, climbing easily round the front of the formation. Our pilots opened fire as it crossed their front, but equally without result because the range and elevation were both too great. During the reconnaissance this was the one chance our pilots had to bring their front guns to bear; afterward the enemy pilots flew too high and dived only from behind the formation.

Like a trailing shark, the strange two-seater followed the 1½-Strutters, taking station high up behind them and out of range of their Lewis guns. Three Halberstadt Scouts joined the two-seater. Two Albatros Scouts saw the 1½-Strutter formation from below and climbed rapidly to join their compatriots. All six then attacked from the rear. But the 1½-Strutter pilots kept excellent formation and their observers opened accurate fire. No enemy pilot used his superior speed, climb and manoeuvre to press his attacks home. All veered away before reaching 100 yards from the sting in the Sopwiths' tails.

When nearing Tournai at least six more scouts, fast and of an unknown type (they were the new V-strut D.IIIs of Jasta 30), climbed up singly, until the odds against the Sopwiths were at least 12 to 7. The main attack began as the Sopwiths turned on to their homeward course at Tournai. Bethge swiftly shot down 7806 flown by Blake, 24, from Darlington; he and Brayshay (his observer, from Birmingham, who would have been 30 in three more weeks) were killed. The Sopwith formation, still unbroken, was weaving, diving and zooming to avoid attacks and return the fire. Two collided, whether by accident, or because one was hit by enemy fire and fell on the other, may perhaps never be certainly known. The wreckage of A1093 and A2381 fell, ripped fabric and splintered wood, amid which four men died either before or when they hit the ground: 19-year-old Marshall from Huntingdon and his observer, Truscott, 22, son of a former Lord Mayor of London; 34-year-old Campbell from Toronto and Edwards, 26, from London.

Cock and his observer, Murison, said they saw the two colliding aircraft being attacked from below by a scout that climb-turned to avoid the falling wreckage, at which moment Murison fired 50 rounds into it at 30-yards range. He said it broke in pieces and fell on top of the wreckage of the Sopwiths. Air gunner 2/AM Perrott, flying with Newling, claimed he shot a second enemy scout down out of control from 50-yard range, but did not see it crash.

After a 45-minute route battle against enemy aircraft reported to be 'vastly superior in speed and climb' four of the 1½-Strutters (including the two carrying cameras) returned to St Marie Cappel airfield with 11 good photographs of their objectives. Read thought his crews had put up a splendid fight to gain these pictures and bring them back. No doubt the reconnaissance was a success in the eyes of the staff also, but there is no record of any appreciation from either the wing or brigade commanders. Those then in the squadron had an impression of frigidity in the downward relationship from brigade to squadron level.

RFC staff officers of WW1, who themselves ran no risks in the static conditions of the Western Front and who lived in relative luxury, too readily regarded their fighting men as disposable digits. Could a basic reason for prohibiting squadron commanders from undertaking offensive flying have been that this provided front-line cover for the unrisking rear echelon staff to shelter behind? Otherwise, why make disposability cease with field rank?

Read was always solicitous for the welfare of those who served under him. Some of the senior RFC officers appear to have misinterpreted this into a belief that Read could not regard casualties with an equanimity equal to theirs. Read knew as well as anyone that war cannot be fought without casualties, but what he appreciated better than many was that the efficiency of a victorious war can be measured by the formula : Number of casualties x Duration of the war. The economist might add another factor: x Total monetary cost.

The blood price paid for that reconnaissance was high. But, in WW1, reckoning at RFC HQ was by the relative volumes of work done by the RFC and the GAS, not by percentages of air-crews (or aircraft) lost. That being so, RFC pilots reasonably could look to be provided with aircraft at least equal in performance to those used by the enemy; but often they were not. No matter, complaints were not allowed from fighting men; they were the prerogative of the staff.

Senior officers never approve of the 'man who talks'. It is their prescribed duty to reprimand him. But had Webb-Bowen been more like Trenchard, warm-blooded and appreciative, he could have eased the mental stress of some of the flyers serving under him who, in the vacuum of his silence, found it hard to suppress their feelings. One, anguished after return from that reconnaissance by thought of the men who had been lost because of enemy technical superiority, spoke in the hearing of the general and said: 'Some people say that Sopwith Two-Seaters are bloody fine machines, but I think they're more bloody that fine!' and his words brought about his transfer to Home Establishment with loss of acting rank.

Leutnant Joachim von Bertrab of Jasta 30 claimed four Sopwiths on 6 April 1917. Faulty aircraft identification was common to both sides and the serial number of one of his claimed Sopwiths was that of an RE8. But Pecq, between Tournai and Roubaix, where two of his claimed Sopwiths fell, coincided with the position over which the two 1½-Strutters of 45 Squadron collided, so it must be assumed that he claimed he shot down both. His third Sopwith on that day appears to have been 7665, of 70 Squadron, which fell at Ath, in Belgium. The official German victory list gives him a total of five, which makes his four in one day the more remarkable.

But retribution was to come. On 12 August 1917 von Bertrab, flying an all-black Albatros DV with a 220 horsepower Mercedes engine, two guns and 1,000 rounds of ammunition, tried, unsuccessfully, to shoot down one of our observation balloons. Mick Mannock, in a one-gun Nieuport scout of 40 Squadron, cut off his retreat at 2,000 feet, wounded him in both arms and one leg and forced him down at Neuville St Vaast, where his Albatros turned turtle when landing and he was taken prisoner of war. After treatment for his wounds he was transferred to Taunton, in Somerset. At least he survived, with an Iron Cross to show for his services to his Kaiser and Fatherland. But Hans Bethge, a regular officer who rose to command Jasta 30 with the rank of oberleutnant, and having a score of victories to his credit, was shot down and died of wounds on 17 March 1918, on the very day, had he lived, that he would have received the *Orden Pour le mérite*.

Strikes in factories at home cut short the supply of 1½-Strutters and it became impossible to maintain the full strength of the three RFC squadrons using them in France. 45 Squadron was notified that for a time its 1½-Strutter strength would be cut to 12, but it would receive six Nieuport two-seaters to keep its aircraft total at 18.

The 1½-Strutter was already obsolescent, but the Nieuport was obsolete. 46 Squadron, a 2nd (Corps) Wing unit in the same brigade, had been withdrawn from artillery operations with Nieuport two-seaters and was currently re-equipping at Boisdinghem to become an (Army) scout squadron flying single-seater Sopwith Pups.

The Nieuport had two close-coupled cockpits, its 110 horsepower Le Rhône rotary engine was superior to the Clergêt, and it had a strong steel undercarriage. These were its only good points. Cockpit view was bad, its controls were heavy as lead, its performance dud. I measured a top speed of 80 miles an hour at the full 1,225 rpm. Ceiling with war load was only 8,000 feet. The fixed tailplane was not adjustable; fore and aft trim was supposed to be obtained by altering the incidence of the small lower wings about the base of their interplane V-strut. These wings were behind the centre of gravity, but even at their maximum incidence I found the two Nieuports I flew were always tail-heavy when carrying an observer with gun and ammunition.

It was impossible for Nieuports to do the work of 1½-Strutters. Read posted two Nieuports to each flight and restricted their use to line patrols.

I learned to spin on the defective Nieuports by accident.

One day when the sky was full of heavy clouds, McArthur and I went off on two Nieuports to make a north line patrol. He led the way upward through a narrow gap. Following him, but to one side, I flew into cloud. Tail heaviness increased, the air-speed indicator needle swung back, speed swiftly rose and I fell, completely out of control, earthward, through the cloud. When I came out of the cloud and by the earth's horizon below me saw I was spinning I moved the controls and came out into the resulting dive. Three times I tried to follow McArthur through those clouds, but every time my badly rigged Nieuport stalled, spun and redelivered me into the clear air below the bottom of the cloudbank.

McArthur came back to see what had happened to me and found much amusement in my continued efforts to follow him upward. When he realised I could not climb through the clouds without spinning he signalled to me by hand to follow him at a lower level and we carried out the patrol below the clouds. From then on spinning meant nothing to me.

We flew Nieuports on line patrols for about three weeks. They were useless for any other duty. One damaged in landing was replaced by another that was wrecked and written off. When the remaining five were flown back to the Aircraft Depot and exchanged for 1½-Strutters no one shed tears over them.

Chapter IV

LIMIT OF VISION

No. 45 Squadron received orders to prepare another squadron site at St Marie Cappel airfield. A position diagonally opposite was inspected and approved. Four Bessoneaux wood-frame, canvas-covered hangars were delivered and erected, squadron headquarters and photographic huts built, hardstands for workshop lorries and transport made with pit-props. Each operational flight's mess was in a marquee; the squadron headquarters flight mess had to make shift with an army bell tent. When all was ready, 45 Squadron was told to move over, and 20 Squadron, being senior to 45, was given our former quarters. Its transport drove in the day after we moved and a day later, on 16 April 1917, its FE2d pushers landed from Boisdinghem.

We were not overjoyed at being turned out of warm huts and sheds in mid-April of a cold spring to work, live and sleep under canvas, without even floorboards to cover the sodden grass that soon became mud under our trampling feet. If 20 Squadron had not proved to be the magnificent squadron it was on its pusher biplanes and, in the autumn, on Bristol Fighters, we should never have forgiven them. As it was, our chagrin was short-lived, and soon we were proud to share the airfield and co-operate with 20 across the lines when our patrols met, or worked together, as they sometimes did.

The tension under which Major Read had worked and lived during the six months since he had brought the squadron to France dug deeper roots into his psychology when he found that his seniors' attitudes remained inimical, whatever he did. On his own initiative he decided to leave the RFC and return to the Dragoon Guards to gain the cavalry experience in war which so far he had not had. On 24 April he departed to rejoin the cavalry, and Major H. A. Van Ryneveld, MC, and Order of the Nile, who had put up an excellent show when flying in Palestine, became CO. During the few days of change-over we had seen the two majors walking together from headquarters office to workshops, flight hangars, transport, and headquarters mess, engaged in earnest conversation, Read short and wiry, Van Ryneveld tall, loose-limbed, sallow-complexioned.

After he took over, our new CO called a meeting of pilots and observers in the pilots' room on the edge of the airfield. It was the month we who were the RFC called 'Bloody April'. At that juncture, casualties in the RFC in France were running at the rate of 600 per cent per annum. We knew they were heavy, but not how heavy; perhaps Van Ryneveld was aware of the rate; if he were, he gave no sign of it.

He sat on the edge of the table by the window. Before he spoke he looked round the room at the eyes intent upon his, at the countenances of men used to the chances of flight, to the crack and woof of Archie, to the crackle of machine-gun bullets about their ears. They stood close together in the small room, dressed in motley garb – regimental tunics, RFC maternity jackets, sweaters; silk scarves, woolly scarves; leather flying coats wound tight about them, buttoned up, or falling loose; sheepskin thigh-boots, knee-length flying boots of fleece-lined leather with suede tops, slacks and shoes, or breeches and puttees. Some had just returned from an early-morning flight; others were about to set out in the row of graceful Sopwiths lined up on the airfield outside; the remainder were detailed for afternoon patrols. The late April sun shone through a break in a cloudbank and flooded the end of the room with light.

Then, by means of model aeroplanes made out of bullets threaded on wires projecting from wooden stands, Van Ryneveld demonstrated on the table formations and changes in formations and fighting tactics, explaining verbally what he wanted us to understand.

He turned from his models to his audience.

'It's a "perfect case for Mrs Clark", he said in his soft Boer drawl, using a favourite quote of his. 'I would get you escorts if I could, but I can't, so we must do the best we can. There is no point in my following the footsteps of your previous commanding officer because that would do no good, and' – he smiled whimsically – 'you might then get someone who was worse even than I.'

He looked at every face.

'So, let's do our best, boys. I'll help you all I can in every way.'

Every patrol, every reconnaissance, would be personally supervised by the CO before it went off. He would show every pilot his place in the formation by means of the bullet aeroplanes before the start. This was something new. Under the regulations it was the nearest he could get to actual leadership.

He went on, 'I know the COs of the scout squadrons and, although I can't get you an escort, I'll ask them to tell their boys to keep a look-out for you whenever they've got a patrol detailed in orders to go across the lines at the time you go out.'

He made a good impression, but in reality there was little more he could do than Read had done. Scout squadrons usually flew to specified times and patrol beats; but we, frequently engaged on photography, often had to stand by for suitable weather, sometimes for hours, occasionally for days; then, when the chance offered we had to leap into our cockpits and start off towards the break in the weather. So co-ordination with scouts was difficult, a matter of chance under the prevailing system. I never experienced it while flying 1½-Strutters.

On one such occasion early in May each day dawned with a steady drizzle from low clouds that trailed their skirts along the tree-tops. Day after day we stood by. We wrote letters. In the evenings we played bridge, listened to the gramophone or occasionally held sing-songs in the flight messes. The floors of our tents became mud. Towards the end of the bad spell we tired of the monotony of it all and in the evenings ran down to St Omer in a tender for dinner. There were some jolly little parties, the hotel being a recognised meeting place for members of any of the squadrons within a reasonable distance. One met friends and exchanged greetings and received invitations to visit squadrons. On our return to St Marie Cappel about 11.30 p.m. we found a visitor awaiting us from 19 Squadron. The tender that had brought him had gone on to Bailleul to visit No. 1 Squadron and he had to await its return to pick him up before he could leave. He was an old infantry friend of mine and had been at the Lincoln College course with some of us.

We opened some bottles and our pianist sat down at the piano in the marquee. We had to put our guest to bed at one o'clock. His tender had not returned, and he had succumbed to too much port, having wrongly believed it to be a 'safe' drink. We ourselves retired soon after this. When his tender came we could not wake him. We carried him out to his tender and laid him on its floor on greatcoats and we heard later than he did not awaken on arrival at 19, but was carried to his bed there and slept it off.

I had little sleep. At 4.30 a.m. the batman came into my tent.

'Wake up, sir. It's a fine morning. I've brought you some cocoa.'

He lit the lamp and I tumbled out into the damp before dawn and pulled on flying kit over my pyjamas. The hot cocoa warmed me. I swallowed some biscuits and in the greying light of dawn walked down the muddy footpath from the paddock, where our tents were, to the airfield. Four

1½-Strutters were lined up with their mechanics standing by. The sun came up into a sky too pale in colour to promise a continuance of the complete absence of cloud.

We left the ground at 6.15 a.m. on an offensive patrol. My observer was not my usual flying comrade, but flew with me because his own pilot was on leave. He was still feeling the effects of the bottles he had helped to consume the night before, and was very morose. I wondered what he would be like if we met Huns. We climbed in formation to 10,000 feet. At 8,000 the cold sobered my observer completely and he began to talk to me through the speaking-tube. For nearly an hour he told me stories from his repertoire of humour, with his head buried within his cockpit to keep out of the air blast in which it was impossible to make oneself heard through the speaking-tube. Outside the cockpit the wind rush whipped one's words away instantly.

Great clouds formed rapidly below us, making it impossible for us to achieve our object. Our leader fired the white Very light signal for a washout and we returned downward and westward towards the airfield. At 6,000 feet my flying companion's voice ceased. I looked back, but could not see him. When we landed he had again become alcoholically quiet and was in a worse state than when we had left the ground. Yet all the time we were above 8,000 feet he had been most amazingly energised.

By this time I was thoroughly into the swing of squadron work. The Huns were very busy on our front. Work in the air and on the ground was becoming ever more intense as the wet of winter and early spring gave place to summer.

Our 110 hp Clergêt-engined 1½-Strutters' top speed in full war trim was 95 mph at 1,325 rpm at low heights. With these low compression engines our speed fell rapidly as we climbed and at 10,000 to 12,000 feet (our usual operating height) it dropped to about 80 mph. At the beginning of May 1917 Strutters fitted with 130 hp Clergêts began to arrive in France. The actual power increment was not as great as these power ratings indicate but it did give us a slight increase in all-round performance.

Our rotary engines were heavily worked. They developed many minor troubles during flights – broken valve springs, valve rockers, and ignition wires, the last often causing additional shorting as the engine revolved and the broken wires fouled others; defective oil pumps, defective air pressure to the fuel system, blued cylinders denoting worn or broken obturator rings; magneto defects and faulty sparking plugs; the shearing of studs.

Sometimes there were major troubles – broken pistons, a cylinder blowing off (and in its going damaging the aircraft), internal ball-races breaking. The engines required a great deal of attention to keep them going. Complete overhauls were frequent. Our mechanics worked splendidly to keep the aircraft in service, often working all night to change an engine or carry out some major airframe repair. All praise to them for the cheerful way they carried on with their tiring and uninspiring work, without thought of strikes and increased wages, and usually glad they were not in the trenches.

1½-Strutters were delightful aeroplanes to fly and beautiful to look at. On the ground, when taxiing out to take off, they looked like brown butterflies; in the air they were alive and full of grace, charming companions of the clouds.

Spring and early summer of 1917 were marked by much cloud. There is beauty in clouds. Artists have sought to catch their fleeting changes and they have often succeeded. Photographers, too, have essayed this difficult task, but most have failed because of deficiencies in perspective.

Those who possess a pleasurable sense in the prospect of the beautiful must have noted the magnificence of sunset cloud effects; become reminiscent, sometimes, over one in particular when the circumstances of the occasion mellowed the harder thoughts of life so that they viewed the glory of the west in the tranquillity of contentment. Each succeeding sunset upon which they gaze reminds them of the peace and wonder of that other and its companion thoughts.

There are other aspects of clouds seen from the ground; a blustering day in spring when the scud drives low above the trees and the rain stings in pitiless, whipping streams; dirty weather, a day for closed doors and a blazing fire.

To the early airman cloudland was a new world. To an imaginative few it became an enchanted land, the fairyland of childhood's daydreams come true.

To the fighting airman in France clouds meant much more than to any other. They meant the chance to stalk and trap, or the possibility of being taken by surprise. Their absence or presence spelt the call to flight or to stand by on the ground. To the two-seater, bent on work in the low levels of the sky, they sometimes meant life or death, the chance to escape, or fierce and sudden terror, for the man who says he has never been frightened in the air in war is either a liar or a moral coward.

To the airman who flies in time of peace, clouds rarely cause more

than discomfort, but very occasionally they may mean death, for there are
clouds that menace the airman with turbulence; in mountainous country
and in the tropics there is a spice of peril in their presence. But more often
they add much beauty to the empty sky.

I saw one cloudscape extending to the north-west like an ice-bound
sea, smooth, barren, unpeopled, dead. The lunar landscape can be no more
terrible to look upon. On its far edge a range of jagged mountains raised
peaks in silhouette against grey sky. Nearer, a cloud island, deep brown in
colour, was shaped like Ireland. As I watched, its colour changed to velvet
blue. Huge-based, pinnacled cloudbergs, which had broken from the
distant mountains, drifted past on either side of my Sopwith. I climbed to a
height level with the highest peak and the view towards the sun, previously
hidden, was as the glory of a garden on a misty summer morning. But
it was a garden that was upside down, like a reflection in a lake. Against
a background of sombre browns, colours as of brilliant flower beds were
laid out with a disregard of practised horticulture – pink, saffron, golden-
yellow, hyacinth, blue and green. Grey walls enclosed both sides and
screened all view of everything that lay beyond the garden.

In and over such cloudscapes our Sopwiths danced above the fighting
front, from the sea to La Bassée, over Lille, Tourcoing, Seclin, Roubaix,
Valenciennes, Tournai, Ghent, Bruges and Ostend, taking photographs,
making observations of enemy movements, fighting and patrolling the
undefined battlefront of the air. Under, through, among, and over the
clouds we flew; dodging, when we could, the shell-bursts from the AA
guns, avoiding fighting when our orders were to observe and photograph,
seeking combat and the driving eastward and earthward of enemy aircraft
when out on fighting and defensive patrols or as escort to reconnaissance
or artillery observation aircraft. Then there was romance among the clouds;
thrill and glamour in the swiftness of the aerial fight; freedom in the air
above the rack and torture of wire and sap and trench, gas and mortar and
barrage.

We had to train our eyes to serve our senses of smell and hearing, for
the continuous sound and smell of our own engine and its exhaust filled all
our immediate presence to the exclusion of more distant smells and sounds
– except when the dull woof of an Archie burst came near below us, or the
loud sharp detonation of a dangerously close one sent us rocking in the
swirling air, or the graver menace of an enemy's machine-gun bullets came
around us in a crackling stream of sound. When these things happened

we had to watch more closely still, to note the grouping of the AA bursts, or the position of the attacking aeroplane. But it was the pre-hearing vision that meant so much, for it was the keenness of eyesight in spotting the Hun afar off that enabled his eventual attack to be prepared for and met. The chief danger was to be surprised, to be shot down (perhaps out of the sun when its light blinded one's vision) before one realised that an attack was in being. Tail-swishing helped one to see better against the sun. Among the stratus and cumulus clouds we danced, our engines humming rhythmically, our aeroplanes rising and falling in the air waves as we flew along together in formation.

Cirrus mackerel sky was frequently above us. It gave the AA gunners excellent visibility and then our progression was through an expanding trail of brown-black shell-smoke, patent to everyone. On one occasion, I, at the rear of the formation, found myself so concentrated on by shell-fire that I was cut out from the formation. All the guns immediately sighted on my aircraft. As I flew after the formation I saw a convenient cloud. In ignorance I turned straight into it. It was full of moisture and opaque. I could see only a yard or two around me, but the AA gunners sighted on that cloud and filled it full of high explosive. Bereft of vision, but not of smell of the acrid fumes, I felt the Sopwith rock and heave amid the violent explosions, and I realised I was an aerial ostrich burying myself in a cloud. I opened the engine full out, eased the nose down slightly, and came out into the blessed sunshine.

There, half a mile away, were the Sopwiths of my flight formation, and I flew straight on at full speed to rejoin them. I looked back at the cloud and saw the last of the shells burst just on the edge of it. I would like to say that Archie blew that cloud clean out of existence, but that would be an exaggeration of fact, although not of feeling. This incident happened on one of my first trips over the lines and it taught me that a cloud may hide the aeroplane from Archie, but the cloud itself is an excellent target. I never repeated the mistake. (Today, with radar sighting, there are no clouds to hide in but the diabolical thunder-heads.)

During this period we were engaged on fighting patrol work. The patrol areas were laid down in orders and were defined as north or south offensive patrols, and north or south line patrols. The offensive patrols were always led by the flight commander or next senior pilot in the flight and were usually from three to six strong. The line patrols consisted of one or two machines and were frequently undertaken by fairly recently-joined pilots.

The line patrol was considered a soft job of work and a good way for new pilots to gain experience before they had to go farther across the lines.

My observer and I, flying on a north line patrol, saw a Hun flying alone and, making for him, I opened fire with my front gun. He turned eastward all out. German AA batteries opened fire on us and put up a barrage between us and their aircraft. We could not catch him and I circled to the north. It was a marvellously clear day. The visibility was perfect.

We were flying east of Ypres and the Archie shells that burst around were not uncomfortably near. Looking round the sky I could see no other aeroplanes to worry about and glanced downward to the ground. Straight below – although we were three miles east of the trench lines – lay the silver ruins of old Ypres, its stagnant moat and the stretching canals running ribbons across the country. Ahead was the coast of France and Belgium, with its yellow fringe of sandy foreshore. So close that it looked preposterous was Ostend, while farther inland lay Bruges. To the right front the yellow fringe ran north for miles to the islands off the Dutch and German coasts. To the left front was the real wonder.

There England lay, with that comforting shallow of green sea mirroring between. Her white cliffs stood out in prominence and the land swept away from the cliffs to the right and left. To the left, dimly seen, lay the Isle of Wight; to the right the land ran out in a curving sweep around the Forelands before nestling back into the Thames estuary, where it was lost in the haze which extended from Gravesend Londonwards. In the Channel a convoy of ships moved over the sea, a tiny, black destroyer foaming ahead of them in wide curves.

The crack of a shell close behind us made me turn quickly. To the south the fighting line lay smeared across the fair face of France like the trail of a giant snail. Near Soissons the smoke of a continuous barrage mingled with the dark haze which lay below the sun-line and obscured the view beyond. Continuing the turn in a circle I swept the sky. There was no enemy aircraft to be seen. I checked our height. We were at 10,000 feet. We must have viewed the geometrical limit of vision, the distance at which a straight line makes tangent with the round earth. It struck me as curious how the more distant places – the islands of Borkum, Merkel and Vlissingen, the Isle of Wight and the North Foreland – appeared tilted up at an angle, while the shipping in the Channel looked as though it was sailing in the sky. We felt as though we were flying in the centre of a huge balloon with the sky and sea and earth painted on the outside of its transparent but all-enclosing sphere.

The patrol time was over and we were free to return to the airfield. Yet we lingered a while, attracted by the splendour of the vision. Reluctantly I shut the engine off and glided slowly westward. Even Archie did not consider us worthy of further attention, or perhaps our solitary, silent glide escaped his notice. Apart from our idly turning propeller, the whole world appeared somnolent. Even Ypres was unshelled, its roofless walls standing like a host of ghostly cenotaphs in silent testimony to the inhumanity of war. Down, through thousands of feet, we glided towards the little airfield that lay just beyond the field of slowly ripening corn. Down to a second breakfast and a host of unbelievers who thought that we had dreamed, or that we romanced, about the length of visibility.

That same afternoon the visibility failed and clouds came up from the south. The weather turned bad, with heavy clouds and rain. We could do our work only by snatching whatever spells we got.

About this time a weekly illustrated magazine carried a page of photographs of British ladies. One was the teenage daughter of an Irish peer. Her studio portrait displayed the full face and shoulders of a serene, blue-eyed blonde. The tranquillity of her expression was such that she might have posed as a goddess of peace, an anodyne to all the blast and thunder of aerial war.

I cut out her picture and framed it behind a discarded piece of the transparent material that was used in the 1½-Strutter for an upper centre section window to give the pilot who sat beneath it some upward view. Thereafter, before flying on ops, I pinned the picture on a space upon my instrument panel. Many times, while Archie shells crumped around and enemy aircraft sparred for advantageous positions or departed to their airfields after engagements, the eyes of that ingenuous young face appeared to gaze serenely at me no matter what happened in the world outside the cockpit, and I derived an equal tranquillity through (I suppose) some inchoate, quasi-hypnotic response.

One day, when I forgot to remove the picture after landing, I lost it to some other admirer and never found it again. But I have never ceased to feel a sense of gratitude to the unknown young lady whose reproduction portrait flew with me so many times over the enemy-held lands and whose youthful features are still imprinted on my memory. She will never know the joy and solace her picture gave an unknown pilot, nor that she was to him a visual reason for the turmoil of our lives, that hers might remain peaceful. I hope it did.

One evening in a normal wind we started out six strong on a north offensive patrol. We crossed over Lille at 6,000 feet, flew through our usual greeting from Archie and passed over the chain of towns, Tourcoing, Seclin and Roubaix, climbing gradually to 11,000 feet. There was not a single enemy in the sky. Archie was erratic, at times very close, at others wide of our formation. After three hours and a half we returned to the airfield.

It was lined with figures awaiting our arrival, an unusual sight. One after another we glided down. At a thousand feet up we hit tremendous bumps that sent our Sopwiths up, only to let them drop again, sickeningly. The violence of the gusts was abnormal.

The first aircraft alighted and was immediately seized by mechanics. As I made my approach I realised that my speed over the ground was abnormally slow although I was maintaining a high air speed; and I was sinking rapidly to the rough ground outside the airfield. I opened the throttle nearly to full and the thrust from the propeller restored the gliding angle to normal. I was third to land and came in low over the edge of the airfield and flew on to the ground tail up, engine on. The Sopwith sat down without rolling forward. Mechanics rushed to hold her and just before they caught her I had to give her full throttle or she would have been blown backwards.

One by one the remainder of the formation landed. It was a memorable sight to watch each pilot come down in the normal way, then suddenly realise that air conditions were far from normal, and use engine and judgment to meet and counter them.

All six Sopwiths landed safely, almost unemotionally, in a 60 mph gale, a wind that blew in a steady sweep about one and a half times as fast as the landing speed of our aircraft. In spite of conditions which would have cancelled the patrol had they prevailed at the start, the spectators were disappointed in their expectation of thrills; which simply proves how some things can be performed with greater physical ease when the mental state is not obsessed by their evident difficulty. I am certain the patrol's return would not have been crashless had all the pilots been aware of the wind speed. The unusual conditions explained the clean-swept sky, the erratic shooting of Archie, and the absence of Huns during our patrol.

I had met Forrest at Upavon and when he joined 45 Squadron, two days after me, we shared the same hut and, now, on the other side of the airfield, the same bell-tent. On 7 May 1917 he was sent out on a single machine defensive patrol. After patrolling alternately north and south above the trench lines for 90 minutes he and his observer, Gunner Lambert, were both somewhat bored with inaction. They still had half an hour to stay on patrol.

Suddenly they spotted the white bursts of British AA shells. Forrest turned the old Sopwith, No. 1075, slowly, as was her nature, towards the white puffs. She climbed wearily upward. Near Dickebusch Lake he and Lambert spotted the enemy, two Huns approaching our lines, just above the shell-bursts.

The 1½-Strutter drew nearer. Her fixed front gun was useless. The enemy were too high. Her nose could not be pulled up to train the gun. Forrest flew under them to enable his gunner to open fire with the rear Lewis gun, which could be fired upward from its Scarff mounting. He trusted the AA gunners to stop firing when they saw his Sopwith close to attack.

But our Archie gunners may have considered themselves superior to 1½-Strutters in action against the enemy, for they did not withhold fire. Their shells burst below the Huns, right on the level of the 1½-Strutter. Unheeding, Forrest carried on with the job.

Lambert sighted on one of the Huns, flying about 200 feet above him on his left. As the first few rounds rattled out above his head from the upturned muzzle of the Lewis gun, Forrest held his Sopwith steady to enable Lambert to shoot straight. After six bursts of fire the Lewis jammed. Simultaneously Forrest felt the Sopwith shudder and almost at the same instant saw a shell burst white overhead. As Lambert began to clear the jam he felt the Sopwith wobble. He had just time to see the Hun fall out of control when his own machine turned over sideways and Forrest heard Lambert shout: 'God! Look at our tail!'

Forrest looked over his shoulder. The tailplane was crumpled like a half-closed concertina. The British AA shell had smashed it in its upward passage. The shell was time-fused, not percussion, or this story would never have been told. As the machine turned over, a second shell passed through its fuselage, half-way between Lambert's cockpit and the rudder. It carried away what remnant of control the first shell had left, and burst 200 feet above them.

Forrest pulled at his elevator controls but nothing happened. His rudder was jammed. Only the ailerons worked. The nose dropped. He could do nothing about it. The machine's speed increased. Forrest switched off his engine and closed the fuel cock. He could do no more. Lambert crouched in his cockpit. Shot down by their own artillery, they were falling earthward, unhurt, in a half-wrecked machine.

Gradually the Sopwith's attitude changed. The uncontrolled machine raised her nose higher and yet higher. The earth disappeared. She hung on her back, upside down. Without shoulder straps, the two men almost fell out. They held on for dear life. They shuddered at the thought of that 9,000-foot fall to earth.

The 1½-Strutter dropped her nose. The earth came into view again. She dived and levelled out. Neither of her occupants had ever looped before. This, their first loop, was an uncontrolled one. Forrest was impotent, a mere pawn in the game of destiny. His own and his observer-gunner's lives were cradled in the cockpit of chance.

No. 1075 looped again of her own accord. The two men clung on while her nose rose above the horizon and self-steered an erratic course across blue sky and white cloud in a dizzy circle.

They held on more grimly still, volitionless to help or hinder while she hung on her back, suspending them upside down 8,000 feet above the earth.

A bang behind sent a tremor down their spines. They thought the fuselage had broken and that next instant they would hurtle downward in the final plunge to earth. They had no thought of how a parachute each might have saved them, for RFC aircraft crews had never had parachutes and perhaps it is true that you never miss what you have never had.

But the fuselage had not failed. The bang they had heard came from Lambert's four unused 97-round drums of ammunition falling from their boxes. While the 1½-Strutter jerkily cleared the second loop these drums rolled down the fuselage and lodged at its tail end, where their weight partly balanced the aeroplane (because the tail of an aeroplane carries a down load in flight). This converted the aircraft's first wild plunging and looping into lesser oscillations of diving, zooming and stalling.

From 8,000 feet they began to fall in this softer repetitive sequence. Neither man could alter it. In such crises time is immeasurable. Forrest was uncertain how long the descent took. It may have lasted from eight to fifteen minutes. There was time to curse the Archie gunners who had not ceased fire. Lambert had come from the gunners to fly. His own brethren had done this to him. There was time to wonder how long the precariously restored partial stability of their crippled machine could continue. If the drums moved, what next? How would their own fall end? Might the final stall occur at a height from which they would be dashed to earth like a stone? Or be so low that they might almost make a landing, or crash lightly, and survive? With dilated eyes they watched the ground under their undulating Sopwith coming slowly nearer. For good or ill, their suspense was almost over. A moment more would decide their destiny. Yet even so they could not know their fate until 1075 made contact with the earth.

Their 1½-Strutter flared out, zoomed, hung stalled for a moment, then dipped her nose. The earth rushed up. Each man braced himself for the crash he could not prevent. Their aircraft began the next flare-out too near the surface. Just before she hit nose in, her undercarriage wheels struck an iron fence. Her fuselage cartwheeled over it and nose-dived into a disused gun-pit. Her wings, crumpling on the edges of the pit, absorbed the shock. Inertia twisted the fuselage over. With her nose resting on the bottom of the gun-pit the 1½-Strutter lay motionless, a complete write-off.

Forrest and Lambert emerged from the wreckage, physically unhurt, without a scratch. But few men can pass unscathed through what these two endured mentally. Both made a gallant effort to fly again with the squadron but their nerves were too badly strained. Forrest was invalided back to England. When I went on leave I visited him where he was recuperating in a convalescent home for officers and was glad to see him almost restored to his pre-crash self-confidence. Lambert remained with the squadron, but transferred to ground duties.

The enemy machine that Lambert fired at fell on the German side of the lines. Its fall was seen from the British side, but not its fate, because its point of contact with the ground was hidden from surface observation. Its crew might, or might not, have had the same luck as that of the crew of the Sopwith.

When Read commanded 45 Squadron he was always disappointed that there were so few definite victories in combat. There was gallantry enough, but little was positively confirmed which could bring the award of medals. During his time the squadron gained no decorations. About seven months after the squadron arrived in France, the first came for an individual deed of gallantry.

Captain C. H. Jenkins, 19, of Ealing, joined the squadron on 9 April 1917, to command 'B' Flight. He had previously completed a tour in France from the end of 1915 into 1916 with No. 9 Squadron. On 20 May 1917 he led one of our offensive patrols at 11,000 feet north-west of Lille. He saw four or five enemy scouts about 500 yards away. They made a half-hearted attack (or was it a feint?) and Jenkins led his formation at them, firing at the nearest, when about 200 yards off, with his front gun. Suddenly one enemy dived almost vertically at Jenkins' machine from about 2,000 feet above and in front, while two more came at him on his right. Jenkins tried to train his front gun on the diving German, who, closing fast, fired tracer to within 50 yards before pulling out of his dive.

Jenkins' observer was 21-year-old Eglington, of Maidenhead, a pre-war Guys' freshman. He emptied a drum of Lewis into the German aircraft as it passed over his head. Two hundred yards astern it crumpled, and fell completely out of control.

Jenkins told Eglington he had been hit and turned his 1½-Strutter towards the British lines. Suddenly the Sopwith lurched. Jenkins had lost consciousness. Eglington climbed out of his cockpit, crawled over the fuselage on to the lower wing, slippery with castor oil blown back from the oil-exuding Clergêt engine. Standing in this precarious position, clinging to one of the half-struts with one hand, with the other he manipulated the pilot's control stick and succeeded in directing the machine safely over the lines. He brought his seriously wounded pilot down near Neuve Eglise. But Jenkins died three days later. Eglington, who had behind him two years of trench warfare with the infantry, during which he had been twice wounded, was decorated with the Military Cross.

The squadron's only Distinguished Conduct Medal was won for an action of remarkably similar kind.

Pioneer Smith, of Maida Vale, London, had been two and a quarter years in France with the Royal Engineers before transferring to the RFC as an air gunner wearing the ribbon of the Military Medal on his tunic. But he had no stripes on his sleeves. Many did not hanker after them. There is more privacy in the humbler position. It avoids the glare and limelight that inevitably discover the exalted of this world – and there was (and is) much exaltation in the matter of stripes. When a temporary private was commissioned and returned to the same battalion, his one-time lord and master, the platoon sergeant, met him and saluted. But his congratulations were droll.

'It's very nice, sir,' he said, 'to see ye with a star on your airm. I'm just thinking, though, that anyone can be an officer, but it's no' everybody that can become a sergeant.'

Pioneer Smith had been interested in aeroplanes for a long time. He quickly distinguished enemy from friendly, inquisitive, scouts. Above all, he learned to hold his fire until he had a good, close target. His nerves were not of the sort that caused a man to blast off at long range and warn the Hun that the aircraft carried a sting in its tail. He shot to kill. After some trips with experienced pilots he was considered good enough to crew up with a new one.

Pender, a 23-year-old Scotsman, educated at Dollar, was commissioned in the 4th (Territorial) battalion of the Seaforth Highlanders soon after war began. He had been twice wounded in France and promoted to captain in his regiment before transferring to the RFC wherein he ranked as a flying officer (a subaltern) although he wore three pips. He came to 45 Squadron on 24 July 1917, having flown solo for 26 hours, including seven on 1½-Strutters. He had a lot to learn about aerial warfare.

Once, starting on a flight from St Marie Cappel, he flat-turned at 400 feet, spun, recovered, and actually touched the ground with his undercarriage wheels as he levelled out; but he climbed up again and carried out his assignment. On 11 August he went off on a three-machine line patrol, with Smith in his rear cockpit. Captain A. T. Harris, 'C' Flight commander, was the leader, but he had to land five minutes after starting. Ten minutes later the minor fault was rectified and he again took off, but never found the other two Sopwiths and completed the two-hour patrol alone.

When Harris went down, McMaking, from Southsea, took over the leadership and Pender followed him. McMaking had been flying in France for about five months, three of them with 45 Squadron. With him flew Corporal Jex, who had been with the squadron only a few more days than Pender. This patrol was typical of the squadron's method of teaming pilots and observers and sending them on line patrols, on which the comparatively inexperienced Pender and Jex could learn without too much risk, for a line patrol was considered 'a pretty cushy job of work'. Usually it meant a monotonous beat up and down, north and south, over our lines of trenches, or at most about a mile on the enemy side, with no particular excitement to offer. It was our least exacting duty.

At 6.35 p.m., only 15 minutes after leaving the airfield, McMaking led the two machines across the lines over Deulemont. They were flying at 4,500 feet, just under the clouds that almost completely covered the blue sky. They could see nothing but the grey mist above; below lay the tortuous trench-lines, dull brown under the translucent cloud.

Two Albatros Scouts, deadly-looking devils in camouflage war-paint, rose rapidly from their aerodrome and climbed quickly, pulled by their big Mercedes engines. They reached the film of cloud that straddled the sky and flew inside the mist that such cloud really is. It was just possible for the pilots to discern landmarks and keep their bearings. They flew west and when they reached the trench-lines turned south, completely hidden from above and below. Yet they themselves could see enough to keep their machines straight and watch for a chance to pounce on some unwary Britisher. Suddenly, through a gap in the clouds, they saw their prey half a mile ahead and about 300 feet below. They opened out their powerful engines and rapidly overhauled the slow two-seaters. Simultaneously their snouts dipped. They rushed out of the cloudbank, straight towards the 1½-Strutters, for the crews of which it came as a surprise attack.

The twin guns of each Albatros spat forth a double stream of bullets. The almost continuous streaks of tracer smoke and metal hissed around and into the two roundel-marked, drab-painted aeroplanes. Perhaps exultation rose in two German hearts at the thought that those Englishmen below must feel the menace of the huge, black crosses and the red-painted snouts. But almost before such thought was born, they heard the crackle of bullets spitting around their own ears. They could not change course out of their dives quickly enough.

The unmistakable crackle of the four Spandau machine-guns was the first warning the four men had of the Huns' approach; which shows their tactics to have been wrong in flying so near the cloud belt. It laid them open to surprise air attack; but had they flown lower they would have been exposed to ground fire from the infantry. It was a choice of evils.

McMaking instantly swerved and split-arsed to avoid the deadly stream of bullets, yet was not quick enough to prevent a torn gash in his wings and tail fabric. Jex was swift on the trigger. The sharp staccato of his Lewis drowned the sound of the enemy bullets and when his burst of fire ended the Albatros was falling. It burst into flames 2,000 feet from the ground and crashed on the canal to the left of Deulemont.

McMaking went down and flew up and down that part of the line. He and Jex saw the wreckage of two enemy machines, their own and another four fields away, but there was no sign of Pender.

The less experienced Pender did not swerve as quickly as McMaking. His reactions to machine-gun fire were not yet automatic. During the moment of thought before action a bullet passed through the main petrol tank between the cockpits and wounded him seriously in the back. Smith was quicker. He had his gun trained on the Hun in a flash. His aim was deadly, the range too close to miss.

Pender fainted and slumped back before he had time even to throttle his engine. The nose rose, the 1½-Strutter stalled, then fell in a spin, whirling madly with engine full on. Before Smith was jerked from his feet he saw the Hun spinning down above them. Then he turned his attention to his own machine.

He knew instinctively what was wrong and he knew how to right it. He had lain along the fuselage on the way home from previous jobs and handled the joystick. He knew all the gadgets. Pilots had explained them to him on the airfield.

Now his one thought was to get hold of the controls. He crawled down the four feet of thin plywood between the cockpits and tried. But Pender was a big man and his head and shoulders were in the way. He was unconscious and Smith could get no answer from him.

Smith knew the 1½-Strutter was none too strong to stand up to the strain of that mad, earthward whirl. He must act at once.

He climbed out on to a wing and clung to the strut in front. His mouth was blown open by the hurricane of wind. He could hardly breathe. The lower wing and fuselage were slippery with the slither of oil that rotaries continually threw out from the exhaust valves. He felt the slipstream blasting him from his precarious foothold on the spinning machine. He lunged forward with one hand to grasp the strut in front, missed, and almost fell overboard. A cold sweat broke out all over his body. He tried again and succeeded. He hauled himself forward against the blast from the propeller and the downward spinning dive, and then braced both legs against the demon wind-rush. Hanging on like death, with one arm curled around a centre-section strut, he leant inside Pender's cockpit. He could not reach the throttle lever on the far side. He turned a tap... Nothing happened. He tried another and the engine's roaring ceased as the fuel flow stopped. The wind blast lessened. He leant still farther inside the cockpit. He saw the stick was wedged between Pender's legs. He pulled them apart, pushed the joystick forward and was almost thrown again as the 1½-Strutter came out of the spin.

He shook Pender and shouted to him.

Field gunners, with binoculars to their eyes, watched the aeroplane hurtle earthward spinning, recover, and glide. They saw the figure of the gunner-observer out upon the wing; heard him shouting to the pilot.

'Wake up, Pender! For God's sake wake up!'

Pender stirred and opened his eyes drunkenly. He did not speak. He looked stupidly at Smith. His right foot on the rudder bar was veering the aircraft round to Hunland.

'Turn left, sir. Turn left,' bawled Smith.

Mechanically Pender obeyed. They were now going straight, due west, but losing height too rapidly. Smith turned back the tail wheel and they curved into a steady glide... The wind pressure lessened and Smith no longer had to hang on tooth and nail.

They were gliding towards a field of hops, straight at the midst of the artificial forest of poles. Smith shouted to Pender: 'Pull her up, sir. . . . Steady, sir. . . . Now back. . . . Pull her up, sir. . . . Land her!'

Pender's hand followed the words. The 1½-Strutter cleared the hop poles and pancaked on the farther side of them, crash-landing in a field with very little damage. They were not far from Poperinghe and near the 16th Divisional Ammunition Column, whose members had witnessed Smith's courageous action and who rendered immediate aid to both. Captain Pender was sent to hospital and later recovered from his third wound, while Smith returned to the squadron to continue flying and to receive the non-commissioned soldier's equivalent of the DSO.

Chapter V

TOLL FOR THE BRAVE

We had disliked the enforced change from huts to canvas in mid-April, but in summer we were better off. Floorboards arrived after the mud had dried underfoot, yet even in dry weather these improved our comfort. The three operational flights still messed in marquees. On hot days we could roll up the flaps to keep tents and marquees cool. Squadron HQ Flight's bell-tent mess had been replaced by a wooden hut – a status symbol?

Our camp was pleasantly situated. From the hangars a cinder path, inclining slightly up hill, ended at a little wooden footbridge giving access over a ditch to a grass paddock or meadow, the almost square area of which was verged with tall poplars. 'A', 'B' and 'C' Flights' officers' tents were pitched along the east side, near the trees; their mess marquees on the west. HQ Flight officers' accommodation was segregated on the slightly higher south side, the hessian-surrounded officers' latrines on the north. On sunny, off-duty afternoons we carried our camp-beds from the tents on to the grass; there we reclined at ease, drowsily aware of the humming of bees, the low warbling of shade-sheltering birds, the chirping of crickets, and the panting of our camp dogs lying on the grass below us, perspiring through their tongues. Although an order from some high authority had forbidden the keeping of camp dogs and required all of them to be disposed of, no one in 45 Squadron took this order seriously and our dogs continued to live with us. After all, they, too, were volunteers; we had not impressed them.

At intervals the drone of homing aeroplanes would swell louder as they neared us, drowning the humbler sounds around. But, after they had swooped above our camp and turned in to alight with throttled engines, the natural sounds of summer became again audible as those of man's invention ceased. Sometimes artillery, along the nearer parts of the line, made the hot air tremble with the rumble of continuous gun-fire.

On just such an afternoon, great activity was suddenly aroused by the passage of a single enemy aeroplane flying very high, evidently on reconnaissance. Our first intimation of its presence was the bursting of shrapnel shells above us, white puffs against the azure dome. Pieces of shell began to fall around, followed by an ominous whistle that grew louder, until, with a thud, the missile struck the airfield. Fortunately it did not explode. We walked over to the place and found a hole in the ground where it had penetrated. Meanwhile our recording officer advised the Wing HQ that our airfield had been bombed by a hostile aeroplane, but the bomb had not exploded. He was instructed to have the bomb dug up, examined, and reported on as to type and size. A party with spades and no previous experience of bomb disposal work began digging carefully to enlarge the hole. Excitement ran high when one spade struck something metallic. Very gingerly we pulled the object out; and found it was an unexploded British anti-aircraft shell!

Those sunny afternoons at St Marie Cappel were very like the calm before a thunderstorm. The peaceful atmosphere was unnatural. The restfulness was a mockery, like a freak looking-glass which, mirroring the actual, throws it back distorted, grotesque. It was a boon to be unimaginative; a sore trial to have an introspective mind and a brain which analysed the wisdom of the human powers that, to all seeming, directed one's destiny: and a curse to meditate appreciatively on the personal values of the fighting comrades by whom one was temporarily surrounded, their sorrows, joys, triumphs, failings, jealousies, and great sacrifices. Sometimes one or another would lift the veil of secrecy behind which humans enshroud their emotions and deliberately tune in the intentioned transmission of thoughts by words; then one understood that beneath the martial garb, and more powerful than the laws of discipline, were human desires and aspirations, and the remembered relations with that other life moving in parallel in some home in a part of Empire, near or far away, and its interconnection with the ever-fateful present. For one was part of a civilian army, a nation in arms, dressed outwardly in khaki, but thinking inwardly in terms of mufti, knowing that one day the guns would be silent and the uniforms discarded. Even as the tumult of a day of rain, wind and thunderstorm can be succeeded by the peace of evening, so would this war pass away in the years to come.

We were not (as were some squadrons) greatly given to sing songs at the piano; but sometimes, when Selby vamped the hit songs of the time, we did sing. Nor were we much attracted by the indigenous songs of the RFC. We preferred our gramophone and the music of the masters, whose voices and orchestras were recorded on the records that we had. Those going on leave were expected to bring back at least one disc.

Carleton, a 26-year-old pilot, was our principal music lover, and I have always felt grateful to him for the solace provided in our spare moments by his choices of records that otherwise might not have been heard at St Marie Cappel. Apart from hits from popular musicals of the day, such as 'The Cobbler's Song' from *Chu Chin Chow*, he introduced records of Schubert's Unfinished Symphony, 'O Star of Eve' from *Tannhäuser*, songs from *Omar Khayyám* 'Myself When Young' and 'Ah! Moon of My Delight', arias from *La Bohème* 'Your Tiny Hand is Frozen' and 'Musetta's Song', *Madame Butterfly* 'One Fine Day' and other operas; and songs sung by Peter Dawson and John McCormack. I learned quite a lot about the love of music from Carleton. One favourite was a variant song, accompanied by Hawaiian guitars, and as I write I can still hear the sobbing notes of that version of 'On the Beach at Wai-Ki-Ki'. How I should like to have all those records now, recordings that were made before the days of electric (and electronic) recording, of singers whose methods of voice production were different from those of today and much more natural. I still picture a meadow, a clear sky on a summer's night, a full moon tracing long shadows of bordering poplars across grass half-ringed by pallid bell-tents, and this melodic magic transmuting the harsh reality of guns and aeroplanes into a transient but inconsumable beauty of sound.

Throughout the preceding months the intensity of our work in the air and on the ground had constantly been increasing with the lengthening daylight hours. The thunder of war overrode almost all else! Our patrols, our reconnaissances, our escorts to Corps aircraft engaged on long-range shoots, our encounters with Archie and our brushes with enemy aircraft, were all leading the demons of war to greater outpourings of men and material on both sides. Our losses were replaced by other men and new machines.

Our damaged aircraft, shot through by bullets and flying pieces of exploding shells, were repaired. The holed tanks, the shattered spars, the cut longerons, the torn fabric, were made good by men who worked long hours both day and night to keep our aircraft in fighting trim. The overworked engines which gave trouble were whipped out and overhauled, and spare engines fitted in their place.

From the beginning, 45 Squadron pilots and observers had done their best to engage the enemy. But the squadron had arrived in France when the air superiority attained by the RFC during the early stages of the Battle of the Somme had waned with the introduction of new types of enemy fighters which overthrew the temporary advantage the DH2s and earliest 1½-Strutters had gained. Against this changed background the 1½-Strutter's initially promised value rating, which had been based on the merits of its design and layout in comparison with the obsolete British types it outshone when it was first produced rather than on its own performance or those of the enemy aircraft it was soon to be pitted against, may have been justified for a few short weeks; but as a direct result of the introduction of these new German scouts it declined before the 1½-Strutter had properly started its war career in France. Its active service use continued, however, for more than 12 months, long after its real worth as a fighting aeroplane had vanished.

Thus 45 Squadron's first 10 months in France lay in a period when the advantage in *matériel* was in enemy hands and the possibilities of 1½-Strutter crews succeeding in combat were correspondingly lessened, with no reduction, but the opposite, in their own casualty risks.

For a long time after the squadron first went into action its crews fought combats that proved indecisive. One enemy aircraft was described as having been seen 'crashing downward', others were 'driven off' or 'driven down', 'driven down in a vertical dive', 'smoke was seen to issue from the fuselage', another 'dived smoking' and yet another 'dived steeply and was lost to sight', one 'turned sharply away and apparently went down', another 'nose-dived and side-slipped 2,000 feet'. None of these combats comes into the confirmed victory list.

In almost all of these early encounters, the range – up to 400 yards – was too great to achieve success. The aircrews did not then realise that in the air the single machine-gun was really a close-range weapon. From the often unsteady and always moving gun platform of a 1½-Strutter it needed a lot of luck for any burst fired at over 100 yards to be fully effective, and when the enemy held the initiative because his aircraft were faster in speed and climb it was seldom easy for the 1½-Strutter pilot to close the range, whereas enemy pilots could dart in and away again at their own choice.

The frequent stoppages of the observer's free-firing single Lewis gun and the unreliability of the Ross interrupter gear used during the early months to control the pilot's single Vickers' firing through the propeller's arc contributed their quotas to the poor combat results. This Ross gear was, I believe, developed largely by a flight sergeant of another name whose RFC flight commander was named Ross. It reduced the Vickers machine-gun's rate of fire to about 300 rounds a minute, but had the advantage of leaving the normal ground trigger on the gun and when we found ourselves in a really tight corner we fired the gun direct without the gear and doubled our fire power; although bullets then hit the revolving propeller, that was less vital than being unable to fire fast enough at a fleeting target. It was quite common for a machine to return with up to 20 holes through its propeller from its own bullets. The propeller then had to be scrapped, but I never came across a case of propeller failure in the air due to this.

When our propellers were scrapped they were of no further value to the RFC, but the beautiful wood, usually laminations of walnut and mahogany, was converted into various ornamental objects; bosses became mounts for clocks and aneroid barometers, or were sometimes turned into tobacco jars with wood base and lid and knob lifter made from broken blades; tips became photograph frames; on parts of broken blades amateur artists painted scenes of combat between our and enemy machines; if the remains of a blade were long enough, a handsome walking stick could be turned from it. A different kind of souvenir was made by threading leather washers from metal caps of two-gallon petrol cans on to a length of heavy gauge piano wire, the ends of which were tapped to take a nut. The leather washers were compressed by tightening the nuts against a metal washer at either end of the wire and the laminated leather was then turned on a lathe, with its diameter decreasing from one end to the other, and finally polished. A handle attached to the thick end and a ferrule to the thin evolved a splendid walking stick, its rather heavy weight its only disadvantage. I never discovered how the petrol tins were kept gas and fuel tight without washers, but probably the washers used were scrounged from tins scrapped because of leakage.

If the making of these articles was not according to the book, it did no harm, because the materials used were scrap, their conversion maintained fitters' or carpenters' skills and gave them spare time occupation on an airfield where there was then all too little recreation or entertainment. The article was usually given to the pilot from whose machine the broken or bullet-riddled propeller was removed, and was seldom or never the product of a request by him. The work showed the admiration and esteem of a devoted air mechanic for the man who flew and gave life to the machines on which the ack emma worked and it strengthened the bond that existed between the flying and non-flying members of a unique corps.

From late October 1916 until early May 1917, 45 Squadron certainly destroyed only three enemy aircraft; two more might have been destroyed but these cannot be confirmed. In this period 23 pilots and observers were killed and five wounded in action, three were accidentally killed and one injured. That was not the period of our heaviest casualties; this was about to come, with the air war then rising to fever pitch.

Were it not for the high value of its other work, the squadron's early record in the fighting role, for which its 1½-Strutters were supposed to have equipped it, would be a depressing one. But the chief duty of 1½-Strutters was strategic reconnaissance for Army HQs. Because they were classed as fighter-reconnaissance aircraft they were expected to carry out this work without fighter escort other than that which could be provided by the machines of their own squadron. No. 70 Squadron appears to have been an exception in this; it was in the special RFC HQ Wing coming more under the direct control of Trenchard and its 1½-Strutter formations sometimes received fighter escort, but 45 Squadron did not. On occasion we provided escorts for Corps machines engaged on short tactical reconnaissances, we made continuous patrols over and beyond the entrenched infantry and were sometimes employed on ground attack in direct support of the ground forces. Most of our combats were the direct consequence of executing these duties and occurred during them, with none more bitter than those that our reconnaissance formations had to fight.

At the stage when real air fighting began to make its effect felt, RFC losses were very heavy relative to losses in RNAS squadrons operating on the same front. General Henderson, the first commander of the RFC in France, and simultaneously its Director-General at the War Office in London by proxy, was asked why the RFC losses were so much greater. He did not mention inferior equipment, but attributed the difference to the longer training of naval pilots. Questioned further, he expressed the view that short training in the RFC was a consequence of the number of casualties and not the other way round; which seems, on reflection, to be a case of heads you lose and tails I win.

Pilots who went to France with only the brief RFC standard training of the time discovered after they reached a first-line squadron that their training had been quite inadequate and during their early weeks on operations they had to learn what they did not know (and could not do) at the risk of receiving the chop from more experienced enemy pilots flying machines of better performance and armament. There can be no question that too short training caused many casualties, nor that these casualties put greater strain on the training organisation; this, together with too ambitiously rapid first-line expansion, prevented the period of training from being lengthened to give pupils more flying experience before being posted to combat units. Pilots who were retained temporarily to serve as instructors, or who were posted to squadrons forming at home before going overseas, were luckier, because their flying experience was extended before they were required to enter the arena of the fighting fronts.

In 45 Squadron we did our best to rectify this, and compared with some squadrons' casualties, we appear to have met with some success, even if not as much as we could have wished because of our 1½-Strutter equipment. Every new pilot was given as much extra training as an operational squadron had time to give. Every new 1½-Strutter pilot or observer was given a personally conducted tour of the battle area in the rear seat. Whenever possible an experienced observer or pilot was always sent up with a raw pilot or observer on his first few action flights. When crossing the lines the new pilot was never put at the rear of a formation, where he was wide open to a sudden enemy attack. Instead, he was allotted a place in the vee immediately behind the leader, with other aircraft behind to guard him until he had overcome the tiro's too often fatal inability to see enemy aircraft during his first few engagements, in the course of which he became so involved in following the formation leader's wild gyrations that he had never a fraction of a second to spare for anything else.

Some squadrons put the new man at the rear, where he was most easily picked off by the wily Hun. This was a wrong and unfair practice. Had 45 Squadron not taken its common-sense precautions, our casualty list, heavy though it was, would have been proportionately greater; in this respect there can have been no better squadron for any new pilot to join.

In those days, when the only aptitude tests were full-scale, the ability to learn varied widely. Thus the aeroplane produced that most modern psychiatric study, the airman in the air. And the WW1 airman in the air was often the Dr Jekyll of a Mr Hyde upon the ground. He lived a dual life: One, the normal life of the average individual; the other, the aloofness of the life aerial, cut off from all communication with the ground and other aircraft, with the added thrills of war thrown in. On the ground, more often than not, he was a very human person indeed. In the air he was... Yes, what was he?

To him an aeroplane in flight was simultaneously a chariot of frail mortality, yet, paradoxically, a thing of beauty and of wonder, a feminine creation with caprices and personality, a charming creature to be coaxed and won, but over which no brutal force could ever hold sway. In the air, she (for an aeroplane is undoubtedly feminine) was his companion to the exclusion of all else. By her sweetness and response, and her birthright of the beautiful skyscape whither she bore him, she bred a new man; and by her instant remorselessness in action against brutality she inculcated in him a new nature, teaching him, more and more every time he sought her company, that he had to learn to understand her ways.

In the early days of RFC work in France the air arm was new. It was at a stage of evolution from the exhibition aero-acrobat, the cross-country prize competition, the toy of the enthusiastic amateur and a few naval and army officers, into no one knew quite what. It was not taken seriously. The use of the aeroplane in war was not comprehended by many and its inception as an offensive weapon was delayed, and misdirected when it came.

It is easy in turning over the pages of air history at the beginning of the Great War to see the errors, easy to picture their results from the casualty lists in later years, easy to frame another picture had the policy that controlled British aircraft design (including engines) been more far-seeing, easy to note the lack of vision that held our air progress in check. But, at that time, when ideas of field armies and wars of movement were changing into the realities of trench defence and a war of attrition, the then undefined place that aircraft were later to assume must have been terribly hard to visualise.

Some pilots and observers fought many combats, but never succeeded in bringing down, confirmed as destroyed, an enemy machine. Others did, in varying degree. The difference between the one and the other is too subtle to analyse. In what proportions should one attribute the differences to relative flying skill, natural aggressiveness, hatred of an enemy race, patriotism, egotism, the love of competition winning, keen eyesight, speed of visual and muscular responses, markmanship, courage, the lust for glory or rewards, the luck of time and chance, the ability to seize the fleeting opportunity? Nor do awards made reflect initial analysis, because there was no similarity of standard for the submission of recommendations; as much as modesty varied among the fighters, some senior officers were most free with recommendations while others were the opposite. Yet some men stand out from among their fellows.

Lubbock was the first outstanding fighter in 45 Squadron. From its first days in France in October 1916 he was frequently in action, attacking enemy aircraft whenever he saw them, but he was rarely able to close to short range and both he and his observers had much gun trouble. His combat reports were always modest, yet his aircraft were often badly damaged by enemy fire, involving him in numerous forced landings, and on one, even when half his tail plane had folded back, he managed to crash-land without hurt to himself or his observer, Austin. He may have shot down several enemy aircraft, but there is no record of a positive victory until 6 March 1917, when he led three 1½-Strutters across the lines near St Eloi to take photographs. One flown by a Canadian, Captain MacKay, had to go back from near Houthulst Forest with a faulting engine and Lubbock thought he had recrossed the lines safely. But on his way back MacKay was overtaken by five Siemens Schuckert D.Is, the Germans' deliberate copy of the successful French Nieuport 17 scout. Believing them to be Nieuports, MacKay took no evasive action. His error was not surprising, because these blatant copies of the French aircraft had just reached the first line and were not known to the Allies. Their surprise attack riddled MacKay's 1½-Strutter with bullets and mortally wounded his observer, Greenhow. Flying and aileron balance wires were shot away, both tyres punctured, a longeron cut almost in half, wings and fuselage holed like colanders, MacKay's flying cap ripped by a bullet. He dived across the lines and landed his tattered machine at 41 Squadron's hangars at Abeele airfield. Greenhow died minutes later. MacKay had to be invalided from shock.

Lubbock and Thompson, Marshall and Lance Corporal Perrott, were also attacked by the Siemens Schuckerts, which Marshall reported as Nieuports. Two of the enemy scout pilots dived too far and passed beneath the Sopwiths. Both observers fired as they passed, then one German fled eastward, leaving Lubbock and Marshall free to blast the other from close range with their front guns. Marshall's trigger cable to the Vickers' firing-bar broke while he was firing, but he pressed the knuckle joint and kept his gun firing. The German pilot dived steeply and a British AA battery saw the SS scout crash on the enemy side. Lubbock's engine stopped. He forced landed near Abeele. That evening Read wished he had 18 Lubbocks in his squadron, a pilot who had been in more fights, taken more photographs, and shown greater keenness for both activities than any other. He was 'always on the ball'.

When MacKay and Marshall insisted (Lubbock did not) that their attackers were Nieuport Scouts, Read telephoned de Dombasle, commanding No. 1 Squadron at Bailleul, which flew them on our front. De Dombasle was hurt at the suggestion that his pilots could have attacked our 1½-Strutters and, of course, they had not done so.

It almost seems that Lubbock's fate was preordained. At the beginning of August 1916 when 45 Squadron was required to throw off a nucleus at Sedgeford in Norfolk to form 64 Squadron, Lubbock was posted to 64, a squadron that did not go overseas until a year after 45 went. But the Wing posted Lubbock back to 45 a month before it flew to France. Then, four days after the Siemens-Schuckert fight his 'B' Flight was scheduled to go to Cormont for a week's gunnery course, and he and Marshall went ahead by road on 8 March 1917 to make arrangements. Next day Wing HQ substituted 'A' Flight for 'B'. Rain and snow stopped all flying on 10 March, but on the following day Mountford's flight flew to Cormont and Lubbock/Thompson, Marshall/Truscott, Bowden/Stevenson left St Marie Cappel airfield at 9.30 a.m. on a photographic line patrol. A few minutes later Marshall forced landed near the airfield with a broken valve-rocker arm.

Lubbock and Bowden went on, began their patrol at 10.15, and Thompson took five photographs of required objectives. At 11.07 two Albatros D.IIIs attacked them over the Ypres salient. The fight lasted for five minutes, but the 1½-Strutters were outmanoeuvred by the faster swifter-climbing scouts with their twin forward-firing guns. Yet from the ground, one of the scouts was seen to fall out of control in the enemy lines. At the same moment Lubbock's machine broke up in the air. Its fuselage fabric trailed out behind as it nose-dived into the ground, close behind our front line trenches on the Ypres salient. The other D.III pilot attacked Bowden, shot him through the head. As he fell over the controls his Sopwith swerved, nose-dived, the wings folded back, and it plunged down into the Ypres moat. Both observers fell from their cockpits as their machines went down.

German gunners shelled Lubbock's wreckage, but the Army retrieved his body. The exposed plates were salved with the camera. Bowden's body was recovered when his smashed 1½-Strutter was pulled out of the moat. All the bodies were taken to No. 10 Casualty Clearing Station at Poperinghe. That night our squadron carpenters made four coffins, affixed brass plates engraved with the ranks and names of four more men of a lost generation, and squadron transport bore them to 10 CCS. Next afternoon, in the presence of all available officers of the squadron, and most of 'B' Flight, our gallant dead were buried at Poperinghe, alongside Greenhow.

Until the advent of air power, there had been no military formation such as an air squadron, that sent into battle only a fraction of its members, and those its leaders, with the sole exception of its overall commander who, at the time when Lubbock died, was restricted to administrative duties. This remarkable aspect of a 1916–17 air squadron – the years when air combat first became potent – evoked contemporary references to 'knights of the air' and 'the chivalry of air combat'. Sometimes there was evidence of chivalry, but more often there was just the sheer bloody murder of the head-hunter. Even today, more than half a century later, many amateur grapevine historical societies exist solely to collect and collate information about the WW1 air head-hunters, their tallies, arms, mounts and methods, a form of hero-worship that is as strange as it is highly devotional.

Greenhow was 19, Bowden just 20, Thompson and Stevenson were 21, and Lubbock 23. All their names are forgotten by the ace-hunting historians. But Lubbock, although never mentioned in the list of aces, as a man justified the existence of that too often derided educational Mecca, Eton College. So many take the wrong view today. It is not the privileges of any class of society, but the failures, when there are any, to show due results from privilege, that should be attacked. Lubbock did not fail. His character was of the kind that made England great, that alone can maintain her greatness in a changed and changing world. Lines that Chaucer wrote in the fourteenth century might have been penned as an epitaph perhaps for each of the five men who now lay silent in a row at Poperinghe, but certainly for Eric Fox Pitt (known, not to the squadron, but in his family as 'Yay') Lubbock, son of a man of wide achievements, Lord Avebury, and, to judge by her letters, of a wonderful mother:

> . . . there was his son, a young Squire,
> Of twenty year he was of age I guess,
> And he had been some time in chivalry
> In Flanders, Artois and in Picardy,
> And borne him well. . . .

Belgrave, of 'A' Flight, who came from Chinnor, in Oxfordshire, succeeded Lubbock as the squadron's most aggressive fighter. He had been commissioned in the 2nd Oxon and Bucks Light Infantry in February 1914, joined the squadron in France on the last day of November 1916 and his first combat report, with Thompson as observer, told of an indecisive encounter on Christmas Eve. An exponent of front-gun fighting, as Lubbock had been before him, neither did he neglect opportunities for his observer to engage the enemy. His last combat for the squadron, fought on 27 May 1917, featured in his 15th combat report. The narrative quality of his combat reports varies greatly and sometimes descends to bathos. Positive claims of actual destruction of enemy aircraft were not made in any of them, but he (with his observers) is believed to have shot down two in flames, four out of control, and to have driven down others.

All WW1 combat reports are very variable. In Belgrave's time with 45 Squadron they were the original writing of the participants, and their literary quality, discursiveness or brevity, not to say precision, differ widely. Each participant wrote his own version of the same engagement on a separate form. Later, it became the practice for squadron headquarters to edit, even rewrite, combat reports, and when these were collective they were usually (but not always) signed by all involved in them; sometimes only the squadron commander signed them. The later combat reports are much more decisive. Anyone making a study of these documents should bear in mind the changing background to them.

Belgrave, the first pilot in the squadron to be decorated, was awarded the Military Cross on the very day he was posted home for a rest 1 June 1917. He returned to fly SE5as in 60 Squadron and was killed in action on 13 June 1918 after gaining a Bar to his MC and (some say) with 15 victories to his credit, a figure I can neither confirm nor alter.

After 18 days' attachment to RFC HQ to pin-point aerial photographs, Emery returned to England on 26 April 1917, to train as a pilot, the only one of the 13 original observers to do so. Five of the other 12 were killed in action, two by active service flying accidents, three were wounded in action, and two voluntarily gave up flying and returned to their infantry regiments. One calendar month after Emery went home 22 of our observers had been killed, wounded, or were missing, and of the last most were dead. Then only two of the originals –Carey and Vessey – remained in the squadron. Both had been recommended for return to England to train as pilots. Why they had not been relieved I do not know. They had earned relief. Had they survived another month, at most, they would have gone home; but they did not survive.

When fighting men philosophically said a man was safe until the moment he met a bullet with his name on it, what was the sublimal force they recognised and connoted by this remark? And why should some have been aware, and others ignorant, of the impending arrival of the named bullet?

It was at this time, at St Marie Cappel, that I wrote the following impressionist picture:

He had been out, constantly at work, for over eight months and the strain had begun to sap his nervous well-being. The order to go home to learn to fly as a pilot might come any day within the next month.

Then his pilot turned ill, not seriously, but badly enough to prevent him flying for three weeks. Whenever possible the same pilot and observer always worked together. Because they knew each other's methods this produced both confidence and efficiency. Thus for a time it was unnecessary for this observer to fly, and his Flight Commander told him to have a well-earned rest. Before his pilot could resume flying it was expected that this observer would receive orders to return to Home Establishment.

The previous autumn's prowess of the 1½-Strutter had steadily waned with the advent of more powerful enemy machines. Her fate was certain. She would be superseded as soon as another type was ready to usurp her place. But the later type had not yet been produced. Meanwhile, the arduous and dangerous work of supplying information about and obtaining photographs of areas far behind the enemy lines must continue. It mattered not that the type of machine was obsolete. That was unfortunate. Those responsible were doing their very best to hurry on the production of better and more powerful machines. In the interval, men, the finest products of their race, had to sacrifice themselves in their obsolete machines to the ruthless God of War. They started out on a job of work knowing well that the odds were against their safe return. They took their lives in their hands and carried on. They were brave men who showed the highest form of courage. And this particular observer was one of the bravest of them all.

The respite was a godsend to him, for his nerves were worn to shreds. During the last month his eyes had become sunken and his complexion had changed from fresh to sallow. He was but a travesty of what he had been. Coming off a show, even when there had been no particular excitement, his hands shook and his eyes were dilated.

He was naturally introspective and possessed of a vivid imagination: Two evil companions in war. During the eight months just passed he had seen almost all of his original comrades killed – several had gone down to earth in flaming, smoking planes that writhed and twisted as they fell, things of horror.

Yet he was the type of man who would not give in. A month before he knew that he was beaten. The doctor had wanted to strike him off flying then. But he only answered, 'And what about my pilot, Doc? Do you think I'd let him go up with anyone but me? How would I feel if I stayed on the ground and one day he didn't come back? No, Doc, I keep on flying as long as he does, unless my warrant comes through for Blighty.'

Which shows the real love that often existed between pilot and observer who had been through flying fights together. They felt themselves as indissolvable units of the one machine.

One would have thought, however, that now his return to England seemed so certain his brow would have cleared, his tattered nerves have strung taut again. But no! His eyes remained dull, with a haunting sense of tragedy, and his nerves remained broken. In the mess one evening he announced to one of his most intimate friends that he would never again see home. His life was already forfeit to the machine that had claimed so many of his comrades. In vain his friend tried to cheer his melancholia. It was hopeless.

The observer ran over a list of names that were only names to his friend. To the observer they were men; men who had gone before; men that the machine had claimed to earn her fame and write her name, in blood, upon the roll of successful war machines: To him the machine had become a goddess that demanded blood upon her altar. The time would come when the sacrifices she compelled, especially the burnt offerings, would evoke horror in the reader of history. But, meantime, only those who served her realised the awful nature of her sway. He most of all. Under this mental cloud he lived each day, for he knew within himself that ere the idolatry that had kept her in power for so long was glutted he, too, would give himself, a witting yet powerless victim. The luck which had seemed his did not continue. After a few days the doctors said he might fly again if necessary. When the time came he did not hold back.

McArthur was one of the older members of the squadron, and he had been with it from its training days at Sedgeford. He had flown many gallant reconnaissances and patrols, but absolute success in combat had somehow always eluded him.

On the afternoon of 9 May his formation of five 1½-Strutters (which should have been eight had engines been reliable) flew across the lines and over German-held territory on a south offensive patrol. Simultaneously Schaefer led his Jasta 28 from its airfield at Marcke-sur-Lys, between

Courtrai and Menin. The two formations clashed between Menin and Warneton. Some of our aircrew said there were 11 Albatros Scouts. One of our most recently-joined pilots, whose youngest brother many years afterwards would become Air Chief Marshal Sir George ('Bertie') Mills, flew behind McArthur. He was a Woolwich-trained regular of the Royal Field Artillery who had been an observer in No. 8 Squadron from the end of 1915 before going home to learn to fly in 1916. He received his pilot's wings on 9 April 1917 and, in the hasty way of that bloody month, joined 45 Squadron four days later. Flying with him was 2/AM Loughlin, an Army private who had been with 45 for only six days as an air gunner on probation. This teaming was contrary to the squadron's usual practice of matching experience to lack of it and why it should have occurred is a mystery. Perhaps the practice, as I knew it, grew from the roots of bitter knowledge, a way all too common in war. Perhaps it was thought that Mills' time as an observer gave him experience which he had not quite acquired as a pilot.

Mills was badly wounded by Schaefer's first attack. When he slumped over his controls his 1½-Strutter fell out of control and crashed. Loughlin was thrown out, injured, made prisoner of war, and for the rest of his life had to wear a surgical boot, for which he received a 30 per cent disability pension. Mills died of his wounds and injuries in enemy hands.

This, Schaefer's 26th victory, was gained nine days after the lanky pilot was awarded the *Orden Pour le mérite*, Germany's top fighting decoration. He scored four more before he was killed on 5 June 1917. He certainly had the greater glory during his brief life and as a successful air fighter his name is found in most books that tell of the air aces of WW1. But if we compare his total span of usefulness to the world with that of the unknown Loughlin, who passed the magic three score years and ten as one of Schaefer's more fortunate adversaries, the balance swings away from the romantic Schaefer, for the world owes more to Loughlin. The unknown factor in the equation of this comparison springs from the folly of a war that destroyed Schaefer at 25, and Mills before he was 20, when both were ripening to live useful lives.

McArthur got away, partly through his flying skill, partly through the heroism of his observer who, although mortally wounded and with his right hand partially shot away, continued firing with his left hand and drove the nearest scout down. Then McArthur succeeded in spinning away from two other attackers and, by a miracle, his machine hung together despite the wires that were shot away. He landed on Bailleul airfield. Senior was rushed into the adjoining hospital without delay, but he died there and we buried him in Bailleul cemetery with the honour which his brave soul merited.

McArthur returned to the squadron and wanted to carry on in spite of an armour-piercing bullet which, after passing through a longeron and penetrating the rubber heel of one of his flying boots, had ended by puncturing the hard part of his heel to a depth of three-eighths of an inch. The doctor told him not to be a fool, gave him an anti-tetanus injection, and sent him home on a week's sick leave.

When he returned the inevitable question arose. It could not be eluded. Who was to become his new observer? He did not want to split up existing partnerships. But to a flight commander, leader of formations across the lines, an inexperienced, newly joined observer was useless; moreover, it required experience to take reconnaissance photographs accurately and successfully.

There was only one choice, that of the only experienced observer available. Even if he did not want to fly, because he desperately needed rest, he could not help himself. He had to volunteer. He could not hold back and brand himself a coward. That he never was.

An over-worked observer, when kept too long on his nerve-shredding task, might picture himself sitting in the observer's cockpit, his shoulders hunched against the blast of the slipstream. His picture might, or might not, be prophetic. It is useless to theorise, hopeless to conjecture. But by the very thought of that constant, nerve-racking vigil, his eyes would feel already strained. There, in front of him, he could see the trembling tail plane floating in the invisible air, the rudder's crescent, just discernible, protruding to the left. All around him was the empty air; above, the vaulting dome of sky with its burning sun; and, thousands of feet below, the earth with its little dolls' houses and tiny fields in varying shades of brown. He shuddered as he thought of its remoteness. God! How far to fall. Then, in a flash his empty sky would fill with diving horror. Out of the sun, up from the earth, out of nowhere, swarming like locusts, they peopled his dreams. Things of ugliness, with snouts of vile intent, they closed around him with lightning swiftness. He raised his gun and sighted on the nearest – ra-ta-ta-tat! The others closed. He fired, sighted, and reloaded with feverish energy. He heard the crackle, menacing and merciless, about his ears. He felt a sudden stabbing pain, a mistiness, a choking, a smell of escaping petrol, of scorching paint and varnish ... nothing.

If he knew fear, McArthur never betrayed it. He was a man who would go anywhere. Carey knew this and knew also that by volunteering to go with him he relinquished all hope to ease of mind.

On 27 May 1917 Carey went up with McArthur on an eight-machine central offensive and photographic patrol. Mountford, as senior flight commander, with his observer Vessey, led. McArthur was deputy leader. Both carried cameras. Both returned almost at once and landed with engine trouble. McArthur was quickly away, but had to land again. Both finally left 30 minutes late. This delay disorganised the formation. One of the eight machines crashed on Bailleul airfield, its occupants unhurt. Three could not reach Mountford's 13,500-foot height and patrolled apart.

Near Roulers, Mountford fired a red Very light and the four Sopwiths dived at seven Albatros Scouts seen ahead 500 feet below, scouts that were painted red, green, green and blue, and blue and red. While churning the air in the uncoordinated mix-up of a swirling dogfight, crews saw one scout spinning with splinters ripping off its fuselage, a second spinning down (these might have been the same one), and two out of control. Fitchat saw an unidentified Sopwith, that must have been McArthur's, in difficulties. He dived at one attacking Albatros and, with his observer, Hayes, forced it to abandon its quarry, in order, itself, to escape, apparently undamaged. Mountford broke away from the fight, his engine punk from a stuck-up inlet valve back-firing into the carburetter. He beat his way back across the lines, landed at Abeele airfield carrying the chief objective of the patrol, 18 photographs exposed by Vessey. Fitchat and Hayes, Sergeant Cook and 2/ AM Shaw, returned to St Marie Cappel, but in the end only Fitchat out of these four survived his tour with 45 Squadron.

That evening McArthur and Carey were posted missing. All we then knew was that their 1½-Strutter had last been reported as seen at 12,000 feet about two miles east of the enemy trench-lines. But a few days later a German aircraft dropped a message reporting them dead. It gave only the serial number of their aircraft, named it a Sopwith, and stated their ranks and surnames.

It is now known that their A8226 fell near Ypres, not far over on the German side, as the 13th victim of the guns of Offizierstellvertreter (Acting Officer) Max Müller, then in Schaefer's Jasta 28, a Bavarian who began his air fighting career as a non-commissioned officer under Bölcke, lived to score 36 victories, become an oberleutnant, wear at his neck the dazzling jewel of the *Orden Pour le mérite*, and command Jasta 22. But at Moorslede, on 9 January 1918, he leapt to death from his own blazing Albatros fighter, shot into flames by the guns of an RE8 flown by Zimmer and Sommerville of 21 Squadron.

In 45 Squadron two original pilots and one observer were now left. On 12 June 1917 two of these, Mountford and Vessey, flew to No. 1 Aircraft Depot at St Omer. Returning in A8299, just after three o'clock, they were gliding through a gap in the clouds to reach St Marie Cappel airfield. At about the same time, six 1½-Strutters took off for a photographic reconnaissance, each climbing singly through gaps to join into formation above the clouds. They passed through heavy rain at 3,000 feet, which an atmospheric inversion of temperature prevented from dropping to earth; otherwise their start would have been cancelled. Watt and 2/AM Pocock in A8244, ascending through one gap, were skirting a pillar of cloud when they collided with 8299 descending round the same pillar from the opposite direction. From the airfield we heard the crash in the air, saw the wreckage fall to the ground and ran to it. It did not burn up. But all four men were dead.

This left in the squadron one original member, Geoffrey Hornblower Cock, who had been given command of 'B' Flight after Jenkins was wounded on 20 May 1917, and promoted to captain from that date.

Cock was tall, good-looking, always immaculate in his RFC 'maternity' jacket. He had a slight stutter. The monocle he carried was not an adornment, but a necessity for one defective eye. In 1914, when 18, medical officers refused him for the King's Shropshire Light Infantry and in 1915 again rejected him for a commission in the Royal Welsh Fusiliers. These two rebuffs would have deterred most men, but Cock entered the 28th London Regiment (Artists' Rifles) Officers' Training Corps in December 1915, passing thence to a commission in the RFC in June 1916. In both cases a doctor and a medical orderly looked the other way while Cock 'did a bit of fancy work with his monocle'; they also proved remarkably understanding when filling in the medical forms.

After the Oxford course, Cock began his elementary flying at 25 Reserve Squadron at Thetford, joining 45 Squadron at adjacent Sedgeford on 25 July 1916 to raise his flying to service standard. Gaining his pilot's wings on 7 September, he flew to France with the squadron in mid-October with 7 hours dual and 37 hours 40 minutes' pilotage entered in his log-book. He (as did all who flew these frail machines) damaged his quota of 1½-Strutters while developing into the squadron's third leading fighter in succession to Lubbock and Belgrave.

Cock flew 97 sorties over the lines and his personally kept records add up to 19 victories for himself and his various observers, of which he regards 15 as certainties. Squadron records show six out of control from his front gun and from his observers' two in pieces, one in flames, two out of control, one damaged and three possibles, two indecisive. By whichever score-board one reckons, he must have been the most successful combat pilot who ever flew the old 1½-Strutters – aircraft which were akin to the sailing ships of Nelson's time – into battle.

His success came from handing his 1½-Strutter like a scout and using his front gun as much as his observers used theirs. On 9 May 1917, when flying tail-end Charlie in a six-machine offensive patrol near Seclin, he saw four Albatros Scouts behind. He fired a Very red light and without waiting for anyone, turned instantly. Reaching the enemy first and using his Aldis sight, he fired at two scouts while closing from 120 yards and saw one dive, spin, and fall completely out of control. Then he swerved to let Murison (a volunteer from the Machine Gun Corps and an extrovert who fancied himself behind a Lewis against any number of Huns) have a go at others who were diving at them. Eighty rounds from Murison hit a grey scout in the centre section at 50 feet. It collapsed. From further bursts of fire it folded up and fell to pieces. Beneath the combat report a senior officer, whose initials are illegible, wrote: 'This is gallant but is all against orders and common sense.'

On 16 June 1917 Cock was awarded the second Military Cross to be won by a pilot of 45 Squadron.

BUTTERFLIES OF WAR

At its Headquarters at St Omer General Trenchard accepted command of the RFC from General Henderson in August 1915. At the end of March 1916 his HQ shifted south to the château of St Andre, near Hesdin, because battle emphasis was soon to be on the Somme. RFC HQ moved back to its earlier Moyenneville château at St Omer early in June 1917 when the main British thrust was about to fall on the northern sector.

Trenchard, a prodigious worker, found time to visit his squadrons at surprisingly frequent intervals. He visited 45 Squadron on 15 March 1917, not for the first time while Read was in command. Early in June, when Van Ryneveld was there, Trenchard came again to St Marie Cappel, no far cry now from his St Omer HQ. Before he left, pilots and observers of the squadron were asked to gather round the general without any formality, on the airfield, away from the office, hangars and boundary, where his spoken words would carry to them alone.

'Boom', to give that popular and universally-admired leader of the Corps his nickname, which none ever dared to use to his face, spoke earnestly and with obvious feeling. I cannot from memory quote the precise words he used, but the substance of his talk rings clearly down the intervening years.

'I know that your machines are old in type and outclassed by the enemy's latest fighters,' he said. 'I have worked and am continuing to work to hurry on the new machines which are being produced to replace those which you are using now. You will get them just as soon as ever I can get them for you. I know you have had a bad time, but in the few days which lie ahead there is going to be a battle and our aeroplanes will help largely to sway the issue with our forces on the ground. That is why I have come to see you today, to tell you of the impending attack, and to ask you to carry on and do your very best, knowing that I sympathise with the difficulties under which your work is carried out and that I, in my turn, am doing my very best to help you to become equipped with later type machines. I know you will do your utmost when the time comes and that when I say go, you will go with all your might, and so keep the sky clear of enemy aeroplanes even right behind the enemy lines.'

There were no questions, no clearer definitions of what we should have to do, or on which part of the front the attack would fall. Clad as we were in our usual variety of garments we saluted and dispersed to wherever duty or relaxation led us.

On the pleasant evening of 4 June 1917 a few of us decided to walk to Cassel, the little town on the hill two miles away, to have dinner at the hotel as a change from the marquee mess. Forrest's place in my tent had been taken by a newcomer, a 20-year-old Canadian named Bennie, a quiet type, of Scottish descent, fairish hair and rather less than medium height. I asked him if he would care to join us. But he looked up with a quiet smile and answered simply, 'No, thanks, Mac, I've got some letters I want to write.' And I left him sitting placidly on the edge of his camp-bed.

When we returned at about 10 o'clock he had just finished writing and stood up, stretching, as I entered the tent. Very, very quietly he spoke.

'I've written a couple of letters and gone over all my kit,' he said. 'If anything happens to me tomorrow, Mac, will you post the letters for me and see that my kit is sent off to the two addresses where I've labelled it to go?'

I said I would. But what words can one utter at such times? Christ knew the loneliness that precedes predestined end of life when he went alone into the Garden of Gethsemane and prayed. There is one journey everyone must make alone.

Soon after, we turned in. Beyond the narrowing vee of the tent opening tall trees shut out all but a tiny strip of sky where pale stars sparkled, disrobed of rain or mist. Cool, sweet air came in under the upturned flap at the bottom of the bell tent. On his camp-bed opposite me my half-tent comrade of the past three weeks slept peacefully. In the distance a cock crowed throatily.

Next morning eight graceful aeroplanes stood at the edge of the airfield. Overhead the brazen sun of a hot summer day drove heat-waves down upon all our world. A number of inert mechanics sprawled inverted in the shade cast on the ground by the outspread wings. Not a sound broke the sweltering silence.

No cloud flecked the blue vault of sky. This was a day fit for the joys of summer – a day on which to recline in somnolent ease upon the sandiest beach fringing the mirrored pool of ocean, or to dream upon a grassy couch beside some melodious brook weaving a tortuous course through scenes of rustic beauty. But, instead, eight graceful aeroplanes outlined the raw edge of a large, flat expanse of ground where once crops had grown, where now the surface was scarred by the passage of the iron-clad tail skids of taxiing aeroplanes.

Away to the east small blobs hung motionless in the sky. After observing them steadily for a minute or two they appeared to move uncertainly up and down. But they were quite stationary, those distant kite balloons. It was the heat swirl in the air that imparted their apparent movement to the eye.

A group of men gathered outside the pilots' and observers' hut at the corner of the airfield – 17 in all. Sixteen of them carried flying kit; the 17th was the squadron commander, who was speaking.

'Well, you know what to do, eh, Charlie?' he asked.

'Yes, sir,' Charlwood replied in his slow, soft, Sussex voice.

'We've got to get the photographs of the railway station and return as quickly as possible.'

'Yes, that's right. Don't waste any time. Get your height, go straight over, get the photographs, and come straight back. I'm sorry I couldn't get you an escort. Can't be done.'

The squadron commander paused and glanced round the circle of faces. They were grim. There was not a smile on one of them. The job on hand was no 'cushy' one. It involved a trip to the town that recently had become the squadron's bogey: Menin. The very sound of the name was ominous. They had been there before; often; but, mostly, when they had come back, someone did not return. It meant running, or rather flying, into a perfect hornets' nest of Huns, for the biggest concentration of enemy aircraft was now on this sector of the front. It meant... but they all knew precisely what it meant. Van Ryneveld's wide lips curved into a wry smile that was characteristic. He slid off the small wooden table on which he had been sitting and stood up.

'Come on, chaps, time's up. The very best of luck.'

All the squadron's single guns firing through the propellers' arc were now operated by the Sopwith-Kauper interrupter gear. Kauper had come to England from Australia at about the same time as Harry Hawker and had joined the engineering side of the Sopwith Aviation Company. His gun gear gave the Vickers a faster rate of fire than the Ross and was more reliable, but this improvement was too slight to convert the inferior 1½-Strutter into equality with enemy fighters carrying twin forward-firing guns and having swifter speed and climb.

Pilots and observers donned flying caps, gloves, goggles and leather coats as they walked over to their machines with the clumsy movements imparted by thigh-length sheepskin-lined flying boots. It was hot on the airfield, but it would be cold at or above 10,000 feet. They climbed into their open cockpits. After wriggling down into his basket-work, leather-cushioned seat, each pilot loaded his front gun and made preparations for engine starting. Each observer, standing in his cockpit, tested his Lewis gun and Scarff gun-ring for free movement. Speaking-tubes were rapidly fixed and connected.

Van Ryneveld glanced along the line of machines. All were ready. He raised his hand. At the signal the mechanics swung the propellers. One after another each engine thrummed into life. Their note rose to a roar as the pilots ran them up on test.

In succession the 1½-Strutters taxied out and took off. Up above, they were soon in formation. Van Ryneveld watched them swing off north-west to gain their operating height. When they disappeared to specks he walked slowly back to the squadron office, his hands deep in his pockets, his brow furrowed, his head bent. No squadron commander relishes sending off his men to a task that he is himself forbidden to do. When he reached the office he entered and crossed to the window. He stood silent, looking out for a long minute. What thoughts passed through his head he confided to none.

In a few moments under the hour the formation crossed the lines. It took that time to reach operating height in formation. There were no Huns in the sky. The 16 men flying east subconsciously hoped that the sky would remain empty. But all the time they scanned the circles of space around them; above, level and below. There were no clouds. Their eyes behind their tinted goggles were screwed up to resist the glare of sun and the thin stream of cold air that penetrated the fur and leather. And then, suddenly, their gaze concentrated. Thousands of feet below they saw a cluster of tiny things moving across the earth carpet. They would have escaped an untrained eye. But every one of the 16 men knew them for what they were, a loose formation of enemy scouts climbing rapidly to intercept them.

They were still several miles short of their objective. They glanced ahead at it, then again at the Huns below. It was even odds on reaching it before the inevitable scrap began. Charlwood ignored the Archie bursts that left a wake of smoke hanging in the sky to mark their course. He led the formation straight towards the place. He knew it was their one chance. He must risk the possibility of Archie splitting up the formation. The other pilots saw his move and grimly they stuck to their places. None had had to fall out with engine faults. Straight ahead, damn Archie, was their one thought. They hoped by the concentration of fire from their rear guns to keep the Huns at a discreet distance while the photographs were taken and then fight their way back. It was their only chance to succeed. If it failed? They bunched up as tight as any formation had ever done. And Archie neither split them nor hit them, which just shows the tremendous element of luck in Archie.

They circled over Menin railway station at 11,000 feet and at the same time the first Hun reached their level. He was a large, wicked-looking, all-red Albatros with black wheels. A big-nosed, heavy-shouldered fellow with two machine-guns firing forward. He did not attack at once, but contented himself with a short burst at them from 400 yards to test his guns. The bullets whistled harmlessly past several 1½-Strutters. Then he climbed above and behind them, followed by his comrades.

In that breathless instant Charlwood's observer, Copeland, buried his head inside his cockpit, sighted down the peephole, and exposed his plates. Relying on the seven other 1½-Strutters for his own machine's protection, he completed the job carefully, methodically, so that there should be no mistake. When he looked up again the sky above him was full of Huns, all of the very latest chaser type. The 1½-Strutters were up against the famous circus, the vaunted German Jagdstaffeln.

Amid the roar of his engine and the rush of wind past his open cockpit, Charlwood heard down the speaking-tube the murmur of Copeland's voice, 'I've got the photos. Get home.'

An inlet valve broke on Charlwood's Clergêt at that moment. His was the only machine with a camera. The photographs were the object of the flight. He had no alternative but to beat it for home with 10 photographs of Menin station and its environs. He swung round westward. As though it were a signal for attack, the Huns dived.

Leading them, the brilliant red machine came rushing down, spearhead of five pointed straight at the centre of the formation.

The pack followed.

The formation was perfect, every machine in its place. Not one blinded the fire of another. Each observer, tight-lipped, grim-faced beneath his goggle-mask, stood or crouched in his favourite attitude for handling his gun to the best advantage. It would have been impossible to have had a better formation to guard Charlwood's now defective 1½-Strutter with its precious photographs. But the Huns, outnumbering the formation by two to one, recklessly (or perhaps contemptuously is the word) dived straight at and into it. It may have been their superiority in numbers, or perhaps their faith in their greater fire-power against ours, that produced such absolute confidence.

With their faster speed and manoeuvrability and four times the number of trainable guns, the Huns ought to have annihilated the British formation and felled the photographic machine.

There were too many Huns for each observer to pick out one. Probably several rear guns concentrated on one Albatros, for one went turning and twisting down like a falling leaf, apparently to a certain crash. With the escort protecting his tail, Charlwood flew as fast as his uncertain engine would allow, nose down, westward, towards the lines.

Three Huns came right into the formation, led by the red Albatros. Others came down on the west of the formation, failed to intercept Charlwood, but splitarsing round, forced some of the two-seaters to turn north. In less than two minutes three 1½-Strutters were falling to earth. One dived vertically out of control, temporarily, at least. Another emitted a little wuff of blackish smoke, sideslipped, a tongue of flame curled from her, and an instant later she fell flaming, a thing of tortured horror, from which there was no escape. The third was a ghastly sight. One second she was a beautiful aeroplane, a creature graceful in her element, yet frail. The next she did not exist. A growing cloud of black smoke marked the place where she had lit up with a lightning flame.

No pilot or observer of the remaining 1½-Strutters knew which fate befell which of their fallen comrades. They did not even know who had gone down, for their 1½-Strutters carried no individual recognition mark, as later machines did. In the furious tempest and hot concentration of the dogfight there was no time to observe much detail, certainly none to note the four small digits of the serial number on the rear fuselage or fin of another aeroplane. Not everyone saw all three 1½-Strutters go down under the hammer of the first enemy attack. Visual opportunity could absorb no more for those who did, because in the mental paradoxy of the aerial dogfight, the fleet passage of elongated time, too much happened too quickly for the contestants to perceive more than a fraction of the whole.

The scrap was a long one for aerial fighting. It occupied 23 minutes. But the real scrap, the initial dogfight, was over in less than five. In the other 20 a running fight to the lines took place.

Charlwood, losing thousands of feet in height, shook off his head-hunters and, reaching St Marie Cappel in 20 minutes was first home, with his exposed photographic plates intact.

The remaining four 1½-Strutters of the escort were scattered across the sky at varying heights. Newling's was badly damaged; his observer, Corner, wounded; chased and harried by four Huns, Newling just managed to cross the lines, then crashed because there was no petrol left in the holed tanks. Firth's main petrol tanks were shot through and by a miracle did not make him a third flamer; he came back hedge-hopping low over the ground until the gravity tank ran dry and he crashed at St Sylvestre Cappel, near 11th Wing HQ, without hurting his observer, Hartley, or himself.

The last two were separated for a time, each scrapping three Huns. Then their luck brought them together and helped to save them, after almost proving their undoing. Frew, to avoid one Hun and attack another, dived, then swerved upward in a climbing right-hand turn with his front gun blazing. Simultaneously, to dodge two Huns behind and attack one below, Macmillan swirled violently over to the left in a vertical bank and sideslip while his observer, Webb, let rip a drum from his Lewis at the lower Hun. Frew, zooming upward, and Macmillan, coming down, missed collision by sheer chance. Bare inches separated their wingtips. They were close enough to recognise each other despite the masking of their faces by leather and fur. And, as they missed each other, two of the six Huns went down earthward, falling out of control. Having found each other, the two stuck together. They travelled west whenever the opportunity offered. When the four Huns closed on them the observers fired a burst at the nearest and the two pilots splitarsed round and opened fire at them with their front guns. These tactics did not appeal to this particular clutch of Huns. Every time the 1½-Strutters' noses swung round at them they steered off to a safe distance and Bunty and Mac splitarsed west again. Possibly the Huns, after seeing the two-seaters miss each other by inches and put down two of their comrades, thought they were up against hot-stuff pilots. How were they to know it was a miracle the two did not crash? When still three miles east of the enemy lines the two pilots, as if impelled by one thought, although they had no means of communication, Immelmanned in the same second and zoomed up at the four Huns who followed them, like sharks after a ship for the meat that offers. Instantly the scouts turned east. The 1½-Strutters followed them for a mile with their single, front guns spitting at them stutteringly. Then, with ammunition from both guns all but spent, the two-seaters turned west again and crossed the lines at 9,000 feet. Both machines bore scars of combat. Frew's rudder and elevator controls were partially shot away. He crashed when landing on the airfield. Dalton, Frew's observer, who had fired at one Albatros at very close range during the dogfight, reported it became enveloped in black smoke and then burst into flames when the pilot put the nose down.

It was a bad day for the squadron. Three machines missing, three crashed on our side. Three pilots and three observers missing, one observer wounded. On the credit side, ten photographs of the objective gained. But if our senior commanders had had any sense, or better still personal experience of what they ordered us to do, they would have organised a combined operation with the Nieuport Scouts of No. 1 Squadon, for Menin was well within their range. Had this been done our combined force would have inflicted heavy casualties on the enemy and reduced those we suffered. But Higher Authority was wedded to the idea of rover patrols of scouts at times defined by them and would not depart from it because they thought that this protected the Corps machines engaged on artillery observation, gun ranging and trench photography. The same thought trend persisted into WW2 until losses compelled the RAF descendants of WW1 to learn sense.

Not until the messages came in from the two machines that crashed outside our airfield did I know for sure that my little tent comrade, Bennie, had not been wrong and that I would have to post the letters that he had written on the previous evening when we went out to dine at Cassel. God grant that it eased him to know that he was going, for he went forward bravely as though he was unafraid of the road he had to travel, as though he knew whither he went, and that the end of the way was good.

Next day our planes filled the sky. Patrols of different types of aircraft were detailed to operate at all heights from the ground to upwards of 20,000 feet and from our 1½-Strutters on low patrols we could see nothing in the air but British planes above and all around us. The enemy were driven back and held and on the ground free movement was devoted to the culmination of prepared plans.

Early on 7 June 1917 the Messines Ridge mines were blown and the Battle of Messines began, the first operation in the long series of engagements of the Flanders offensive which lasted until 10 November that year. This was the battle of which Trenchard had spoken to us on our airfield. During morning, afternoon and evening British planes flew over the battle area. The fighting scouts drove enemy planes far back behind their trench-lines, thereby adding to their ground disorganisation and contributing materially to the success of the infantry. Our squadron patrolled at heights from the ground upward to 12,500 feet, and took battle-area photographs from a thousand feet.

During the late afternoon thunder clouds gathered, and lowered, athwart the sky. A cool wind rose from an ominous calm. The tree-tops surrounding our camp bent before the sudden swirl of its onrush. And then, as suddenly as it had come, it died away. It left behind an atmosphere that seemed charged with omen. A great unrest was in the heavens. The noise of the great god Thor reverberated throughout the land as continuous thunder bespoke the oppression that afflicted nature. An hour later the storm passed. The sky overhead cleared rapidly. The sun shone over the cloud cumuli that bestrode the western horizon. Eastward, the land looked bright.

The hum of our engines broke into the quiet of the evening. One after another our five aeroplanes swept upward from the ground, things of beauty that rose to float serenely across the blue patch of sky above the airfield. Once, twice, we circled, then flew away eastward. A thunder of sound broke out anew. But it was the thunder of man, the paean mouthed by war. Away to the east, where lay the trench-lines, an outpouring of smoke proclaimed the conflict that was in progress. In a few minutes we were above the battlefield. Our leader swung round, and we floated northward, above the warring hordes.

Five thousand feet below lay the tortured world. Dirty brown in colour, it writhed and twisted, as if in living agony. Seared masses of tumbled earth huddled close together, forming one great scar, no, a living weal erupting fountains of mud and human flesh; at intervals, great warts protruded, the huge craters of exploded mines. Over all this cancerous excrescence of war, little sparks of flame leaped and sank and died in continuous reincandescence; and the pounded earth spouted at their torturing recurrences. A thick pall of greenish smoke shrouded the spectacle in the semi-gloom of a mystery our eyes could not penetrate and that only those of us who had served in the trenches could fully comprehend.

Westward, flickers of natural lightning pricked a peculiar pattern above the background of land and a whitewash of low-lying cloud. Another bank of cloud moved slowly eastward, obscuring our vision outside the vicinity of the battle area. Above this second bank undischarging thunder-heads towered ponderously, and in and out among their changing channels floated and danced our graceful aeroplanes, bearing tiny atoms of humanity, remote from war on earth.

The scene below was oppressive to look upon, its Goyaesque malevolence firing the imagination. One knew, yet found it impossible to realise, that the pigment of that impressionist picture painted on the earth's surface for none but those who flew to see and witness was composed of thousands of men struggling for dear life, one against another, opponents without personal quarrels, who had never met until now. A terrific thunder of sound, the visual evidence of which we saw as if it were a silent movie, all the time was bursting in their ears, as the storm of metal hissed over and about them, imperilling life and limb. A mile above it we were so detached as to be able to view the whole battle-front of ten miles in one comprehensive glance, a picture too big for us to see in detail. Emotions of individuals involved in it were outside our ken. Ours was as the unimpassioned, all-embracing viewpoint of an overall commander of great armies; but ours were not as his emotions either; for we had no participation in his personal triumph from a cruelly won victory, neither had we any need to share his fear of the abysmal personal consequence of possible defeat.

The echo of it reached us as we floated over it. The thunder of its tumult came to us, faintly, through the loud-voiced music of our engines. Great, invisible shells hurtled through the air around us, rocking our frail machines by the fury of their onrush. They screamed past us, unseen, unheard; but the hidden menace of their passage was presaged by the waves of air that made our aeroplanes dance like frightened horses.

Around us, on our level, now writhed the thunderclouds. They were unclean things to gaze upon. They reared lurid heads at us; they stretched forth huge, curling tentacles to enfold us as we danced; they were ugly, those great cloud monsters, green and ragged. As we came yet closer they seemed very devils, for our engines' music changed to spluttering terror, and our dancing, carefree aeroplanes shuddered and recoiled from their ogreish touch. Then the sun was blotted out by them and we seemed to be poised, in a viridescent atmosphere everywhere vibrating from the tremors of gunfire. We saw the flickering lights still stabbing at the earth, a churning mess of tortured land, a veritable inferno. Very, very gradually the lower cloudbank crept over the battle area. The earth became vague, then vanished, as if a veil had been drawn over its face.

Our five graceful aeroplanes danced alone in a world of cloud-land. We seemed then to awake to consciousness, to realisation of a fantastic nightmare, the vividness of which remained in the turbulence from the passing shells that still rocked our frail machines and the shivering sensitivity of our wings to the remoter shock-waves of the continuous barrage that haunted us through the throbbing music of our engines.

One after another we nosed our way westward in the fading light. One after another we dipped downward into the cloud that wrapped its shroud about our wings and fuselage. With our engines shut off we glided quietly downward and homeward, back to the warmth and comfort of our mess and tents, acutely conscious of the luxury of the way in which we rode to war.

Although our squadron had had a busy day, when dusk fell we had lost only one machine. It had been shot down before breakfast amid the hail of metal hissing through the air above the ground where shell, machine-gun and rifle played their part in the thickest of the fighting. It was A8296, flown by Dobson, just short of his 24th birthday, with Davies a year younger and a Welshman with the forename Gwynonfryn, as observer, who had dived at enemy troops on a road just behind the German lines. No one saw what happened, but the New Zealand Division of the 2nd Anzac Corps found the remains of their 1½-Strutter on the road west of Deulemont three days later. Their bodies lay close to it and the Anzacs buried them there on 10 June. Dobson had been with us for 56 days, Davies for only a fortnight.

By this time I had become one of the senior pilots in the squadron. Postings to Home Establishment and casualties had gradually decreased the numbers of those who were senior to me, even though it was noticeable that most of the casualties occurred among the less experienced pilots. It could be asserted confidently that if a pilot survived his first month in France he had a very good chance of a long life, barring accidents and ill-luck. But in his early days lack of skill as a pilot, ignorance of the appearance and habits of enemy machines, ignorance of how to dodge Archie, and inability to orientate the trench-lines and weave through ground-fire over the enemy back areas, all made the new pilot figure most frequently in the casualty lists.

In the process of working up to seniority I had reached the stage when I led patrols and escorts, and my observer was the one selected to carry the camera and take the photographs while the remaining aircraft in the formation served as escort to our photographic machine. On the day after the Messines Battle began, my observer, Webb, took 36 photographs of the desired objectives.

Flying the 1½-Strutter straight and level, with the observer bent over the camera in his cockpit, gave both Hun and Archie excellent opportunity to concentrate on the photographic machine. The escort was no sinecure so far as the Hun was concerned, but it could do nothing to give any protection against Archie.

On some flights we found occasion to amuse ourselves at the expense of Archie when not involved in photography. We found we could outwit the German gunners by using a new formation manoeuvre which we had recently developed. Each machine flew at a slightly different height in the vee so that each pilot had his own particular piece of sky. (Previously the pairs of machines stepped up from front to rear in the vee had flown at common lateral levels, and the complete formation could make only a wide sweeping turn.) With our new formation the leader simply executed a fast vertically banked turn when he wanted the formation to turn about. The machines behind him did the same in precise order, turning outward from each other. The completed manoeuvre placed the formation in the same order of machines facing the opposite direction except that the leader's left-hand following aeroplanes had become his right-hand followers and vice-versa. This way of turning the formation was too swift to be anticipated by the artillerymen. Sometimes we spotted the gun-flashes of an Archie battery and went down at the guns and gunners, firing with our front gun, then zooming upward in a climbing turn while our observers let drive at them with their Lewis gun.

Chapter VII

ODD SCRAPS

The first German Jagdgeschwader was formed on 23 June 1917. It had Nos. 4, 6, 10 and 11 Jagdstaffeln under the overall command of Rittmeister Manfred Freiherr von Richthofen.

If not before, Webb-Bowen ought to have changed his policy of withholding escorts at the beginning of July 1917, when the new Jagdgeschwader moved north from the Cambrai to the Courtrai area and British squadrons in Webb-Bowen's brigade faced a much greater concentration of German fighters than before.

The spotlight on the aces of the Richthofen Geschwader was skilful, maintained, and still continues; but it was, and is, delusory, because it concentrates on their tactically defensive combats and never illuminates their strategic failure. The theatrical glamour of air combat is as fascinating as the scoreboard of a game, but it was not the real war for which the RFC continued to work, maintained the offensive, and was never denied its objectives other than occasionally and locally and never for long. But RFC losses were augmented and the Jagdgeschwader's diminished by the British brigadier's refusal of escorts.

On 7 July 1917 No. 45 Squadron sent a six-machine photo-reconnaissance to Wervicq, led by Cock. His observer, Ward, exposed 21 plates at 10,000 feet over the required area. As the formation returned the Richthofen Circus (as the RFC dubbed the Geschwader) attacked it. Nine Albatros Scouts came down from above and another nine zoomed up from below, with perhaps a few more around. The 1½-Strutters fought to bring their photographs back and reported several Albatros going down but there was no chance in such a *mêlée* to watch them to see what happened lower down, for too many attackers were coming in repeatedly against each Sopwith. Two of the six Sopwiths fell in flames: Hewson, who came from Ararat, Victoria, Australia, was 22 and had been with 45 for three weeks and had not flown nine hours on 1½-Strutters when he arrived; his 30-year-old observer Snyder, who came from North Kitchener, Ontario, had been with us four days longer; 20-year-old Gleed had been a pilot for nearly 10 months and had flown 50 hours on 1½-Strutters and as much again on other types when he had joined 45 Squadron only eight days before; his observer, Fotheringham, was 26, a Canadian from Ottawa and McGill University, and had been with us for two and a half months. They were shot down by 26-year-old Leutnant Hans Klein of Jasta 4 and Vizefeldwebel Lautenschlager of Jasta 11, near Houtem and Wytschaete. One was Klein's 14th victory, the other was Lautenschlager's first and only one. But 45 Squadron brought the photographs back to St Marie Cappel.

Next day Richthofen was hit in the head by a bullet from the Lewis gun of Woodbridge, an observer in 20 Squadron, flying in an FE2d from St Marie Cappel, and but for the defensive tactics of the Germans, Richthofen would have finished the war alive as a prisoner. Instead, he landed on his own side of the lines and was soon under military medical care at Courtrai. On 13 July Klein was slightly wounded and on 19 February 1918 was again wounded, this time in the right hand. Klein survived the war, but Lautenschlager died on 29 October 1917 north of Houthulst Forest when a German two-seater mistook his Fokker Triplane for a Sopwith Triplane and killed him.

In June 45 Squadron had been fully re-equipped with 1½-Strutters powered by 130-horsepower Clergêts; these engines were unable to increase speed appreciably, but they did raise the height at which the ageing 1½-Strutters could operate. This did not help when patrols at lower heights than could have been attained were laid down in orders.

The squadron was ordered to make a photographic reconnaissance of Menin on 22 July 1917 at 15,000 feet. Van Ryneveld tried to prearrange with the CO of No. 1 Squadron that his Nieuport Scouts would rendezvous at that height, but the arrangement came to nothing and our 1½-Strutter crews saw no Nieups.

The squadron crews were not told, but it may be assumed that the mounting pressure of German opposition was the reason why Webb-Bowen and Van Ryneveld went to the front line that morning to watch. Did Van Ryneveld perhaps think this ground-to-air view of events might persuade Webb-Bowen to reverse his stubborn rule against escorts; or was it merely the senators witnessing the contest of the gladiators in the arena?

The formation was strengthened. Eleven 1½-Strutters started, led by Cock. Three had to return with the troubles that Clergêt engines were heir to. Eight flew on, in perfect formation; four carried cameras.

Disparity exists about where the fighting began. Charlwood, a very reliable pilot, and his observer Selby said it started over Messines. Another report mentioned a large shell bursting into a white mushroom of phosphorus above the formation when over Menin and this, it said, attracted the enemy aircraft. The Jagdgeschwader maintained a daylight look-out watch from Courtrai and doubtless special signals were fired by forward batteries. German combat reports named from south-east of Zonnebeke to near Kortewild as the area of their engagements.

All who returned to St Marie Cappel estimated enemy strength at from 25 to 30 Albatros Scouts, some of a newer and larger type. It was a mixed bunch of DIIIs and DVs that dived into the perhaps too perfectly aligned 1½-Strutter formation, which was quickly broken. One Albatros came too low and passed between Firth's and Charlwood's aircraft. Firth opened fire with his Vickers from closer than formation distance and after about 12 rounds the German pilot appeared to be killed and the Albatros went down out of control. But, simultaneously, two more Albatros from behind killed Firth's observer, Hartley, and riddled the aircraft. With his main tank shot through and its air pressure at zero, Firth broke away, turned on his gravity tank and, although hunted by four of the enemy, escaped and scraped over the lines. He landed with his dead observer at No. 1 Naval Squadron's airfield, in an aircraft fit only to be returned to the Aircraft Depot for repairs. Two days before, Hartley had received permission to wear the observer's badge which, unlike the pilot's wings, could be gained only through operational service. He was 20, had been through Sandhurst during 1915–16 and afterwards served with the Royal Munster Regiment in France for six months before transferring to the RFC; Lancashire mourned another son.

Four Albatros came down on the tail of another 1½-Strutter and Leutnant Alfred Niederhoff of Jasta 11 shot Deakin and Hayes down. Other 45 Squadron crews last saw their A1032 falling in flames near Menin; Niederhoff said it crashed south-east of Zonnebeke, which sufficiently tallies. Deakin, another Sandhurst graduate during the early part of the war, was commissioned in the 10th Jats, Indian Army, and had been up at Oxford before the war; he had never served with the Army in the Field and he came to us only a fortnight before he died, with a total of 40 hours as a pilot, 16 of them on 1½-Strutters, the son of a Worcestershire county family. Hayes, 21 and a year younger than Deakin, was a Londoner before volunteering to be an observer. He had been with us just over three months. But Niederhoff did not long enjoy this, his seventh and last victory; Hoidge of 56 Squadron killed him six days later.

During the running fight, Blaiklock, observer to Crossland, claimed an Albatros shot down out of control.

Cock told me his story long afterward. About 30 Huns attacked and the leader's first burst of fire put his, Cock's, engine out of action. After one shot by his observer, Moore's Lewis gun jammed and he could not get it going again because he had let the spring tension down and had forgotten to bring a spare. Five Huns continued to shoot at them all the way down from 15,000 feet and Cock had the luck to set one on fire with his front gun after his engine had stopped, a marvellous feat which he said Webb-Bowen and Van Ryneveld confirmed. The propeller must have stopped where the cam allowed the gun to fire freely. Cock was soaked in petrol from his riddled tank and has never known why his B2576 did not catch fire. Possibly the dead engine saved them from this fate. The left side of his rudder-bar was smashed by a bullet that might have been explosive and part of this bullet penetrated his ankle (and was later extracted with a penknife).

Webb-Bowen and Van Ryneveld, watching from the ground, may have been among the last to see B2576 come down, with five Albatros snarling at it, like a pack of hounds after a disabled animal. They did not see the end, because Cock's Sopwith passed below their line of sight while still struggling with its pursuers. Cock crashed on a trench-line which he thought was about half a mile from Warneton. His shot-to-pieces aeroplane fell apart. He and Moore were taken prisoner.[1]

Leutnant Otto Brauneck claimed this for his ninth victory. But he, too, did not long survive this triumph. The new Camels of No. 70 Squadron killed him four days later, two before Niederhoff, and before he had scored again.

The broken 1½-Strutter formation, scattered and leaderless, fought back to the lines, and the survivors crept home. German records that I have seen name no fighter pilot killed on 22 July 1917; so, presumably, those believed shot down survived, as did Cock and Moore.

This was the only reconnaissance from which the 1½-Strutters of 45 Squadron failed to bring back photographs, and in this sense it was a victory for the Circus. What Webb-Bowen and Van Ryneveld thought of it has never been revealed. Squadron records tell nothing either, because our

---

[1] Cock and Maurice Moore remained in the RAF after the war and became group captains. In that rank Moore commanded the RAF at Narvik and was drowned when the *Scharnhorst* and *Gneisenau* sank the aircraft carrier *Glorious* during the final evacuation from northern Norway in 1940. Cock survived WW2.

1½-Strutters were superseded so soon afterwards that little time remained in which operational orders could show whether or not the brigadier-general had changed his policy. Perhaps this early supersession offered a timely opportunity to avoid the admission of any change.

On that same day, after his fourth visit to the British Armies in the Field, King George V issued a Special Order of the Day: 'But be the road before us long or short, the spirit and pluck which have brought you so far will never fail, and, under God's guidance, the final and complete victory of our just cause is assured.' Squadron orders conveyed the message to all; and also announced the transfer of Charlwood from 'C' to 'B' Flight to take immediate command in the room of Cock. In 1917 promotion came quickly in combat squadrons.

Apart from these main engagements, these battles of the air when the numbers of aircraft engaged were great and the fighting fierce, there were many that were different. When the active-service pilot, looking back upon his varied hours across the lines in France, takes the trouble to think, it must strike him that he was in many odd scraps. Odd, in this case, does not imply peculiar or out of the ordinary. It is used in its other sense, as one uses the expression 'odds and ends'.

Such scraps had no definite beginning. They were not planned. Their origin was somewhat obscure. Sometimes they had no very definite finish, when, to use the accepted term, they were 'indecisive'. At other times, the end was just as certain as the beginning was dubious. These were the scraps ('scrap' was the pilot's expression for an aerial fight) that the pilot, or the formation, just fell into at a time when there was very little doing. Their usual vigilance, perhaps, somewhat relaxed, they suddenly found themselves mixed up with several enemy machines equally tranquil of mind.

The expression 'machines tranquil of mind' may seem strange, but it is easily explained. A pilot, thinking of his accompanying machines, invariably knew them by the occupant. For instance the leader of a formation, looking back to see how the formation was holding together, mentally noted the position of the several machines. He said to himself, 'There's Browny on the right, Mick on the left, and Bill tucked in behind. That's all right.' But when he thought of a Hun machine he knew nothing of the man inside it. Nevertheless, since an aeroplane in the air did betray the temperament and personality of the man in the cockpit behind the controls, he always talked of a Hun aircraft as if it were a human being. It was natural to do so.

A formation on offensive patrol was, as a rule, on the look-out for a scrap. Then, the responsible task of the formation leader was to use his skill, judgment, and, above all, his wit and common sense, to manoeuvre his formation into the best possible position for a united attack and the speediest defeat of the enemy machines. Methods adopted varied with the circumstances, because, as in everything connected with flying, conditions changed with lightning rapidity. It needed a cool and steady head, and all the skill of a Nelson or Drake, to lead a formation of fighting scouts into successful aerial combat. Then there were the long reconnaissance formations which, for the sake of the valuable information they sought, avoided unnecessary combats; this, again, was a job for a master of his craft.

Rumours of the impending change in our machines had been current ever since 'Boom' had made his speech to us just before the Battle of Messines Ridge and whenever we went down to No. 1 Aircraft Depot at St Omer to collect replacement 1½-Strutters for those written off, we scouted around to look at any new types. I disliked the DH5 at sight and hoped it would not be it we should receive. I liked the look of the Camel, and being from the Sopwith firm it appealed to us who had been flying their products. The Camels we saw had the same engine as our 1½-Strutters, which meant we should not have to learn any new engine tricks, and we were glad when we heard that we were to have Camels.

Van Ryneveld flew one from 70 Squadron to St Marie Cappel late on 24 July 1917. Three days later he and Harris flew first and second Camels from No. 1 Aircraft Depot. These first Camels were used as practice mounts by our senior pilots. Before any did so Van Ryneveld insisted that he must first demonstrate his ability to spin his 1½-Strutter over the airfield. This was a wise precaution that may have played a part in the complete absence of personal accidents during the change-over period. I had learned to spin on the Nieuport 2-Seaters and had often spun the 1½-Strutter, but, as with the others, I dutifully spun my 1½-Strutter above the airfield for the CO to see before I flew the Camel. When coming in to land in the 70 Squadron Camel, John Firth could not make the engine pick up when he saw he was undershooting; he came down outside the airfield boundary and wrecked her.

In the early morning of 28 July I flew the squadron's first 1 AD Camel. It was my second flight in a single-seater scout and quite different from my first such experience at Upavon months before. The Pup was smooth and stable, mellow like old wine. The Camel was a buzzing hornet, a wild thing, burning the air like raw spirit fires the throat. This fierce little beast answered readily to intelligent handling, but was utterly remorseless against brutal or ignorant treatment. Possessed of a sensitive elevator control she reacted swiftly to slight fore and aft stick movement. I spun her and she fell earthwards in a mad whirl.

Her fuselage was short. She was tail heavy, so that one had to press the stick forward in normal flight because there was no tailplane adjustment. Her rudder was too small. The gyroscopic action of the rotary engine in her light wood-and-wire framework forced her nose down in a right-hand turn; once this began the rudder could not bring the nose up again. To make a swift right-hand turn without losing height one had to apply left rudder the instant the manoeuvre began and push on full rudder before full bank. Then the Camel turned very fast, far more swiftly than to the left. It was mainly on this ability that she won her fame in fight, for the heavier stationary-engined German scouts could not turn as quickly and, when they were engaged at close quarters, the Camel could make three turns to their two in a right-hand circle, in spite of her relative inferiority in climb and speed at even moderate altitudes. But, let the ham-handed or inexperienced pilot pull the stick just a little too far back while turning all out and the Camel would flick quickly into a spin, which was the pitfall of many a novice and, could be a death-trap at low heights.

After my first Camel flight and still before breakfast I was standing by on the sunlit airfield, with my 1½-Strutter, awaiting reports of enemy activity. The squadron office telephone bell rang. The Recording Officer, told of some enemy aircraft seen near Warneton, told me. I jumped into my cockpit. White, one of our observers who had just got his badge, jumped in behind. We trundled off towards Armentières, then round by Warneton, and over to the east of Comines. We drove two observation aircraft eastward, then ran into five enemy two-seaters escorted by several scouts and had a long-distance skirmish at odds of 10 to 1 well east of the lines. But there was no sign of the enemy aircraft above our trenches, which we were supposed to deal with. Probably they had departed before our arrival.

After lunch I went to St Omer by tender and flew back a new Strutter. Its rigging was poor and needed attention from our riggers.

In the evening I made a second practice flight in the same Camel, and spun her down so fast for 2,500 feet non-stop that when I came out the whole landscape appeared to be tilted upward to my still spinning vision and I sideslipped for 400 feet with the horizon askew, yet appearing mockingly level, before I was able to fly straight again. Never did I fly another aeroplane that spun as fast as the Camel for so little loss of height. She could complete one turn of a spin in a drop of 100 feet. No wonder I was giddy after 25 rapid revolutions and needed the height loss of four more to restore my equilibrium. Aero-medical specialists were to investigate this sort of thing later, but at that time their research had not begun.

Comparatively slow delivery of our Camels involved our squadron in the continuance of our work on 1½-Strutters, and during this time we had occasional practice flying on the Camels. No. 70 Squadron, more fortunate than ours, had moved back to Boisdinghem and out of action to re-equip, while No. 43 Squadron was engaged solely on line patrol work pending its re-equipment with Camels.

31 July 1917 was a zero day in the Flanders Offensive. One of the series of Ypres battles began with the Battle of Pilckem Ridge, which resulted in the capture of Westhoek on 10 August. Our squadron was engaged on special low reconnaissance work and during one trip I dived low and with my observer, Copeland, fired about 300 rounds on huts and stationary transport at a little place called Korentje. From our two-seater we could spit bullets from the front gun as we dived, then bank and turn and zoom upward with the observer directing a stream of lead downward past the tailplane. But the strain of the work told on our engine and we just scraped over the trenches with our engine cutting out and I landed at No. 1 Naval Squadron at Bailleul.

A few days later, in cloudy weather, a clutch of French Spads dived and fired on three of us. In self-defence we pulled up and pooped off back at them, whereupon they passed overhead, flying north. A few days more and we were again standing by on the airfield awaiting the call of enemy aircraft. In answer to the first call Copeland and I found near our lines an enemy two-seater which we drove east of Lille. He was faster than ourselves and we lost him. Forty minutes after returning to our airfield, and before breakfast, we were off again in answer to another call and had a scrap with seven Albatros Scouts, one of which fell earthward probably out of control. In the evening on a south patrol we flew through dirty weather. Above us were some big FE2d pushers of 20 Squadron and some DH5s of 32 Squadron. During the ensuing three days of patrol work we had some indecisive scrapping with several enemy scout formations and shot up a DFW enemy two-seater. In one of these scraps we suffered a broken foresight on the rear gun and in another we expended all our ammunition. In intervals between shooting we observed and reported large gun-flashes and a fire at Langemarck. On one of our flights we dived on enemy trenches and finished our unused ammunition dispassionately among their occupants, just what we were expected to save our own infantry from enduring. Several times our overworked and overloaded 130-horsepower Clergêt engines gave us trouble with valves and ignition; frequently the wind-driven air pump that kept up the pressure to force the fuel from the tanks to our engines failed to maintain the flow, which meant that the pilot had to keep the pressure up by hand pump. These things all came along in the day's work. There was no need to make special comment on them. They were all entered in the Squadron Record Book in the normal routine of war.

On 12 August my own Camel was allotted to me and I took her up to practise spinning and diving. Next day we arranged a formation practice with seven Camels. After cruising and manoeuvring, the leader was to fire a red light as a signal for imaginary enemy aircraft sighted below, then dive, and all the others were to follow in formation.

Findlay had taken over 'A' Flight after Mountford's death and was formation leader; Charlwood was deputy leader. I was flying at the rear in B2314. After half an hour of climbing and manoeuvring, Findlay led us, at 7,000 feet, northward away from the airfield and fired his Very pistol. I saw the flare curl outward and upward from his aircraft and, as it slowed speed above us, brighten into red flame. Findlay's Camel then curved forward and downward towards the ground.

On the 1½-Strutter we had to exert all our strength and skill to dive forward, for they were very stable aircraft, and resistant to any sudden change in flight attitude. We shoved the stick hard forward, simultaneously turning the tailplane wheel to increase tail incidence. In my keenness to follow Findlay (after only 45 minutes of previous Camel flying) I inadvertently thrust my stick hard against the Camel's instrument board, just as we did on the 1½-Strutter. B2314's response was instantaneous. Her tail rose like a bucking bronco's and threw me head first out of the cockpit. My lap belt, a ridiculous, elastic-sided contraption, immediately expanded, letting me slip through it. I thrust my left hand down to grab hold of the bottom of the seat as I felt myself going. My blind fingers missed the seat but caught the adjusting tap for controlling the fuel rate of flow to the rotary engine which I had screwed off just before pushing the stick forward. My fingers closed around the T-head of the tap, but the acceleration on my body was too much for that flimsy fitment to resist and I was shot out on top of the two Vickers machine-guns, the barrels of which lay along the fuselage deck forward of the hump that gave the Camel its name, with the T-piece in my left hand. To save myself I clutched at whatever projections I could. There I lay, with the windmilling propeller blades almost grazing my nose, until the terrific initial acceleration died out. Then, while literally standing on my head, I had the forces of the partly inverted dive to earth to contend with. Using all my strength I forced myself backward and upward inch by inch towards the cockpit until my right hand found the grip at the top of the stick to use as a handhold with which to pull myself back into the cockpit, ignoring whether the stick could stand this unstressed load or not. With a back somersault over the stick I landed back in my seat. My feet found the rudder-bar. I eased the Camel out of her headlong plunge, having fallen head down for almost a mile. 'Good thing our dive began at 7,000!' I thought.

The formation had dived away ahead. The other pilots' view from their shallower angle of dive prevented them from seeing me in my predicament behind them. They were now far ahead and much higher than I was. The dive had been made with the airfield behind the formation; anyone watching from there saw only the bottom of my Camel against the sky; I, lying on top of my fuselage, was invisible to them. In my fall I was as one who goes over a cliff when others are about, yet no one sees what happens.

When I recovered normal speed I automatically opened the throttle. Nothing happened. I remembered that the gravity tank fuel ran through the same fine adjustment, which I could no longer operate. I could obtain no help from my engine and could not rejoin the formation. I slowed to a steady glide and looked around to find the airfield. I quickly spotted the hangars in the distance; turned towards them, and estimated I could reach the airfield without power. I had a little surplus height at the last moment; rather than use it to try to pull off a clever landing close to the hangars without an engine, I made a couple of S-turns and landed near the centre of the airfield. I climbed out; walked in. Van Ryneveld, standing at the edge of the cinder track, looked severe.

'You ought not to lose your engine when you land, Mac,' he said.

'Not without reason, sir,' I answered, holding out my left hand with the T-piece of the fine adjustment still in it.

'What's that?' he asked.

A brief explanation changed the remonstrance into realisation that it was fortunate that both B2314 and I were whole except for the tap handle. My Camel was quickly wheeled into the flight hangar to have a new fine adjustment fitted. One by one the others came down and taxied in safely.

During our last week of work on the 1½-Strutters the Battle of Langemarck was raging below us and our reports were full of details of fires and dump explosions, train movements and barges on canals, smoke screens and gas, battery positions and shelling. We carried out our work at a lower level than usual and fired at hostile trenches and kite balloons. Archie was good, accurate and determined, but unlucky. Over Ypres, we spotted two Gothas and drove them eastward.

On 18 August Van Ryneveld was on the airfield when a Hun two-seater came over flying very high. All our pilots were out on jobs of work. The major jumped into one of the new Camels and darted off in pursuit of the Hun. It was the fourth time he had chased Huns on our side since our Camels arrived. He had flown the first 45 Squadron Camel to go into action, when, on 9 August, he engaged an Albatros two-seater at 16,000 feet only to have both his guns jam with broken Prideaux links (the disposable aluminium clips that formed cartridges into belts). On his second and third sorties he had been unable to find or catch up with the marauder. Now, for the fourth time he climbed up, up, gaining all the time on the aircraft he could see. He was below the Hun's tail and considered himself still too far off to open fire, when the enemy observer pulled his trigger and scored a lucky burst. A group of four of the stream of bullets centred round the major's heart, all within half an inch. A fifth grazed the side of his head. He shut off his engine and glided downward. He felt that he must fall asleep. But he knew that if he did, it would be his final sleep in which his Camel would carry him earthward in the fearsome, uncontrolled plunge of a machine with an unconscious pilot fallen on its controls. And so he willed himself to stay awake. With skilful hands and strong determination he guided his Camel to a perfect landing on Bailleul airfield. He took the watch from the instrument board and put it in his pocket, for watches left in unguarded aircraft were seldom found again and their safety was a pilot's responsibility. As people ran up to his Camel he climbed out, and said: 'I'm wounded'.

He collapsed. They took him into the adjoining military hospital and his magnificent constitution pulled him through the valley of shadows. When he was fit to be moved he went home to England and we lost a splendid commander whom we all loved.

Captain A. T. Harris, the senior flight commander, assumed command of the squadron. He had come to us from 70 Squadron as a flight commander and was not one of the old pilots who had fought his way to that rank with the squadron. When we lost McArthur, Benge was posted to us to replace him in command of 'C' Flight, but eleven days later was posted home. Harris took his place on 18 June 1917. Harris was an accomplished pilot, with extensive flying experience for that period. He was slim, with fair to ginger hair, very blue eyes, and forthright speech. When he first took over 'C' Flight he flew behind one or other of his junior pilots as formation leader. He said he would do so until he became familiar with the sector we operated over; but possibly he also wanted to see just how well his flight did its operational work. We admired him for that unusual action by a flight commander. A strict disciplinarian, when he first inspected his flight hangar, he saw that NCOs and ack emmas had pinned a number of pictures from magazines, photographs and cartoons to the internal wood framework of the canvas-covered Bessoneaux, an innocent enough anodyne to the unending drudgery of their work. Harris immediately ordered the whole lot to be taken down and the interior of the hangar to be kept clear in future; this did not endear him to the men, who judge quickly between what they regard as essential and non-essential orders. But in such matters he was peremptory. He had an inventive mind and in his Camel fitted a hand-operated mechanical digital counter to record the number of rounds fired from his Vickers guns, with one gun's external moving mechanism operating the hand lever of the counter. He also fitted one in my Camel and perhaps in others. To many his personality was disconcerting, but I liked him. He needed an experienced observer and I volunteered he should take mine, Webb, who had been with the squadron since mid-May and was imperturbable in all situations. I then took on Copeland, whose temperament was less stoic and for that reason in some ways perhaps even more courageous; but Webb was the better for the formation leader.

On the day after Van Ryneveld was wounded we flew out in six 1½-Strutters on close offensive patrol. About 20 to 30 Huns were in the sky, but they would not come near us and their speed made attack impossible for us. At the end of our patrol time we were returning to our lines in formation at 7,000 feet. Evidently with engine trouble, one machine lowered to about 200 feet below the other five. When four miles east of the German trench-lines we flew into shell-bumpy air. These projectiles, aimed at ground targets, screamed past us, throwing off waves of air that rocked our aeroplanes in unmistakable fashion; but we could neither see nor hear them. We flew straight on towards the lines. My gaze was on the 1½-Strutter below and I saw it was struggling gamely on. Then suddenly it reeled upward in the air and shuddered. As it shook, its wings fell off. The unwinged fuselage looked like a coffin. It nosed down and plunged vertically towards the earth and, as it turned over, a huddled object that was the 19-year-old observer, Fowler, from Scotland's Greenock, shot out of the aft cockpit and then with flailing arms and legs began rotating as he fell. His pilot, Ross, a 24-year-old Australian from Melbourne, fell in the fuselage. Long after the fuselage and Fowler had vanished we saw the wrecked wings drifting down like crumpled brown paper, the uninscribed epitaph to a horrific scene; and my questing mind wondered by what process of predestination were they picked on by an insentient shell that was not even aimed at them and that carried onward unexploded, an invisible harbinger of destruction? Parachutes might have saved both men; although they would have become prisoners of war, they would have had a chance to live, instead of none.

That same day a Special Order of the Day came to us for the information of all ranks. It was a translation of a telegram, of eight days earlier date, addressed to Field Marshal Sir Douglas Haig from General Korniloff, Commander-in-Chief, Grand Quartier General, Russia. It read: 'I have the honour to inform your Excellency that by order of the Government I have taken Command of the Russian armed forces. I am convinced that on the re-establishment of strict discipline amongst our troops the Russian Army will devote all its powers at an early date to assist the efforts of the Allies towards the attainment of the common object which unites us.'

But much more was needed to save the Russian armed forces from their headlong course. Their value as an Allied element against the Kaiser's Germany and Allies was already dead.

The work of our 1½-Strutters was nearly over. They had done good work despite deficiencies in performance; but at high cost in men and aircraft. They had fought and photographed, covered and protected the artillery observation aircraft, and aided the entrenched troops. If some of their pilots and observers said that in acting as the fringes of the artillery fleet they were simply used as bait, there is this much to be said in reply: That they were damned fine bait. The idea of human 'bait' may be repulsive to the mental epicure. But only too often it is a necessary part that must be played by some poor, unfortunate actor in that camouflaged tragedy, War.

Chapter VIII

MY LAST JOB ON THE OLD 1½-STRUTTERS

On 21 August 1917 six of us flew on a distant offensive patrol. A new observer accompanied me, a stout London lad named Morris, who had been with us less than a month.

Led by Findlay, we crawled slowly southward at about 8,000 feet, well across the lines. Archie plastered the sky all round us, but we flew onward, treating his familiar greeting with insolence. Archie put up a line barrage between our formation and the trenches. Still Findlay flew south and ignored it. Archie redoubled his efforts by putting up another barrage on his own side of us. Still we flew due south, travelling along an aerial lane bordered by thorny hedges of bursting shells. Then Archie proceeded to be very clever. He gradually narrowed the width of the lane, narrower, narrower; then concentrated every gun within range on that little area of sky where lay the apex of the long triangle, the dead end of the lane. But Findlay knew the game, too. Archie and he had played it often. Just as the shattering burst from the many gun-mouths deafened the ears of the gunners, Findlay swept in a swift half-circle and flew due north. The formation followed on his tail. Fifteen seconds later the dead end of the lane was black with shell-bursts and curling smoke clouds that writhed despairingly in the empty air. Six hunded yards away the formation leader, looking back, laughed merrily.

After a minute's cessation Archie began again, following us northward. Again we swung south. One of the machines next to the leader's developed some engine trouble and began to lag behind. Still the formation flew on. The laggard had dropped back about 400 yards. An old hand would have gone underneath and in front of the leader, then made for the lines and been shepherded back. But Smith was a new boy who had been with us for only a week. With him was Grenner, a qualified aerial gunner, who had come to us temporarily from 20 Squadron two days before. From the rear of the formation I kept an eye on the lagging 1½-Strutter. I saw a solitary Albatros Scout diving from nowhere towards its tail and turned instantly to help Smith. Through the speaking-tube I told Morris to be ready, while I myself fired a burst at the diving Hun. About 100 yards off I swung to give Morris a clear field, because his Lewis had a far faster rate of fire than my

Vickers, and time was important. I steadied the 1½-Strutter and shouted to Morris to open fire. He took a steady aim while I held his platform level. He was a natural marksman.

Grenner, taken more or less by surprise, was wounded in the leg by the Hun. Smith turned right and flew straight towards the lines, with the Hun pouring out lead at his machine without closing right in. As luck would have it, that Hun missed all the vital spots. In spite of his wound, Grenner fired at him and the Hun pulled away from Smith and came nearer us. Morris put a long burst right into him and he disappeared below, going down out of control. I had no doubt Morris hit him and sent him down.

Smith made for the lines as fast as he could. We watched him go west, then veered to rejoin the formation, which had also turned towards Smith and given him escort from some way behind. When he crossed the lines the formation swung east by north to continue the patrol. Smith landed at Bailleul airfield. Another Strutter went home with engine trouble.

A layer of cloud gathered above us, straddling the sky at about 7,000 feet. Although not thick, it was impossible to see through the cloud layer from below or above. Ten miles east and west of us the sky was clear right up to the roof. Our four Strutters flew about 500 feet below the cloud-belt. Archie, for some reason, left us alone. Judging by the poor downward visibility, which veiled the earth in a misty blur, we probably offered little more than the deep-throated purr of our engines for Archie to fire at.

Archie did often fire in the direction from which the sound of an invisible aeroplane seemed to come. Sometimes when he did so he was extraordinarily accurate; more often his aim was exceedingly poor. It was all a matter of luck. Archie accounted for some of our most wonderful pilots: Captains Thayre and Cubbon of 20 Squadron and Rhys-Davids of 56, to mention but a few; men who were super-airmen in scraps, yet who came to an unfortunate juxtaposition in time and space when Archie had fired, perhaps, his 30,000th shell. That was how Archie reckoned his score, averaging out so many shells to each aeroplane brought down. At the end of the war this worked out at something like 30,000 shells fired for each German aeroplane brought down by British gun-fire in France.

It may have been, at the particular time of which I write, that the Hun Archie's shell consumption was above the average since his previous hit. That, coupled with bad visibility making markmanship difficult, might have been his reason for lying quiet. There was no other apparent reason. And the Hun usually loved to brass off as fast as he could load and fire.

One result of Archie's silence was to keep us constantly on the alert. The approach of our 1½-Strutters was usually the signal for all Archie batteries within range to open fire. This was partly because we usually flew at moderate heights, and partly because we always flew in formation, thus offering a good target. We were naturally suspicious at the unusual absence of the familiar 'woof' and 'crack' and 'crumph' around us. We scanned the sky closely and keenly, ready for immediate action. Anything might come diving down out of that cloud ceiling 500 feet above us.

An hour passed without incident, while the visibility gradually worsened. It was just possible to discern the main features of the groundscape below. Our vigilance began to relax a little as our patrol time passed and nothing happened. We decided that Archie's quietness was indeed due to the poor visibility and not to enemy fighters outnumbering our formation's, for when Archie saw his own fighters closing to attack he stopped firing in case he hit the wrong target. He knew that an aeroplane with machine-guns was a far more efficient enemy strafer than he could ever hope to be. And so he left them to it and turned from his guns to his field-glasses to watch with redoubled interest the progress of the vivid battle up aloft. Now, after an hour of constant patrolling over enemy-held ground, we decided definitely that Archie was not worrying about either guns or glasses. We did not know why and our ignorance tickled our curiosity. The air pilot likes to know the reason for each tiny detail that colours his aerial life. But, gradually, as the minutes passed, even our curiosity faded into a memory. One day memory would awaken and raise a hot discussion in our mess. Meantime it rested, as a subconscious impression that swallowed wonder and suspicion.

The patrol was almost finished. If anything, the cloudbelt overhead had thickened. Findlay turned in a wide sweep, making a last detour over the southern area of patrol before going home.

Suddenly, with the swiftness of the air, a machine dived headlong from the clouds. It rushed towards our formation and dived beneath it. A second after, another plane came hurtling down from cloudland. It, too, made for the underside of our formation. It was a British scout, a Sopwith Triplane. Down from the clouds it rushed in a straightaway dive. Fifty feet behind it, squarely on its tail, entirely engrossed in the pursuit of its prey, came a big, ugly, heavy-shouldered, green camouflaged Hun, with small black crosses in white circles, pouring forth a deadly stream of bullets.

The triplane pilot saw our friendly formation and dived for its

Right: The author, 1918.
Below: Camel in camera-gun's bull's-eye, Chattis Hill.
Bottom: Maurice Farman Shorthorn (the Rumpety) shows off its undercarriage.

Opposite top: Upavon aerodrome.
Opposite middle: Sopwith
1½-Strutter. Author taxies in at
Upavon.
Opposite bottom: Forrest practising
with a camera-gun at Upavon.

Above: Sopwith 1½-Strutter up a tree.
Below left: Garratt and Carey in flight
in 1½-Strutter.
Below right: Brownell demonstrates
full flying kit of the period.

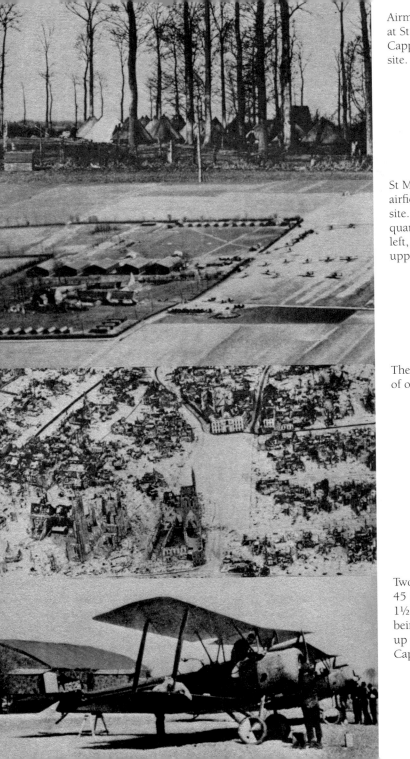

Airmen's camp at St Marie Cappel second site.

St Marie Cappel airfield first site. Officers' quarters lower left, airmen's upper right.

The silver ruins of old Ypres.

Two 'C' Flight 45 Squadron 1½-Strutters being tuned up at St Marie Cappel.

Top: Train halt in France en route for Italy. From left to right; Moody, the author with Beattie, Black, Brownell, Dawes, Watts, Carpenter and Child.
Above: The cockpit of a Sopwith Camel scout fighter.

Top left: From left to right; Selby, Carey, Cock, Vessey and Bennie at the officers' camp, St Marie Cappel.
Top right: From left to right; Author (just out of shot), Bush, Firth, Williams and Ross beside the pilots' hut, St Marie Cappel.
Left: The author with McArthur and Bramwell at Chattis Hill.
Below: 'A' Flight Camels lined up for patrol, St Marie Cappel.

Top: Crashed 'C' Camel after being brought in to Istrana airfield. Left to right; Corporal G. Warren, 2/Lt C. E. Howell, 1/AM E. Hyde.
Above: Members of 45 Squadron (left to right; Williams, Watts, Moody and the author) with two Italian pilots at Istrana. (*Imperial War Museum*)

Top: 'V' Camel after a
down-wind landing at
Grossa airfield.
Above: DII Albatros
fighter captured intact.
Right: The author's
favourite Sopwith Pup,
Chattis Hill.
Right bottom: DV
Albatros.

protection even as his comrade had successfully done. But his straightaway dive proved his undoing. The Hun, which I now recognised as a DFW two-seater, poured in a raking fire on what amounted to a relatively stationary target. The Hun pilot did not see our formation below him or, if he did, his blood was up, and in the heat of the chase he flung caution to the winds that rushed behind him.

All this took less time than it takes to read. One instant it was not, and the next it was!

As the first triplane came down from the cloud ceiling our formation immediately swerved into a rotating circle. This was our 'line of battle'. Like the ancient defensive square, it offered the maximum fire effect and, at the same time, covered each individual machine front and rear by the rear and front guns of its immediate neighbours in the endless swirl of machines.

The first triplane dived below us safely, then climbed and joined in our formation. The second one was harder pressed. He made his bid for it and, as he came, I saw his plight and dashed out of the swirl towards him, pulling my nose up at his Hun aggressor. I fired a few shots before my B2583 stalled and its nose flopped down again. As we stalled I kicked on rudder and shoved the stick hard across in a skidding turn and shouted down the tube to Morris: 'Hun above us, shoot!'

Morris crouched low in his cockpit with his Lewis gun in sighting position. As I straightened from the skid he aimed just below the nose of the Hun aircraft. At the first whipping crack from Morris's gun I steadied out and held the 1½-Strutter firm as a rock.

The triplane dived out of sight below our wings. The DFW followed close behind. Morris opened fire at a range of 50 yards with his target closing at a relative speed of 100 miles an hour. The Hun's headlong dive after his quarry brought him almost to the muzzle of our crackling Lewis. He flew right through the stream of bullets, and they raked his fuselage from nose to tail. His forward impetus carried him on underneath us and we lost sight of him for the moment, just as we had lost sight of the British scout he hunted.

We were about 400 yards from our formation. I circled round to rejoin it. As I banked over in the turn I glanced down. Some 2,000 feet below us a camouflaged aeroplane was falling earthward out of control. It fell almost vertically, nose down. And, as it fell, it developed a curious, uneven, flicking turn, the certain sign of an aeroplane absolutely out of control. I pointed him out to Morris.

We descended in a spiral, Morris and I, watching the doomed machine. When it was quite close to the ground, just how close it was impossible to tell from our height, a tiny, licking flame appeared from the middle of its fuselage, followed by a trail of smoke. Its end was sudden. It fell in a headlong dive and crashed sickeningly nose first into the ground. During his fall I felt a strange mixture of pity and triumph within me. I was thrilled to see him go down; but I would have liked him resurrected on the ground.

Somehow I felt a sense of danger. I looked up. A second Hun was diving on us, at our blind spot, quarter front. I swerved down and away just as the DFW opened fire and his first burst missed us. I hoicked up in a fast climbing turn. As the old 1½-Strutter answered her controls, I shouted down the speaking-tube to Morris, who was still intent on the crash and the ground below, and unaware of the danger above. We had been almost caught napping, and our formation was too far off to give us immediate help.

'Fire on that blasted Hun above!' I yelled.

Morris did not even answer. He spotted the Hun at once and swung his gun into position. He knew what to do, exactly. And to give him time, even as I shouted down the tube, I sighted my own gun while I shot upward with the speed gained in the downward swerve. As my sight centred with the necessary deflection I pulled the trigger.

Pop-pop-pop-pop! stuttered the Vickers.

The Hun zoomed, pulled upward by his big Mercedes engine. My few shots passed unpleasantly close under him, but not for long could I hold the 1½-Strutter up at a big angle before her nose dropped in a stall. Her engine was not powerful enough.

The instant our nose dropped I jammed the controls hard over in another skidding turn (turns which in post-war flying days came to be known as the essence of crazy flying). I saw the angle of Morris's gun in my little mirror. I saw the Hun turn over at the top of his zoom for another dive at us and allowed for both. I steadied the Strutter.

'Fire!' I yelled in my excitement. But my words were cut short by the rapid staccato of our rear gun. Morris saw his tracer smoke right into the fuselage a foot behind the pilot. Then, just as his gun got going, it stopped. He had fired five rounds, one more than I.

'Damn!' he shouted.

The word was carried away in the slipstream and borne across the heavens. He cursed himself for a blinking fool as he removed the empty drum. In the excitement of watching the first Hun fall he had completely forgotten to refit a full drum. There had been only five rounds left in the one on the gun. These five did not kill the Hun. The bullets probably just missed a vital part of the DFW. A full drum would almost certainly have got him. But the chance was gone, for, as Morris's gun ceased firing, the Hun dived. I turned and dived after him, but there was no comparison in our speeds. The heavy-shouldered Hun went down vertically at over 200 miles an hour. I fired a few parting shots from my single Vickers, then flattened out. A minute later the Hun eased out far below us, heading due east, nose down, engine full on, at a pace we could only envy but never equal, in the language of our squadron 'beetling for home, tail up, wind up!'

We turned west and fell in below the rest of the formation. A little way over our lines the leader fired the washout signal; a white Very light. The formation broke up, each pilot choosing his own method of going home, some flying straight back to the airfield, others stunting on the way.

Morris and I glided slowly down with the engine shut off, so that we could talk with ease. And, as the Strutter glided smoothly, delightfully downward, Morris spoke.

'I say, old man,' he said, 'I'm beastly sorry about losing the second Hun. I am a ruddy fool.'

'Oh! It's all right, laddie,' I replied. 'It's a pity, but anyhow we did give him a thorough scare.'

As we neared the ground I turned on the fuel. The engine roared again and swallowed up our laughter at the thought of that German going home all out from an old 1½-Strutter.

After landing, Morris and I went to the squadron office to report. All combat reports were then signed by Harris, as temporary squadron commander. We made our claims and naturally expected confirmation from other members of the patrol, who were only some 400 yards away at the time each Hun was shot down.

Pilots and observers of the patrol said they saw a British machine go down after diving from the clouds. They could not confirm having seen a Hun go down then. They saw only one machine fall, as did also Morris and I.

No. 1 Naval Squadron telephoned our squadron office that a new pilot of theirs had been shot down while our patrol was on the lines; did our squadron know anything about it? The place they gave was where we had had our scrap. This made confusion worse.

I protested that we would never shoot down one of our own machines and asked the recording officer to ring up our AA and ask if they saw the scrap. The RO could not get them; but a message came in from our Field Artillery that an aeroplane was down on our side in the vicinity of our second scrap; they were unable to identify it.

Because of the conflicting evidence, Harris said I had better go off in a tender to the place, and find out whatever I could on the spot. Rumour spread around the squadron that Morris and I had shot down one of ours. John Firth, meeting me just going off after discarding my flying kit, said: 'I hear you've shot down one of our Tripes, Mac'.

'Don't you believe it, John,' I answered.

'I don't!' he replied. Good old John, solid as the family steel.

Poor Morris, left behind, was badly chaffed. He was told he should learn to distinguish between friend and foe before pulling the trigger.

Our driver drove as near to the lines as we were permitted. Then we left him and went forward on foot, over the French *pavé*. It was a lonely road. German guns were shelling it farther ahead. My former infantry experience enabled me to judge this shelling and I walked on until I knew it was necessary to leave the road and make a detour around the part being shelled. Grimmitt told me long afterward that he was astonished at the way I had walked on towards the shelling as if nothing were happening; he had never been in the infantry and that made all the difference. I curved back to the road when we had passed the target area.

Pursuing our way we came at length to the spot where the reported crash lay. Partly buried in the soft soil beside the road was the pitiable wreckage of a once proudly flying plane, crumpled just not beyond recognition as a Sopwith Triplane. I felt a great wave of pity pass over me. I looked upward to the sky where the awning of cloud still stretched across the blue. From above it, down from the sunlight, through that very cloud, underneath our formation, this plane had been hunted, pursued by a merciless machine manned by one whose eyes gleamed along the gun-sight, one whose sole thought was centred in the destruction of this now crumpled plane, whose pilot had passed from the sunlight into the eternal shadow. Could he have held one instant's thought for the youngster he was shooting down to earth? Standing beside the tangled mass of rubbish that had fallen from the sky, I knew that he could not. Just one instant's hesitation, one fleeting sense of pity, might have saved himself from the avenging stream of lead that Morris poured into his plane; for I knew it was no British triplane we had shot and watched fall downward to the ground, but a camouflaged Hun biplane, wearing crosses on his wings. Besides, this triplane had not crashed in flames, and we had seen flames coming from the Hun.

I stood beside the wreckage of N6308, the death-bed of Flight Sub-Lieutenant F. C. Lewis. At 9.50 that very morning he had left Bailleul airfield with Flight Lieutenant Everitt (N5454). They had engaged four enemy two-seaters. Everitt reported fighting until his ammunition ran out. He landed back at 11.10 and reported Lewis brought down by an enemy aircraft at 10.30. Poor Lewis had not lasted long: Eastchurch Flying School on 7 April 1917; Cranwell for advanced flying on 2 June; Dover Command on 23 July; killed on 21 August.

I would a thousand times rather have saved Lewis than avenged him. But war is nature in the wild, the sequence of the snail, thrush and hawk; the swallow and the butterfly; an endless trail of killing.

But the naval triplane's fate was only part of the evidence I had come to seek. I pressed forward to make inquiries and in the front line trenches found my affirmative. Less than a minute after the triplane crashed behind our lines, the front line infantry saw our Hun fall. Down like an avalanche he plunged and broke into flame before crashing about an equal distance behind his own front line as his victim fell behind ours. The infantrymen said I had better hurry back or else remain with them for the night, because methodical Jerry was just about to begin his heavy evening shelling of the roadway we had to traverse to reach our tender. I told them I must go, because I had left two men beside the triplane crash and could not leave them there.

There was no salvage for us to collect. We footslogged back upon the *pavé*. The first shell came over us as we left the triplane wreckage. It burst to the right of the roadway, well ahead. The 42 mm shells whined at regular intervals. I could readily judge their impact distance from us. One of my companions was jumpy and ready to drop into the roadside ditch. When one shell came low overhead he fell flat on the roadway. Another, who had never before today been under shell fire, behaved like most rookies, walking along upright, half contemptuous of the shells, half ignorant of what to do. I estimated which part of the road was the target and when we came near it circled left over the fields until we had passed the area concentrated on, and then returned to the road not far from the tender, the driver of which was still patiently awaiting us.

I reached St Marie Cappel in the evening and told my story. During my absence a signal from 'J' Battery AA had confirmed our Hun, with regret for the delay. It was now clear to everyone that by watching the Hun go down Morris and I had missed the fall of the British machine, while the others in the formation missed the fall of the Hun by their concentration on the circled Tripe-hound.

Which shows how quick was victory and defeat, life and death, in the air. So much was to be seen that much was missed. In the air was the biggest, freest life in the war yet, measured as flying time is tallied, in hours, spent in the air, it was often the shortest.

The French 48th Squadron at Bergues had witnessed the fight with the Albatros that wounded Grenner. Their pilots had been stalking it and saw it go down partially out of control, then dive, break up, and crash. Smith had reported how Grenner fired at the diving Hun and saw his tracers hit the Albatros. Harris told me he had awarded this Hun to Grenner as consolation for being wounded. Personally, I thought that but for Morris, Grenner might well have been dead, and Smith, too. I was certain then and am to this day that that Hun fell to Morris's gun. I had never seen such a natural shot in the air as Morris. His aim was deadly. He had only to pull the trigger on a drum of ammunition to shoot his target down. But he was too new to the squadron for his prowess to be known when Harris signed and substituted Smith's report for the one he had previously signed for us. Ours remained in the squadron file, marked 'Cancelled'. Theirs went to the Wing. In the course of the war it was immaterial who shot the Hun down.

Our last 1½-Strutter operation was an unexciting four-machine close offensive patrol flown on 27 August by our newer pilots and observers in stormy weather, with clouds at 2,000 feet and visibility restricted. One returned in an hour with a broken exhaust valve; the others had little to report at the end of a two and a half hour patrol. Within ten days three of these pilots were killed in Camel actions and the fourth was shot down and taken prisoner two months afterward.

By 1 September we were fully equipped with Camels. Seven of our observers, including Morris, and all our ground photographic staff, were posted across the airfield to 20 Squadron. Not long afterward, Morris was injured when his 20 Squadron pilot crashed on the airfield; but he survived and was invalided home. Two pilots and three observers, who had been out for a long time, went home tour expired, the observers to learn to fly. The pilots were Findlay and Charlwood. Findlay had been with the squadron exactly seven months, Charlwood three weeks less; both had earned but received no decoration for their work. Decorations for the daily dangers of 1½-Strutter operations were pitifully few and bore no relation to the risks run and the courage shown; observers, especially, went unrewarded; fulfilment of routine tasks, however arduous, however dangerous, however well performed, gained no recognition for anyone. Looking back, one cannot but feel that the pilots and observers of the 1½-Strutters of 45 Squadron were shabbily treated by receiving never a decoration for their functional performances. No observer could become a flight commander; that was exclusively a pilot's prerogative.

On 1 September I took Findlay's place as 'A' Flight commander and Wright took over 'B' from Charlwood. We had been recommended by Harris to fill these vacancies, which carried with them the rank of captain. Wright had been in a lot of tough fighting and his Strutter had often been badly shot up and one of his observers had been wounded. On 6 August 1917 he was awarded the *Chevalier de l'Ordre de la Couronne* which carried with it the Belgian *Croix de Guerre*. His decorations, and the three Military Crosses (one each to Eglington, Belgrave and Cock), and one Distinguished Conduct Medal to Pioneer Smith, were not a great reward for all that the squadron had done and suffered in doing it in 10½ months. The single-seater fighter squadrons were the darlings of the gods represented by the top brass, and upon them were showered most of the decorations. It was not until very late in the war that orders were issued that factors other than the spectacular one of number of aircraft shot down were to be taken into consideration when recommendations for awards were put forward. Qualities of leadership, command both on the ground and in the air, ability to instil *esprit de corps*, administrative abilities, too, were then to be taken into account; this gave the squadrons which were not specifically air-fighting units a better opportunity of reward.

When the three 1½-Strutters landed from their last operation Harris led six Camels off on a distant offensive patrol. His formation engaged 11 Albatros Scouts at 12.15 over Moorslede. Harris fired about 40 rounds into one at 20-yard range and we saw it go down out of control. No combat report was filed, but in my logbook appears the entry I made at the time: 'Harris put one on the floor'. About an hour after that combat I had to land at Bailleul airfield with a fuel pressure failure. Wright had to return to St Marie Cappel, with a faulty engine giving him insufficient revs to keep up with the others. When flying home at the end of the patrol Moore forced landed without damage because his main fuel tank ran dry and the engine did not pick up quickly enough on the gravity tank. It looked as if we should still have our problems with Camels, much as we had had them with the Strutters.

The three 1½-Strutter squadrons, Nos. 70, 45, and 43, which went to France in that order, spent 35 squadron months in France and destroyed between them 41 enemy aircraft. Of these, No. 70 destroyed four in 15 months, No. 45 destroyed 23 in 11 months, and No. 43 destroyed 14 in nine months. And the destruction of these enemy aircraft by the 1½-Strutter crews was a record writing more gallantry across the skies of France than the far greater totals achieved by some of the later and more favoured British aeroplanes, the better performances of which turned the odds in the air definitely in favour of the red, white and blue roundeled planes of the British forces.

Chapter IX

OUR CAMELS GET TO WORK

I first met Vaucour as a captain taking over 'B' Squadron at CFS, before his promotion to major in May. He had flown between 400 and 500 hours when our paths crossed again with his arrival at St Marie Cappel on 22 August 1917 to take command of 45 Squadron. Captain Harris handed over to him that day. Vaucour had entered the regular RHA and RFA on 1 September 1914 and served 11 months with the regiment without seeing active service. In mid-July 1915 he transferred to the RFC and within a month was flying in France as an observer with 10 Squadron; a month later he gained the Military Cross. Next he learned to fly and put up his pilot's wings in May 1916. Three months later he was piloting 70 Squadron 1½-Strutters in France, with Alan Bott as observer; Bott later wrote the book *An Airman's Outings*, in which Vaucour featured as 'Vic'. With 70 Vaucour won a Bar to his MC in October 1916.

To follow in the footsteps of Van Ryneveld was a difficult task. But Vaucour, 27, fair-haired, blue-eyed, about 69 inches tall, with quick movements and an alert mind, had a cheerful manner and a happy smile and he radiated leadership rather than command. He soon succeeded in winning the confidence of his junior officers and later gained their devotion. He straightway instituted the signing of squadron combat reports by those personally involved in the combats, with his own counter-signature below. He upheld those who worked for him; in return they trusted him.

With the impending change to single-seaters an easier administrative task lay ahead for him. Our future aircrew strength would be halved, the smaller machines would be simpler to maintain, all our Camels had the same guns and other equipment, did no photographic work, and the squadron needed fewer groundcrew. It became a closer knit unit than it had been in the 1½-Strutter days.

On the day Vaucour arrived we made our début across the line in Camels. We still felt raw in our new mounts while making that offensive patrol over Menin and Lille, rather as if our Camels were inclined to take the bit between their teeth, and we were fortunate in finding the patrol a quiet one.

In the afternoon we had orders to take some photographs with our

remaining Strutters. We decided to escort them with five Camels. The
Strutters successfully took their photographs over Courtrai and we all
turned west for home. Near Zandvoorde we had a running indecisive
scrap with 11 Huns, but no blood was spilt, and we carried the photographs
safely home. What a difference there was in the extra manoeuvre and speed
of the little single-seaters, in which we could turn and swerve all round the
1½-Strutter with surprising ease.

During the next two days the weather was bad and work was confined
to short flights.

On 25 August, while running over the airfield in the take-off, my
wheels sank in soft ground. My whirring propeller struck a large bone,
which the camp dogs had playfully dragged to the centre of the airfield,
and flew to pieces. It might have been caused by cavitation (as some have
since suggested) but I think it was a direct blow, because a Camel had little
propeller clearance with its tail up and less when the wheels sank into the
ground.

In the evening, in another Camel, I was a member of a distant offensive
patrol. In the gathering dusk the air was very full of planes. My engine was
not running well and I was unable to keep up with the formation. Finding
myself alone, I joined two DH5s flying in a northerly direction. When they
continued to fly north, beyond our patrol area, I left them and turned sharp
right over Houthulst Forest and flew south-east. I saw some FE pushers
away to the south and flew towards them. Suddenly a bunch of Albatros
Scouts came out of the evening haze and very nearly caught me by surprise.

I did not see them until I was about 100 yards from the formation of
ten enemy planes. One of them attempted to dive on my tail from about
50 yards. I threw my Camel about and out-manoeuvred him, swerved,
then opened fire with both guns on one Hun who swerved off. Without
ceasing fire I turned my Camel's nose on a second Albatros, who suddenly
fell downward, vertically. I had no time to observe his fall into the ground-
mist, but 'H' Battery AA confirmed having seen him fall. Both my guns
ceased firing. I found one stoppage and one jam and broke off and turned
westward towards the setting sun.

After clearing my guns I flew east again, but the gathering dusk had
emptied the sky of patrolling planes, and I turned home towards St Marie
Cappel with my heart beating faster than usual after having drawn first
blood for the Camels of 45 Squadron.

On the last day of August No. 46 Squadron landed on our airfield.

Earlier in the year they had been in France, but on 10 July they flew to England and were stationed at Sutton's Farm (later called Hornchurch) airfield as one of London's defence squadrons against Gotha raiders. We all turned out to watch 46 come in, for the weather was dud for work over the lines. The little Pups arrived in separate flights and droned around the airfield.

The first two flights alighted safely in formation, but one pilot of the second flight stopped his engine when he landed. Then the third flight glided in and we watched the comedy of their landing, for one of them, gliding in formation, flew straight towards the stationary Pup. The pilot of the latter looked over his shoulder, decided it was unsafe to stay in his cockpit, jumped out and ran clear. A second later one Pup of the last flight landed fairly and squarely on top of his machine and wrote them both off. The second pilot extricated himself from the mess he had created, unhurt, but looking mighty foolish. Coming in formation he had been following his leader down through the drizzle and not looking out also to see where he was going.

Our airfield was then very busy, with three squadrons to accommodate. But 46 did not stay long with us, under 11th Wing, 2nd Brigade. On 7 September it flew to Filescamp (Izel-le-Hameau) on transfer to 13th Wing, 3rd Brigade, in exchange for 60 Squadron, the swift little SE5s of which glided in to St Marie Cappel without incident that day and took over the vacated quarters on the opposite side of the airfield alongside 20 Squadron; and there we three squadrons remained until November, when 45 flew off to entrain for Italy and were replaced by 57 Squadron with DH4s. The only other event of importance on the airfield was 20 Squadron's change over from FE2d pusher two-seaters to Bristol Fighter F2b tractor two-seaters at the end of September.

On 3 September our Camels got into their stride. We were flying patrols of four Camels that day, patrols numerically too weak relative to enemy tactics at the time. Unlike our 1½-Strutters, we took off in formation in our Camels. These had only about half the duration of flight and every minute saved was of value.

I led a north offensive patrol off the airfield at 0815. While we climbed up towards the lines, gaining height, Shields, who had been only three days with the squadron, dropped out and went back with plug trouble. We were not long over the lines before I saw some Huns to the north-east, and turned towards them, climbing hard. Dawes, who had joined 45 on the same day as Vaucour, fell behind in this manoeuvre, and lost us. I pressed on with Heywood, who had been with us since 28 July. He closed up and together we dived at the formation of Huns.

I picked out one and went in to close range before opening fire. I pressed the gun-triggers and saw him fall over Dadizeele. I was right on him and believed that I had killed him, but there was no proof and this could only be named indecisive. The enemy formation dived away and as their dive was faster than ours there was no point in losing height after those Albatros Scouts. In their flight they came across Dawes, who in a scrap with them had his Camel rather shot about over Zandvoorde before returning to the airfield.

I flew southward with Heywood and over Comines saw two DFW 2-seaters. We dived on them, but they saw us coming and flew east before us. The range was too great to do more than merely scare them and we could not catch them.

I swung round westward and scanned the sky, but could see no more aircraft anywhere. Then my last companion left me. I could not tell what had happened to him, and I shall never know. I watched him fly west across our lines in the direction of our airfield leaving me to wonder if his guns were jammed, his engine or fuel feed faulty, or he, himself, unwell. I saw him well westward of our lines before I took my eyes off him and then I was alone. All three who had set out behind me had returned and I was left to finish the patrol by myself.

I flew northward and near Hollebeke saw four RE8 two-seater artillery machines of No. 6 Squadron from Abeele airfield travelling across the lines in good diamond-shape formation. Above me, to the eastward, were enemy scouts. I saw that the RE8s were flying into trouble and, as I fell in behind and above them, flying east by north, I wondered if their leader knew the Huns were there.

Near Tenbrielen the RE8 leader turned his formation northward, probably to fly his photographic stint. Three formations of Albatros Scouts came down on them, five and five and five concentrating on the rear of the RE8 formation. Down on the bloody crowd I dived, straight at the heart of the leading five attacking the rear machine of the RE8 diamond. Flying true, with my guns all set, I watched the round-bellied scouts grow larger as I rushed towards them. When barely 60 yards away the air seemed full of Huns. I pressed the triggers and saw my bullets rip the plywood of one painted body just behind the engine. With wild exulting anger in my heart

I drove at him until we all but crashed, then zoomed upward to determine my next move, while the painted Hun went down in flames. I turned over sideways and went down again, spraying the Hun scouts with short bursts of precious bullets, for my ammunition was running low. The RE8s turned for home. Their rear guns and my wild charge had driven the Huns to a more discreet distance, although the fire-power available from 30 enemy guns had brought down the RE8 flown by Pickett[2], with Sergeant Foulsham as gunner. From behind the three remaining RE8s and to the east of them I dived and zoomed, spraying the Hun formations to keep them at a distance from the retreating RE8s, for I knew from my own two-seater days that such tactics were the best to follow to protect them.

The Huns fell back and did not press home their attack. The three RE8s returned across the lines in safety, lucky to be alive and flying and carrying only one casualty; wounded Bush. After expending the last of my ammunition in a final burst of fire at the Huns, I crossed the lines behind the RE8s, with a recollection of 90 minutes of constant watching and diving and shooting throughout the whole period of that patrol.

Here, with those RE8s, was yet another example of ordering inefficient two-seaters on reconnaissance over enemy territory without fighter escort. I knew no reason why my patrol should not have been briefed to meet those RE8s and give them escort. Their squadron was in the 2nd (Corps) Wing of the same Brigade as 45, so that Brigade HQ co-ordination of its squadron's work for reconnaissance and escort could have been as direct as the reverse process of the confirmation of the fight at Brigade level from my report forwarded through 11th (Army) Wing and that of 6 Squadron through 2nd Wing. The channels of communication existed; yet I was not informed that this reconnaissance was to be made. It was only by luck that I happened to see those RE8s. If (as was even odds) I had been at another part of my patrol line at the time, I should never have seen them, and they surely would have suffered more than the loss of one machine. From this in-coordinate Brigade policy we in 45 had suffered more 1½-Strutter casualties than we need have done. Here was evidence that 6 Squadron was in a like predicament, brought upon them by the continuation of a policy that did not make sense.

Reporting at our squadron office I learned that Dawes and Shields were back. But Heywood, who had been at my side throughout our first scrap

---

[2] Second Lieutenant A. C. Pickett was taken prisoner and survived the war.

and during the driving off of the DFWs, was not. Just as I had wondered in the air why he had left me to go west across our lines, so now I wondered why he had not flown straight home then, I had hoped that he would have been able to confirm my shooting down of the first Hun scout; but, instead, I was left only with my own belief that one enemy plane went down that never was accounted for by our confirmatory procedures. To this day I have never been able to solve the mystery of the disappearance of my flying companion in the little Sopwith Camel, who was posted missing, and subsequently reported killed. I can only assume that something he could correct in the air, such as a gun jam, caused him to cross our lines and that when he had corrected it he came back east again to rejoin me and was shot down either by Archie or, more likely, an Albatros pack of wolves. He had been with the squadron since 28 July and I was sorry to lose him at the age of 21, a loss to the Mancunians. It grieved me, for I felt that I might have followed him and led him home to our airfield, but had I done so the RE8s might have suffered more than they did. During my leadership 'A' Flight lost only two planes in combat with the enemy, and I grieve more over the loss of these two men than I exult (no, that is not the word, for I do not now exult over such things) over the record of 34 planes shot down by my flight during this same period.

On that day 'B' Flight sent off a four-Camel patrol at 12.40. Thirty minutes later these Camels met 11 enemy scouts near Zandvoorde. E. D. Clarke shot one down in flames which was confirmed by Bunty Frew and Flight Sub-Lieutenant Ridley of No. 1 Naval Squadron; in the same scrap Frew sent one down out of control.

At 15.00 a north offensive patrol of four Camels from 'C' Flight led by Harris met about 14 enemy scouts at about 12,000 feet between Ledeghem and Dadizeele, flying in two formations of seven, painted with black and white stripes on the tail and fuselage, and ably handled. Harris dived at one Albatros who was attacking the rear Camel and fired 150 rounds at close range and saw the machine go down vertically in flames and streaming black smoke. Meanwhile Moore had dived at an Albatros on Harris's tail and fired about 200 rounds at it and it went down out of control. McMaking shot down another out of control with a burst of 100 rounds. Clegg, flying the fourth Camel, was shot in the knee and broke away from the fight. He crossed the lines, but before he could land at Bailleul airfield his Camel suddenly nose-dived from about 500 feet and he was killed. Harris's right Vickers cross-fed a round and jammed and during violent manoeuvring his seat collapsed under him, leaving him doubly handicapped. But after the fight the three pilots resumed their patrol and all reported seeing three machines burning on the ground near Ledeghem.

Harris signed the combat reports for that day on behalf of the Squadron CO. Unlike Vaucour's practice, Harris did not have the signatures of the participants over his. His own combat report was later initialled 'T.I.W.B.' and counter marked: 'This sounds good. R.B.' The first initials are those of Webb-Bowen, made without comment. The 'R' of 'R.B' might have been 'M', in which case the second initials would be those of Maurice Baring, the GOC's personal assistant at Trenchard's RFC Headquarters. In 1936 the original report was taken from the file for permanent retention by the squadron and a certified true copy substituted.

With five enemy scouts reported destroyed, plus two possibles, for the loss of two Camels and their pilots killed, and another Camel damaged by machine-gun fire with its pilot uninjured, 3 September 1917 was quite a day for 45 Squadron. But it is difficult to cross-check combat claims of the period against German published losses. The published list that I have seen of German pilots killed is incomplete. I have seen none for pilots wounded. Those who crashed, but escaped slightly hurt or uninjured, leave a wide-open gateway to the unknown. Thus it was often difficult for us to confirm the material result of a combat because we almost always fought over their side. But Leutnant d. R. Vollertsen, of Jagdstaffel 36, stationed at Cuerne, near Courtrai, is listed in the German records I have examined as killed at Tenbrielen on 3 September 1917. He thus appears to have been the pilot of the Albatros I shot down from among 15 Huns when I dived to aid the RE8s of No. 6 Squadron, RFC, and simultaneously score 45 Squadron's first confirmed Camel victory. Other than this I know nothing about Vollertsen: I do not know how old he was, or where he came from, nor what he looked like, whether he was married or single, carefree or perhaps filled with foreboding on the eve of the day he died. The tragedy of air fighting over their side of the lines lay in the near impossibility of our ever knowing the personal equation. Perhaps this impersonal combat was the better way for all of us. I, and the RE8 aircrews who confirmed it, knew only that an Albatros fell. We counted the machine. We ignored the unknown man who flew it.

Chapter X

CAMEL SCRAPS

By this time we had found that our Camels were excellent fighting planes. Although they were slower in climb and speed than the Albatros Scouts, they could outmanoeuvre the heavy-engined German planes on a turn. We seldom had the initiative in a scrap, but we very quickly took it over once the scrap began. This manoeuvrability stood me in good stead on two occasions when the engine cut out dead near the ground, once due to an internal ball-race breaking, for I landed safely in the nearest field each time by simply wheeling to the right.

In the evening of 10 September, flying B3903, I led five Camels of 'A' Flight on the north offensive patrol, which covered an area mainly to the north of Ypres. We had not been long over the lines and were flying at 14,000 feet when I saw over Houthulst Forest an enemy formation of two DFW two-seaters protected by five Albatros Scouts. I had previously arranged, in the event of encountering escorted aircraft, that I should attack with one Camel, while the deputy leader and the other Camels would remain above to protect our tails from attack. On my left was a new pilot, Brownell, a Tasmanian who ultimately retired from the Royal Australian Air Force as an air commodore. He had joined our squadron six days before, having flown a total of 60 hours, five and a half of them on Camels. I had told him that until he became used to flying over the lines and could rapidly spot enemy aircraft as distinct from friendly he must keep right alongside my Camel, do whatever I did, and maintain formation station in all attitudes. My brief experience of Camel operations had taught me that we lost new pilots who did not follow this simple rule.

The enemy were flying south, about 1,000 feet below and ahead of us, well east of their lines, and probably climbing to gain height before crossing the trench-lines on reconnaissance. I swung my formation round above them from the north-easterly course we had been flying and dived at the two-seaters. Brownell came down in station, as instructed. He had seen nothing. He knew only that I dived and he had to keep position. Crossland, Moody and Smith maintained their height to give us cover.

Down I rushed, from 14,000 feet, through the crisp, cold air, watching my Hun through the sights, holding my control stick with both hands, thumbs resting on the double gun-triggers within the spade-handle-shaped stick-top. The observer in my opponent two-seater saw me and I saw him swing his gun to bear. I saw the flash of his shots even as he grew to personality in my sights and I pressed the fateful triggers. At the very first burst he crumpled up and fell backward into his cockpit. My streams of lead poured into the fuselage of the plane, the pilot's cockpit, and the DFW tipped up and over sideways and fell tumbling down to earth.

I looked round for Brownell and saw him close beside me. He had followed me down without seeing the enemy (as blind as all initiates) and without knowing even yet why I had dived, because to keep station he had to fly by watching my Camel as a guide. He had seen my guns firing. Suddenly a two-seater appeared below his Camel's nose. Instinctively he pressed his triggers in a burst of fire.

I swerved to the right to avoid colliding with my target. Brownell followed me. I looked back. A two-seater was falling vertically, with a long plume of black smoke trailing upward from it. 5th Army AA saw it fall in flames. It was impossible to say which of the two it was. The other had disappeared. I was certain that the one I had fired at was mortally hit.

The three Camels above us had kept the five Albatros engaged. After seeing the two-seaters go down, Smith dived and fired into one of the scouts until it fell out of control.

We landed at St Marie Cappel. There I asked Brownell if he had seen what happened to the two-seater he had fired at. He said he did not know. Out of nowhere a Hun had suddenly appeared in front of him, he had pressed his triggers, then swerved to follow me. I could not be sure which of the two-seaters went down at the head of that black plume of burning petroleum. I knew only what I saw and as I could not positively claim the burning two-seater I guessed it would give a new boy encouragement if I gave it to Brownie for his very own. 'Your Hun went down in flames,' I said. It did not really matter which of us had credit for that particular aircraft. But it had to be somebody's. Brownie was immensely bucked for it to be his. He certainly deserved credit for sticking in wingman place with so little experience behind him. In the mess it was regarded with some astonishment that so new a pilot had shot a Hun down in flames.

Next afternoon I led a patrol of seven – Frew, Crossland, Moody, Smith, Brownell, McMaking – again on north offensive patrol. From 15,000 feet the weather below us was misty. One looked down at the earth as if through frosted glass. East of Langemarck I saw some 21 enemy planes wheeling through the mist in a wide ellipse, continuously circling, as gulls fly over a cliff. Among them were the new Fokker Triplanes, the others were Albatros Scouts. Combined, they greatly outnumbered us. I could not determine if they had seen us, but, in any case, I decided to attack. Rocking my wings as the signal for attack, I dived at one of the triplanes, closed right in and, as my bullets flew, saw him dropping below his own formation. The Hun formation was so strong that I knew it would be courting disaster to follow him through it. To maintain height was the essence of strategy. I lost sight of that triplane in the haze as I pulled up from among the Huns to gain breathing space to review the situation, for the Camels had split up when I dived, and it was difficult to see just where they all were amid the many machines milling around in the haze. But I saw that one of my formation who had followed me closely had done exactly what I knew was tactically wrong. While engrossed in shooting at an Albatros he had passed into the Huns' level. Instantly a Fokker Triplane had pounced upon his tail. Now he was in mortal peril.

My gaze concentrated on this one Camel, B6236, flown by McMaking, who was no novice. Although he had come to 45 Squadron about two months after me, he had been in France with the RFC 10 days longer than I had, and he had a score of four to his credit. A burst of bullets made him swerve away from the Albatros he had attacked. I saw the triplane curve in behind his tail and dived instantly at it. Before my sights were centred I fired a brief burst because I knew most Huns reacted to the warning sound of bullets flying near them. This fellow, however, was of a different breed. He looked round at me and I saw his black-leather helmeted and begoggled face above his left shoulder as he swerved slightly to one side then looked ahead again and followed the Camel's tail.

I think McMaking must have been wounded by the triplane's first burst of fire, because he did not use his Camel to manoeuvre as he might have done. He went down straight in a steepish dive, with no attempt at evasion.

I increased speed and pulled closer to the triplane. I was now below the main Hun formation and I heard the splatter of Hun bullets rattling round my ears. Glancing back and upward I saw two Albatros coming down upon me, but above them, Moody, in another little Camel, was treating them just the same and driving them off.

Now I was almost dead upon the buff-coloured triplane's tail. Its pilot looked round again. Possibly the sound of the bullets his comrades aimed at me had alerted him. I was close enough to see (and almost read the expression in) his keen blue-grey eyes behind his goggle glasses and as much of his face as was left uncovered: nose, mouth, chin and shape of cheek. Had I been able to meet them I could have picked him out from among his fellow pilots.

He saw I was dead on his tail and instantly banked and curved to the right while he looked at me just as my bullets spewed forth. My tracers passed close over his central left wing, just outside his cockpit and in line with his head, missing it by inches because of his outward swerve. When my brief burst ceased he looked ahead again. He was a clever pilot.

I saw McMaking's Camel still below him, falling steeply in a gentle curve. If he were already badly wounded (as I believe) why did his opponent not leave him to his fate and turn to duel with me? We were at an advantageous height for the Fokker Triplane for both climb and manoeuvre. Did he think the Camel ahead of him might escape across the lines? Or was it his policy to butcher him right to the ground in order to claim his scalp? I was now alone, our odds were even, and we were on his side of the lines, an advantage to him. Surely he ought to have rounded to engage me? I have never understood his tactics, why he did not take me on.

All the time we fell downward, losing height rapidly, fighting earthward along a pathway inclined at 60 degrees, rushing through the misty air towards the ground behind the German lines.

In my desire to shake that triplane off the Camel's tail I had each time fired a trifle earlier than I might otherwise have done. Each time I had missed a vital spot, but not by much. Damn him! I thought: I'll get him next time.

Out of the corner of my eye I saw a solitary RE8 heading towards us, possibly believing we were all friendly scouts and that he could safely venture east, for the Fokker Triplane had already been mistaken for the Sopwith Triplane by another RE8 whose occupants received the chop by their mistake. I followed the swerving triplane down until I came squarely on his tail. Before I could fire he squirmed out of my sights once more. Again I registered on him, dead. His head did not look round at me this time. Instead, his angle of dive suddenly steepened. It seemed as if I had got him. I increased my dive almost to vertical, barely twenty feet behind him. Suddenly I saw the RE8 about to pass between the triplane and my Camel. Its pilot, evidently realising his mistake, vainly strove to turn away. He had left it too late. His brown wings obliterated my vision of the triplane. For a fleeting microsecond I looked into the face of the horror-stricken observer, and the cockpit in which he stood immobile, his wind-blown mouth wide open as he looked up at my Camel with its whirling propeller so near to guillotining him where he stood, completely helpless. He must have thought my Camel would hit him head on; its whirring engine and propeller tear him to fragments and wipe him from existence. So did I. For an infinitesimal fraction of time I seemed to hang in space while that observer and I saw each other as souls already hurled into the eternal cosmos.

There was but one thing that could save us and only I could do it. What effect it would have I did not know.

Even as I did it I breathed man's shortest prayer: 'My God'. There was no time for more as I yanked the stick hard into my stomach and flashed between the RE8's wings and tailplane as my gallant little Camel answered to the pull. By a miracle we missed a collision, by another miracle my Camel survived the strain. I blacked out momentarily. When vision returned I saw I was spinning inverted from the top of a loop. My Camel fell out sideways when I checked the spin.

I had lost height so swiftly in my downward rush to 4,000 feet that the windmill air pump had been unable to raise the pressure in my fuel tank fast enough to overcome the increased atmospheric pressure and I had had no chance to use the hand pump. My engine ceased to run. Uncertain of the cause, I tried her on the gravity tank. She picked up at once. I turned and scanned the air space.

High overhead I saw planes in the misty overcast, moving like goldfish in a bowl seen through a curtain-veiled window. Around on my level, and below, nothing was visible, no aeroplanes, enemy or friendly, except the interfering RE8 fast disappearing in the mist, westward towards the lines. The triplane and the Camel had both vanished. How could they have disappeared so quickly unless both went down?

The ground below me, indistinct through the mist, appeared free from shell-holes. I climbed and found some Camels wearing the dumb-bell marking of our squadron. Our patrol time was finished and we returned to our airfield in formation; and as I went I cursed the damn-fool pilot of the RE8 who had so baulked me that I did not know what had happened to McMaking. That night he was posted missing and later reported killed. I never knew his end because of the RE8's stupid intervention at a critical moment for my follow-up and further action; for I would have followed that triplane to the ground if need be and who knows which of us would have survived in 45 Squadron's one and only close engagement with Fokker Triplanes?

Several decades passed before I saw photographs in which I recognised beyond all doubt the face of the pilot of the triplane I had followed down east of Langemarck. One photograph showed him standing before his triplane in rough working uniform, looking to his left. In the other he was seated in his cockpit wearing flying cap and raised goggles, and again his head was turned to the left. There were the facial outlines I remembered, the same turning of the head, the same eyes. He was Werner Voss, leader of Jasta 10 in Richthofen's Circus. McMaking was his 47th victim.

I would have liked to have met Voss to discuss the most extraordinary aerial encounter in my experience: to know why he did not engage me, why his dive steepened when I last saw his triplane, making me believe it had been hit. Was the manoeuvre a ruse, feigned for that reason; or was it made to put the RE8 between us, or to avoid a collision with the RE8? And I would have liked to have known the final fate of poor McMaking, whom I had done all I could to save. Voss is usually written up as particularly chivalrous by writers who never encountered him in combat. This is a word with several meanings: one is, an elite fighter of his race and this Voss was; but another is one having an inclination to defend the weaker party. All German WW1 air aces answer to the first definition, but not to the second, for their urge was always to kill their opponents rather than to make them prisoners. Voss was no exception.

But 'he who lives by the sword shall perish by the sword'. Twelve days after our encounter Voss shot down his 48th and last victim in the morning. That evening, just before he was due to go on leave, Voss himself fell, at Wieltje, near Frezenberg, a short distance within our lines, but who flew the avenging sword is another of the unsolved mysteries of the first war in the air. Few aces who fell were killed by aces.

Bad weather plagued us for the next few days. We flew patrols at lower heights, but there was little action on either side. On 18 September I went home on 12 days' leave, during which I did not even notice the reports that Voss was dead.

While I was away Mike Moody led the patrols of my flight and on 20 September he spotted an enemy two-seater near Passchendaele. He and Brownell dived on it, firing one after the other. It turned and dived east. Smith followed it and continued firing at it until he saw it go down in flames.

The first half of October 1917 was marked by a succession of battles. That of Broodseinde began on 4 October. Frew and I went out together on a low flying patrol. A gale blew from the south-west, driving low clouds before it. Our light little Camels were cruelly tossed about in the bumps, sometimes thrown up to the fringes of the clouds at 800 feet, again falling to 200 feet above the ground. We had little control over them. Visibility was bad and we saw very little. The air conditions made the shell-pocked battlefields look even worse to the eyes of airmen bumping through the wind-torn air among the hurtling shells between the clouds and the ground.

The Battle of Poelcapelle was on 9 October; the first Battle of Passchendaele began three days later. On each of these battle days we were engaged on ground strafing, when we always flew in pairs. Our Camels did not carry bombs then, but our twin machine-guns rattled out against troops and transport in the trenches and in the open, on guns and gunners, and all objects that offered us a target. These low-flying jobs offered excitement. Things flashed into view, were fired at, passed behind, and were forgotten with the next target that loomed up. There was an element of uncertainty when the artillery barrages were intense; if caught in the aerial tunnel of a barrage, safe exit could be secured only by flying along the centre of the tunnel. Any attempt to fly out through the shell-walled sides of the tunnel, either towards the guns that threw the shells up or towards the side where they fell to earth, was folly usually repaid by a crash to earth. The possibility of flying a plane unscathed through the barrage was very slight, and for that reason we were always informed of the areas of the massed guns and barrage targets, together with the maximum heights of flight of the shells. The different types of shells were spewed from their guns at different angles and rose to varying heights, thus creating a series of superimposed tunnels through which, at certain definite levels, we could fly in comparative safety. The lowest tunnel was the worst and our rocking flight through it was accompanied by torn wings from fragments of exploding shells and lumps of mud which bespattered our lower surfaces. The terrific buffets of shock waves from the concussions of the exploding shells threw our little Camels about in almost uncontrollable fashion.

I have seen the field-grey-clad German troops throw themselves down into open shell-holes and dig feverishly with clawing fingers as we swooped in pairs upon them, with our fire enfilading their position; gunners drop their occupations about the gun emplacements to scatter into shelter; horses turn and gallop away in terror, dragging swaying waggons along the shell-holed roads until they turned them over in the roadside ditch; marching troops run helter-skelter in confusion to avoid our hail of lead.

The whole month of October was occupied with days of pushes, big and little, British pushes that nibbled into the enemy system of trenches. They looked insignificant enough, perhaps, on the map. To the man in the trenches who carried them through they were big enough to fill the whole of life's horizon. But, then, the points of view of combatant and non-combatant differed. They always will.

The growth of aerial science and the art of flying had pushed the aeroplane right into the forefront of battle. For days, and even weeks, the airmen had steadily carried on their work of reconnaissance, bombing, photographic mapping, and the registration of artillery shoots. In trench warfare they were the intelligence eyes of the staff. Above and around them had buzzed the tiny fighters, clearing the way for the drones. The airman had come into his own as a vital fighting unit. His job was no longer merely that of a spectator and, in a few cases, director of the ground operations. He was a participant, and for that reason airman casualties increased.

On 9 October Brownell and I went out on a south ground patrol. We fired at troops in trenches and in the open, at mechanical transport and gun emplacements. The exhilaration of the rush along above enemy ground at 500 feet and of the swift dive upon suddenly spotted targets can never be forgotten. Down and over, on and up again, through the lower air above the enemy side of the battle area, looking for whatever target offered, with freedom to make our own choice of values, we sped crouching in our cockpits, splitting the air with our wings, racing down towards the things upon the ground, things that must have hated the very sound of our roaring engines and spluttering machine-guns. On our way back we ran into a veritable hornets' nest of ground machine-guns. Their bullets crackled past our ears and, as the crackling sounded louder, we swerved away, turning and twisting to avoid the streams of lead from a dozen machine-guns, the gunners of which sought to bring us down, our only guide the crackle growing louder as the bullets neared us and fading as we succeeded in outmanoeuvring the gunners' aim. We had no ammunition left to dive upon them in retaliation, so we could but endeavour to outwit their aim by dexterous handling of our little mounts.

On 12 October I led Brownell again on a north ground patrol over the area between Poelcappelle and Westroosebeke. Our height varied as we zoomed and dived, but never did it exceed 500 feet. We entered the lowest tunnel of the artillery barrage at the south end and flew through the tunnel to its northern exit. In our dives we lowered almost to the ground. We heard the pounding of the shell-fire through the roaring of our engines and when I neared the ground I heard and felt the thud of mud thrown up by the exploding shells hitting the underside of my lower wings. We fired at infantry in open trenches (as the official report described them) that were nothing but the shell-holes to which the gun-fire had reduced the trenches. All the litter and debris of war lay about that dreadful area: smashed guns, dead and putrefying bodies, broken wire entanglements, mud, filthy water from the rains that flooded that naturally wet countryside, sandbags and torn sacking, broken duckboards, and living men still existing in almost unbelievable conditions of primeval slime in green-coloured shell-holes, men who tried to bury themselves in the filthy mud when we callously dived and fired at them. It was a picture I shall never forget, its title Passchendaele, a hell upon earth. Up, down, rocking, up, down, shooting, zooming, vibrating, amid continuous noises that all but deafened us, we roared over the centre of the battle area and emerged from the tunnel at its other end into air unruffled by the shells and with the groundscape relatively still pure. In Westroosebeke we spotted a small body of troops and dived at them and 300 rounds from our guns made them scatter like Olympic-runners. Next we found a gun firing from an open emplacement. I spotted an Albatros Scout watching us just before we dived upon that gun. He was flying east by south of us and evidently awaiting a chance to cut in when we were not ready for him. I knew it was very difficult for him to dive upon us effectively at our low altitude and so when I spotted the gun I decided to deal with it first and him second. Another 300 rounds from our machine-guns stopped that gun's shelling of our troops, at least for the time, and any let up for them was a respite. As we dived we saw the gunners fling themselves down. We roared upon them out of the blue and sprayed their whole emplacement with our bullets. I flattened out across the ground at 10 feet up and as I opened out my engine she fluffed and refused to answer. Ahead of me I saw green grass and wire, shell-holes, and the usual litter that bespoke the back areas of war. I knew I would not be popular if I landed, even if I were lucky enough not to be badly damaged in the getting down. Then my engine kicked, hesitated, kicked again, missed, then gathered power into its cylinders and pulled me upward into the safety of the air after my wheels had all but touched the surface. I felt hot and cold. As the Camel rose I looked round and saw the Albatros following our wake as though inspired by Samuel Taylor Coleridge. I rocked my wings to warn Brownell, who was slightly misplaced by my engine's hesitation, and we headed for the Hun. He turned at once and made off east. We opened fire upon him, but he would not stay to welcome us at closer quarters and, although we drove him flying eastward, I think our bullets only scared him and did not hurt him. Half an hour after we began our work we saw some men sheltering in a disused gunpit near Oosthoek, upon whom we exhausted our last 200 rounds of ammunition, with what effect it was difficult to judge. We turned westward, hedgehopping above the trench-lines north of the battle zone, flying targets for rifles and machine-guns from the fellows on the ground.

Two days later I flew out by myself in the late afternoon to look for enemy aircraft. I found one hunting an RE8 and drove him off, but could not catch him. But this allowed the RE8 to continue his work unmolested for the time at least. On the way back, after flying through the Archie barrage, I pulled my little Camel up and over in the first loop I had ever made in any plane. It was sheer joy of self-expression. In those days flying was not taught as it was later and all the manoeuvres I knew I had had to teach myself. No one had ever looped me. Looping as a fighting manoeuvre was useless, and I had never troubled to practise it on any of the planes I had flown, although I had made frequent spins and done other tricks. Nor did the other pilots in the squadron trouble much about exhibition flying; we were workers.

During the second half of October and the first half of November we had many scraps in the air above the battle areas of Flanders. We carried on the air war over the enemy's territory. Sometimes we met foemen worthy of our mounts, while again we found victory come easily to our little Camels. Throughout this period there was a tendency on both sides to operate in formations of ever-increasing numbers.

Incidents were many. On one occasion four of us encountered seven Albatros Scouts high up. We attacked and closed, but when we pressed the triggers all our guns gave No. 4 stoppages and we were forced to break off the encounter. Thanks to our mounts' powers of manoeuvre we broke away, chased by the seven Huns who were evidently too surprised to take full advantage of the situation. Our trouble was due to cold contracting the long metal rods operating our gun gears so much that they would not fire the guns. We also had trouble with the congealing of gun-lubricating oils.

A few days later I saw two enemy two-seaters near Houthulst Forest.

Our patrol was six strong and with two of the Camels following me and three remaining above to protect our tails I dived under the tail of one of the German planes and loosed off 150 rounds into it at less than 100 yards. Dicky Dawes and I followed him down until he disappeared vertically among clouds. 'F' Battery, AA, confirmed the enemy plane's fall.

Two days later with a patrol four strong I attacked two enemy two-seaters at 15,000 feet and drove them east from where they were working in the vicinity of Ploegsteert and Zillebeke. Shortly after we found another enemy two-seater in the vicinity of Wervicq and Lille and chased him east of Lille. Then we found another one at Comines and turned him east, but in every case we could not approach close enough for effective shooting, although we drove them from the duties they were engaged upon. They were faster than our Camels and unless we could surprise them we had a poor chance of knocking them down; their observers kept a good look-out and as soon as we were spotted they were off, diving eastward to safety.

When landing at the end of the patrol one of my wheels collapsed and in a flash the Camel turned upside down, leaving me hanging in my belt, head downward, a most uncomfortable position. Very gently I loosened my belt and lowered myself to the ground, a feat that required a certain amount of care. On one such occasion a pilot who loosened his belt too rapidly dropped upon his head and broke his neck.

Three days passed during which we saw no enemy aircraft. On the fourth day six of us were engaged upon a north offensive patrol over the sector Westroosebeke-Moorslede-Gheluwe. We had already swept our area once at 13,000 feet without seeing any Huns. Then I led the formation southward, climbing hard, and when we turned north again we flew at 15,000 feet. I did this because our patrol took us over several enemy airfields and I knew that ground observers would have estimated our height and communicated it to the German chaser pilots. By increasing our height I hoped to gain the initiative when the enemy planes came up, if they did.

Soon after crossing over Menin I saw a formation of eight Albatros Scouts ahead and about 1,000 feet below us. They were climbing hard. We had the sun behind us and I judged that we could reach them just before they gained our level. I opened full throttle and rocked my wings in signal of Huns observed. I glanced behind and saw the whole formation in good position as we raced towards the climbing Huns. They saw us coming and strove hard to beat us to the height. They pulled their noses up until they stalled and dropped and, as they did so, they pooped off a few rounds, perhaps in hope to keep us back, perhaps to warm their guns. My plan of changing height had proved successful and a direct charge was only needed to press it home and take the lead in the ensuing fight. The Huns were stout fellows. With their superior speed, especially in the dive, they could have slipped away, but their only thought appeared to be to get above us without delay.

When I first saw them I felt a tingle of anticipation. Here was the very situation for which I had manoeuvred, and the thrill of that knowledge, coupled with the chances of the next few minutes, sent the blood-stream coursing hotly through my veins. It was seldom we had the height advantage over them. Appreciation of the need for instant and decisive attack at full speed followed in a flash and as I opened out my engine and glanced back at my formation of Camels, my mental attitude became detached from all emotions so that I felt a feeling almost as of boredom creeping over me. This sense of boredom at such times was a strange one, but I suppose it emanates from strangulation of the emotions into an intensity of concentration upon one definite object. It may be the outcome of a mental state which is called upon to encompass a great deal in the swift passage of a short space of time, akin to the emotionless impression one forms when the ultra-high-speed camera reproduces a subject in slow motion. It was probably enhanced by our total inability to communicate with anyone while flying in the aircraft of that time.

We reached striking distance while yet 300 feet above them. They were DVs of twice our horsepower. I picked out their leader, painted in much red, and rushed down at him. Far away lay the brown carpet of the earth, out of focus to my eyes concentrated on my painted opponent. The Albatros grew to tremendous proportions in my sights. I pressed the triggers. Instantly he turned belly uppermost in a roll. My bullets ripped the underside of his rotund plywood body and at the same instant I had to swerve aside to avoid collision with another Camel diving beside me and which, converging in the dive, nearly knocked my left wings off. The second Camel's bullets also sprayed the Albatros and, from the roll, he sideslipped downward as we swerved to prevent an imminent collision. I zoomed up and to the right and found the air thick with swirling planes travelling at speed in all directions, darting hither and thither, and casting shadows upon me as they eclipsed the sunlight, Albatros and Camels shaving past my bow and stern in every attitude of tip-tilted flight. I loosed off a short burst at a camouflaged Hun who passed in front of me and swung hard round to the right upon his tail and let him have a second burst. I got behind the Albatros and let drive with both guns, firing hard. I saw my bullets splashing all around him and saw his leather-helmeted head crouch lower in the cockpit. I was squarely on his tail and a bare ten yards behind him. Both my guns rang out steadily above the tumult of the fight. He dived and I followed him down below the level of the scrap and still raked him with the bullets while the tracer showed the hits. He steepened in the dive, evidently falling forward on the stick and a thousand feet below the fighting flickered into flame. But before that happened I heard the hot lead of a pair of Spandaus playing round my ears. I had followed down too keenly and a Hun in turn had sat upon my tail. I was lucky that he missed me with that first sudden burst that splashed the air about my head. He missed my person only because I had steepened my dive. I swerved and ruddered as the bullets clipped my head by hair's breadths and I saw the wooden splinters flying from my centre section spar and ribs and the fabric ripping into ribbons. The smack of hitting bullets accompanied the crackle of his gun-fire and I swerved again and yet again to miss the deadly double stream until I had the opportunity to flash around upon my right wing-tip in a turn that took me out of my opponent's sights and brought him nearly into mine Then he did not wait for more but plunged head downward for the friendly ground and the advantage that the Germans had when they flew above their territory.

I could not follow him because I saw my upper centre section rear spar was holed and splintered and gashes in the fabric were opening with the wind; even from what I could see of the damage I doubted if the centre section would withstand the strain of a dive, and there might be more I could not see. So, with a parting burst to speed him on his way, I had to watch him go.

All above me my Camels were re-forming after the fight. Anxiously I counted them. They numbered five. Not one was missing. Away above them I saw a formation of Bristol Fighters passing eastward on reconnaissance. Looking down, those boys of 22 Squadron had seen our scrap and saw my Albatros go down in flames.

No other planes were visible around the skyscape. The Huns had gone. Not one of the eight remained to flaunt his crosses in the air that blew above their ground. Our victory was complete and achieved without the loss of a single Camel. I climbed to the level of the others and we re-formed formation. When our patrol time was finished we turned westward and recrossed the lines at height before beginning the long glide downward to the airfield at St Marie Cappel. Because of the numbers engaged in the fight our combat report was signed by Vaucour alone; in it he wrote:

'All pilots state that they never were closer to enemy aircraft, nor had they ever obtained such complete mastery over them.'

That day in that area Leutnant d. R. Walter Lange of Jasta 2, who had scored seven victories, was killed and Leutnant von Gerstenberg of Jasta 11 was shot down wounded.

In the evening, while my damaged Camel was being repaired, I borrowed another and with Clarke, one of the three Old Etonians in 45 Squadron in WW1, went out on a voluntary flight in search of enemy aircraft. Visibility was bad, with a curtain of autumnal mist draping all the sky. We found three Huns flying over Houthulst Forest and drove them east, but could not close to inflict decisive damage. We returned in the gathering dusk and mist, flying low. When we neared the enemy lines a red rocket soared from their trenches and burst into stars. Immediately German AA batteries opened fire and plastered the sky around us with high-explosive shells.

During October when Harris and Wright returned to England, Firth took command of 'C' Flight and Frew of 'B' Flight. Harris was not happy serving under Vaucour, whom he regarded as junior to himself; he had mentioned this to Jack Scott, lieutenant-colonel commanding the 11th Wing, who, it was said, would have recommended Harris to succeed Van Ryneveld had he been aware of Harris's seniority. During rather less than four months with 45 Squadron Harris had scored five victories and had always been a good fighter-formation leader. Wright departed, tour expired, although he had been with the squadron a shorter time than I had. I never understood how this tour-expired arrangement worked; the time schedule was inconsistent; it varied with different pilots. Wright's score was four destroyed, four out of control, and one brought down, and I think the strain had begun to tell because he had been through some tough times.

About this period, because of the increasing numbers in which the enemy fighter formations flew, we patrol leaders began unofficially to arrange between ourselves to collaborate as far as possible when over enemy territory. One day when we were detailed to cover both northern and southern sectors of our Army Front at the same time with two offensive patrols of six machines each, I arranged with Frew that we should co-operate. My southern patrol would fly at a higher altitude than his northern one, guard his patrol if it were involved with enemy aircraft, and reinforce it if the situation required such action.

My end of the line was quiet, but Frew saw four two-seaters over Lille and dived on them and was in turn attacked by enemy scouts. I saw the combat from a distance and flew towards it. There I saw more aircraft above the fight and held them off from diving on Frew's Camels. It was one of those tricky situations in which I had to decide between giving protection or throwing that to the winds to dive into the fight going on below. I saw that Frew's formation was more than holding its own and that it was more important to prevent enemy reinforcement from reaching the combat. But for our prior arrangement Frew's formation might have been overwhelmed. As it was, Peter Carpenter shot one Albatros Scout down in flames and Frew sent another down out of control when it was attacking a Camel, without loss to the Camels. It was a fascinating spectacle to see such a combat from above, with the horizontal windmill of aeroplanes of varied hue threshing the air and revolving as if tied to a central pivot until out of the treadmill one falls and dies, unable to keep up the pace demanded for survival. I have seen no artist's representation of a fight from this viewpoint, which probably was rare; it would have been a marvellous angle for Goya, had he lived in that time, and presented against the carpet of the Flanders landscape it had all the elements for pictorial perfection.

Frew had established himself as lineal successor to Lubbock, Belgrave and Cock as the squadron's most successful contemporary air fighter and in the end he finished up as the top-scoring fighter of the squadron in WW1. He had a slight figure, was about 67 inches in height, with a face sombre in repose that could break into a grin full of fun or a happy laugh. His sense of humour was infectious. He once applied for a new inclinometer for his machine. This was simply a curved spirit level affixed to the instrument panel, the central position of the air bubble in it showing the pilot when he was flying true, without sideslip, whether flying level or turning. It was an instrument that could be destroyed only by a blow that broke the glass. Frew was requested to state the reason for his application and solemnly replied that he needed a new one because the bubble was worn out by the exertions needed to keep it in the centre. His speech never lost its pronounced Scottish accent and he had no desire that it should. He was generally popular and had a happy knack of always landing on his feet.

Two days later we had a most exciting and amusing experience. The weather had suddenly become much colder and very stormy.

Our patrol was delayed at the start by an approaching storm, but shortly after the due time we climbed away into the steel-blue sky above the storm-wrack clouds. We levelled off at 12,500 feet and after cruising round for some time with the biting air filtering into our lungs in cold streams I saw an enemy formation of three two-seaters escorted by four Albatros Scouts to the west of us, near Lille, evidently preparing to cross our lines on reconnaissance.

I manoeuvred to convenient striking distance from them without having been observed. Then I dived into the middle of the German planes, got right on the tail of a fat two-seater and pressed the triggers. One single shot came from each gun, then silence.

Clarke and Brownell came down with me. They pressed their triggers with the same result. We took the Huns completely by surprise and broke up their neat formation. Our 10 machines swirled around the sky in wild rushes and swift turns. Feverishly I reloaded my guns. Again but single shots rang out. The Huns seemed too surprised to open out on us in earnest. Perhaps they thought that we withheld our fire because we were such peerless pilots that we never shot until certain of a kill. We chased them round in circles and must have scared them quite a lot to prevent them closing in on us in sound retaliation. I think the suddenness of our unobserved attack had thrown them into panicking disorder; that, coupled with the closeness of our Camel's snouts behind their spade-shaped tails and the dreaded silence of our guns, made them think we were experts who chose to slaughter them with neat dispatch rather than with excessive shooting. Whatever the reason, we had all the thrills of a realistic dogfight without being able to fire more than single shots, while the shots they fired at us made but a feeble resistance in their defence. Possibly their guns, like ours, were frozen up.

We drove them down in height with the violence of our manoeuvres and presently we broke away. Strenuously I loaded, fired the single shots to warm my guns, reloaded and repeated, while we kept above the retreating enemy formation. Finally I got one gun going. Then I dived and from my single gun fired 200 rounds at one of the enemy scouts, which appeared to wallow faster towards the earth in seeming uncontrol. Their reconnaissance was broken up and we drove them flying, nose well down, east and south of Lille, before we turned and headed for our airfield to tell our armament officer in terse language what we thought about our guns.

In the afternoon we spotted three old RE8s and tucked in above them. We saw five Albatros attempting to molest them and with Moody and Brownell I waded in and drove them off. Their superior speed enabled them to run and they would not turn to close engagement. Without our aid the RE8s would have had a nasty time from those five sharks above the counter-battery area.

On some of our flights when we flew near the top of their trajectory we saw the shells thrown up from the big guns. I have seen them whizzing up, spinning, and slowing, until they seemed almost to stop just as they turned over at their maximum height. Then, falling away to earth, their downward flight, ever increasing in velocity and spin, could be followed by eye for a long way before they dwindled to mere specks and vanished. There followed a time gap before we saw the distant smoke-puffs of the shell-bursts on the ground. It was difficult to know what to do when we saw a salvo of big shells bore their way through the air just ahead and on our level. We had no knowledge of any impending change in trajectory. It was impossible to guess whether the next salvo would pass astern, above, below, or right through our formation. We were no concern of the observing officer who sent the target corrections to the battery. The gunners could not even know how near to us their shells would go. The risk we ran was just one of the possible accidents of war. We simply had to chance our luck and fly on, straight ahead. That way was as good as any other. To be hit by one of these shells was an impersonal fate, useless to the war or anyone, and whenever I saw them I thought of Ross and Fowler, who were done in by them for no reason whatever so far as man was concerned: Where, then, lay the meaning of life and death?

Chapter XI

CASUALTIES

At intervals our squadron boasted a medical officer temporarily attached from the brigade staff but we never had one permanently. Unlike the infantry battalion in which I had previously served in France, we had no padre. Our nearest padre link was at Brigade Headquarters and we had to call upon his services for the committal of our dead who had fallen on our side of the lines or crashed fatally on our airfield. We had no other religious services. Unlike infantry battalions, which came out of the trenches for periods of rest and then on Sundays held church parades, we worked seven days a week continuously. (Our only breaks came in weather totally unfit for flying.) This explains both the more frequent leave periods for RFC flying personnel and the absence of church parades. Our brigade padre's servant, Corporal J. Willey, was an artist in his spare time. He painted RFC aircraft driving down Germans over the Ypres landscape, with kite balloons floating over shell-broken trees, clouds and shell-bursts in the sky. I still have one he painted for me on part of a blade of one of my Camel's broken propellers.

The last in the series of the 'Battles of Ypres 1917' was the second Battle of Passchendaele. It began on 26 October 1917. We flew that day in a strong westerly with low clouds and heavy rain storms. Despite the adverse conditions, we sent out ground strafing, low offensive, and reconnaissance patrols, to attack ground targets, destroy or drive off enemy aircraft, and spot enemy movements behind the fighting area and report them as quickly as possible by writing on a card which we enclosed in a weighted canvas bag with red and yellow streamer tails to be dropped at the report centre on the slopes of Kemmel Hill. This centre was also a post for the observation of the movements of enemy aircraft flying low; a white arrow on the ground, turned in the direction of the enemy plane, indicated the need for our fighters to attack and drive off the marauder.

It was very difficult to write on a message card while flying a Camel at low height in rough weather. The machine's instability, its tail-heaviness, the need for continuous attention to the throttle and fine adjustment controls of a Clergêt rotary engine, to keep a look-out for other aircraft flying about in the rain-swept sky and be ready to dodge machine-gun fire from the ground, made writing those messages a near impossibility; yet somehow we managed to write them. Twice Brownell dashed back with me to the report centre, our Camels swerving jerkily in the bumpy air as we rounded the field where the observers waited for our messages. We flew just above their heads and threw the bags at the centre of the field as we approached it, watched the runners retrieve them, then flew back eastward into the storm-rent skies above the sodden battlefield, where we spotted large concentrations of enemy troops at Gheluveldt-Terhand-Gheluwe and elsewhere, wrote more cards, flew back, dropped them, flew east again.

We flew at 50 feet above the duckboards of the swamps of Passchendaele, and looking down upon that sodden mess of filthy, shell-pocked mud I felt a sudden thankfulness that I was flying and no longer engulfed in the miserable conditions of ground warfare on the Flanders Front. Below us were RE8s shot down by gun-fire, slowly sinking in the viscid fluid that men called Passchendaele. Tanks were swallowed up. Men were drowned or suffocated (which you will) in mud. Duckboards, slippery with the filthy stuff, were their only and insecure foothold. One slip off them and an over-laden soldier sank before the eyes of comrades unable to rescue him. The miles of duckboard testified to our war-trained eyes the terrible conditions prevailing on the surface. Every now and again, when we rocketed past above their heads, we saw the mud-stained British troops stand still and look up for a moment, many of them doubtless envying our swift passage over their slough of mud.

At the time I wrote a brief description of this work which can be read as true, although individual cases might be very slightly different.

The day of attack dawned.

But, long before the dawn, the hum of aero engines being run on test vibrated upward to the stars.

It was the day for the single-seater fighters; they were detailed for 'low strafing'. They were to become the fighting advance guard for the infantry upon the ground. And they were to work, not in big formations, but singly or in pairs. Ever individualists, they were now absolutely so.

With the first grey streaks filtering through the starlight two scouts left the airfield. Borne swiftly along on the half-gale, they rushed away towards the dawn, grey blurs that could be just discerned droning across the dimming stars by accolades of fire flashing from their cylinders' open exhausts.

The hum of their engines was lost in a swelling murmur as of distant thunder, that all knew to be the sound of drum-fire rolling against the wind as the first flush blushed the eastern sky. The four mechanics attached to the two Camels stood silently watching and listening until the fading thrum of the engines came no more. They loved these two machines and the men who flew them.

Far from them, through the half-grey twilight of the opening petals of the dawn, the pilots saw a pattern of fire overlaid upon the field of battle, like a cloth of gold. Little spumes of vivid flame danced and hovered over all the earth. Bigger spurts of fire threw streams of light that flamed into the air and died. The pattern was ever changing, never alike, with gun and shell and mortar drawing the threads for weft and warp. Theirs, from above, was the most wonderful aspect of war. Ugliness and horror were camouflaged in beauty, as if a river of fire were foaming and spraying over hidden rocks and snags. It was the masterpiece of the devil artist of war. Its frame of drifting smoke threw it into weird relief. Overhead, the dawn wrack hazed the stars.

Flying low, the two tiny fighting aeroplanes passed straight into the fury of the inferno. The noise of the drum-fire penetrated even the roaring of their engines. They swung to the right. The barrage was too fierce to fly straight through. They turned southward above the angry mouths of the flaming guns, their frail machines rocking and pitching in the air swirls from the concussions of discharge, rounded the extreme southern end of the barrage, then turned east, and again north. They surged through the invisible air-storm on the enemy side within the barrage. The pilots' eyes, strained to the uttermost, searched the shell-torn earth below. They were human hawks winging to stoop upon the humbler fowl.

The light grew in the sky.

Suddenly one of the machines turned over in the air and dived. The crackle of his guns sounded in the pilot's ears above the other noises of the battle. Down on the earth, where the double stream of bullets struck, a tumbled, shell-cratered line of trenches was filled with grey-clad, mud-stained men. They huddled in their holes, trying to grub themselves deeper with their fingernails. They gazed upward over their shoulders in fascinated fright. The bullets crackled round them in hissing menace. Some of them wriggled and twisted where they crouched, then lay still. On their faces was the imprint of fear, or anguish; theirs were the open-mouthed countenances of the dead in battle, in *rigor mortis* remaining contorted by the suddenness of death, the absence of love and care when departing from life. The rushing, roaring scout-fighter passed over their heads, the bullets enfilading the shell-holes beyond. As the living rose the second machine came down upon them. They flung themselves into the mud of their funk-holes again.

The two aeroplanes screamed at full speed along the line of battered trenches. They zoomed upward at intervals, only to descend in fiercer swoops. The two pilots, crouching forward in their tiny cockpits, followed their tracer bullets downward to the very earth. They sat tense in their seats, concentrating in the every movement of their controls, conscious of the danger of their job, but risking everything.

From redoubts and pill-boxes on the nearer ground machine-guns rattled out against them. They heard the sudden, sharpening, whip-cracking of the passing bullets and the duller sound when some found a billet in the plane. The crackle dimmed as they swerved away, then sharpened as they straightened out. Again they dived. The British barrage had crept forward on to the ground below. Shells burst all round them. Clods of earth and fragments of metal pierced their wings and fuselage. They hurtled downwards for the final burst.

As they zoomed a shell struck one machine and sent it tumbling earthward. The pilot pulled wildly at his joystick. It had no effect. The plane struck one wing first, whirled on to its nose and crumpled up.

The other machine was entombed in the creeping barrage. The invisible shells moaned all around the plane and burst below it on the right. The craft rocked amid the whirling currents of the air. Above, the sky was shut out by a roof of smoke. It was like a living tomb of torment, a picture by Hieronymus.

The pilot did the only thing he could. He dived for the ground, westward for the ground. He prayed that the shells might pass overhead, not short. But, as he flattened out above the ground, the enemy machine-gun barrage caught him. The bullets pierced the fuel tanks, the engine. One tore through his arm. He had no time to choose where to land. In front of him was a shell-hole. There the plane plunged into the soft mud.

The pilot loosened his belt, jumped out, and tried to run onward. Shells whistled and crashed around him, sounding louder now that no engine music dulled his hearing. Still he struggled to run, pulling one foot after another from the clinging mud. His clumsy flying boots made progress more difficult. And as he ran, blood reddened on his sleeve. He stumbled.

A spume of shrapnel burst above him. He lay where he fell.

The light below the clouds increased as the sun heightened to the zenith. On the airfield small groups of pilots hung about. They talked but little. And always their gaze turned eastward, whence came the rumbling thunder of the guns. They were standing by for the next call. But they were also hoping that the missing would come in.

Four mechanics stood outside the corner of one Bessoneaux. They looked disconsolate. Their gaze never left the eastward sky unless the flight sergeant called on them for other duties. Their machines and pilots had not returned. They themselves were almost a part of the machines. It was their loving care that kept them beautiful, that proved their worth in battle. They felt they had lost a part of themselves in the non-return of their Camels. And their hearts stood still for a moment when they thought of the men who flew their planes, who gave their handicraft life. God grant that they might be all right!

The squadron commander came out of the office and approached the groups of pilots. He had a piece of paper in one hand.

'Just come through from Wing,' he said. 'The Army Corps commander wishes to congratulate two of your pilots on the very fine assistance rendered during the first attack. They persistently dived on the enemy trenches and materially lightened our casualties.'

'Damn good!' commented someone.

'Yes,' said the squadron commander, 'it is.'

There was a long pause. As he turned back to the office he too scanned the eastern sky, but there was no sign of a homing plane.

We lost Clarke and Smith that day. Clarke was downed by ground-fire just our side of the fighting infantry and injured when his Camel crashed nose into the mud-holes.

Smith veered too far east, climbed out of the rain to locate himself and was bounced by German fighters (he said) of the Richthofen Circus. He claims to have shot down several before he himself was shot down wounded and taken prisoner. He did not know who shot him down, but a Leutnant von Busse of Jasta 3 claimed a Camel that day for his fourth victory. This might have been Smith, but I cannot be certain that it was.

Smith was wounded in one lung and his left upper arm. His engine stopped. He sideslipped down. The last bullets missed him. He crashed on the German side. Later, when at Ghent, he tried to escape, but was too weak to succeed. After recapture he was held for the duration of the war at Furstenburg, north of Berlin.

Chapter XII

ALL IN THE DAY'S WORK

During October our canvas tents were replaced by Nissen huts. These were to be made more or less bomb-proof by a surround of earth-filled sandbags. This work was carried out by Chinese labourers, who worked happily for the, to them, magnificent pay of a shilling a day and their keep. During the early part of the day they always worked slowly. About three in the afternoon their corporal-in-charge informed them that they were required to fill another 2,000 sandbags before stopping work. Although that number exceeded those they had filled since eight in the morning they then started cheerfully enough to hustle. Sandbags were filled at lightning speed and borne at the double to the spot required. By five o'clock, having filled and placed the number of bags called for that day, they were ready to knock off work.

Then they formed up in the roadway outside our camp, singing weird Chinese songs in high-pitched voices. They seemed very happy as they marched off to the farm barns that served them as billets, grinning, chattering, and singing. Some time later a medical inspection was called, at which we were told it was discovered for the first time that a large percentage of the Chinese labourers were women, and the men and women were all billeted together!

About this time Cardinal Bourne, Archbishop of Westminster, paid a visit to France. He intimated he intended to come to 45 Squadron to see our commanding officer, who had once been his pupil. The recording officer at the time was Captain J. W. Higgins, who had been an observer in our 1½-Strutter days, and previously a Territorial gunner. He was a Glaswegian and a stout Protestant. Vaucour told him, banteringly, that he would have to kneel and kiss the Cardinal's ring. Higgins protested his objection and on the day of the visit kept a watchful eye from the squadron office upon the approach to the airfield. When the Cardinal's car appeared he bolted through the back door and fled to the shelter of the camp. No kissing of the ring for him. But Vaucour received the Cardinal outside his office and dutifully knelt and kissed the ring upon the proffered hand.

Trenchard visited the squadron again, and examined the Camels that were not out on patrol. Beside each machine its pilot stood at attention.

The general's observant eye saw three gun-sights on one machine: the Aldis tube sight in the centre with its rubber-protected rear end protruding through the windscreen, on one side of it the ring, and bead-sight mounted in the usual way with the ring at the rear and the bead at the front, and on the other side the same type of sight reversed with the bead at the rear and the ring at the front.

Trenchard stopped and looked at this unusual trio of sights. 'This is what I like to see,' he boomed. 'Something original. Shows thought, which is good.'

He turned to Firth, who was standing rigidly in front of the wings.

'Tell me,' he said to John, 'how you make use of this triple sight? It might be useful for other squadrons to know.'

'I don't, sir,' replied honest John. 'I just point my nose at them and hose away.'

Trenchard looked disappointed. 'Then why did you fit three sights?' he asked.

'I thought it looked better, sir. More symmetrical.'

Trenchard moved on while listening ack emmas at the rear of Firth's machine barely concealed a grin.

During the last few days of October and the first half of November the luck of the patrols, in which there ran a certain element of chance, did not bring 'A' Flight into the thick of scrapping. We had several encounters with two-seaters and scouts, on one occasion combining with Camels of 70 Squadron and DH5s of 41. We suffered much engine trouble from faulty air pressure, faulty magnetos, crankshaft locking sleeves loose, broken exhaust valves, broken ignition wires. The weather was often bad, on some occasions preventing the Corps artillery machines from operating. If even one of these was out we had to continue our patrols whatever the weather, but if none was able to work we were permitted to return home. The difficulty was that we did not always know and often remained out in weather when neither enemy nor friendly aircraft were up, other than ourselves.

But Mike Moody shot down a Junkers infantry co-operation machine and Hand sent an Albatros Scout down in flames; I drove one down but could not claim more because there were too many machines milling around over Houthulst Forest on that day of better weather to give one a chance to see more. Frew's and Firth's flight added to the squadron's bag in this period with claims for one Albatros and one Rumpler two-seater destroyed, five Albatros Scouts shot down in flames, one in pieces, and another smoking and crashed.

When one writes of claims for machines shot down it means no disparagement of those who made them, but when those machines fell on the other side of the lines we lacked the material proof that would have existed had the fight taken place over our side with the machine falling into our possession even if only as a wreck. Every effort was made to confirm the claims made and they were accepted on the basis of such confirmations. Yet from the records I have seen of German casualties (mostly mortal), and which are admittedly incomplete, I find it impossible historically to obtain from German records evidence of every RFC claim made. Deaths and wounds alone do not provide evidence of enemy losses, for many aircraft on both sides were either severely damaged or destroyed when the pilot and/or observer escaped injury. Thus it is impossible to weigh claims for aircraft shot down in a true balance giving accurate results. It might be that it could be done, but I have yet to find any individual or organisation able to provide a balance sheet. This is one of the unfortunate historical aspects of the world's first air war. It applies to both sides. For example, no RFC historian accepts that Albert Ball was shot down by Lothar von Richthofen, although the claim is made on the German side that he did. One knows, too, that combat reports by Manfred von Richthofen cannot be accepted as strictly accurate even when the aircraft he brought down landed on German-held territory and there is evidence that he did not himself always confirm the facts of his account by interview with his victim when he was available for this to be done.

During this period there is a lengthy list of things observed and reported by our pilots; fires, trains, big guns, spotted; once I saw about four battalions of infantry at the eastern edge of Houthulst Forest; at times we saw formations of enemy aircraft far to the east, one numbering up to 40 and 50 machines, apparently practising some manoeuvres. When leading patrols composed of different pilots we had various skirmishes with enemy aircraft, usually in bad visibility, which made effective results difficult to attain.

On 8 November my north offensive patrol with Moody, Dawes, Montgomery, and Child was made at 8,000 feet above rolling clouds which passed as if suspended between the earth and sky, with open spaces between them at intervals. I saw five Albatros Scouts to eastward at our level. With the afternoon sun behind us I hoped they would not see our approach. But, unfortunately, in the dazzling clarity of the air above the cloud reflector, they did and dropped down among the clouds just before we reached effective range. I guessed their probable position and pushed my nose down into cloudland after them. In the opaque cloud the light filtered through but dimly. I could see a bare yard or two ahead. Suddenly the cloud density decreased, like the sudden clearing that sometimes occurs temporarily in fog. Ten feet ahead, right on my level and so close that my propeller almost touched his wing-tip, an Albatros flew straight across my bows. Before I had time to press the triggers he was again swallowed in the mist. I realised my quest was blind and hopeless and climbed back into the sunlight but all the Huns had gone from there and none returned.

Often our pilots said that Huns dived away from them as if afraid. But in the mental silence of the communicationless air in which we flew and fought we could not know the reasons for many of the things we saw. It was easy to make false assumptions in reflex of our own *esprit de corps*. How could we know when a German formation's time was up, their fuel almost exhausted, or their ammunition near spent? Those five who dipped into the clouds might have hoped we would dive right through the clouds after them and emerge below while they remained hidden in the lower fringes, from which they would pounce and take us by surprise. But if that was their purpose, I was not so ignorant of tactics to be so drawn. The truth is that the German fighter pilots of WW1 were no fools. No more were we.

By now the composition of our pilots had greatly changed. The original squadron that flew to France was drawn almost entirely from the United Kingdom, from the CO down to the rawest 3/AM (third-class air mechanic). Our ground personnel had hardly changed and most of them remained with the squadron throughout the war, for they suffered few casualties and thus required few replacements. After discarding 1½-Strutters we had no non-commissioned pilots. But, increasingly as the months passed, officer pilots from Canada, Australia and, in lesser numbers, South Africa, joined us. At this time the six pilots in my Flight came from Scotland (myself), England (Moody), Australia (Howell), Tasmania (Brownell), and two from Canada (Dawes and Hand). All survived the war. Five between them gained one DSO, four MCs, and two DFCs as immediate awards with the squadron; the sixth shot down in Italy and badly burned, after release from POW went home to Canada and became President of the Toronto Flying Club; two died in flying accidents between the wars; three are still alive. I was privileged, and proud, to be their leader.

When Second Lieutenant 'Spike' Howell first joined my flight in France he was thin and shivering with malaria contracted with the Australian troops on Gallipoli. It was his thinness and gaunt appearance that led Mike Moody to dub him 'Spike', a nickname that stuck. Vaucour was inclined to send him back to England, misjudging his state of health for apparent low morale, but I pleaded for him and Vaucour accepted my plea and Howell remained with us, and later proved himself to be a magnificent fighting pilot. I believe the effect upon his spirit would have been disastrous if he had been sent back to England.

T. F. Williams was a Canadian who arrived late in September 1917 and was posted to 'C' Flight. He was old by our standards, for he was only 18 days off 31 when he arrived, and was the 'daddy' of the squadron. But he was of farming stock, with a strong, wiry physique and quick reflexes and the keenest of eyesight in his aquamarine-blue eyes. Just after lunch on 24 October Frew led a five-machine north offensive patrol, whose members included Williams. In the neighbourhood of Menin at about 10,000 feet Williams was flying above the formation and too far from it when the leader of seven Albatros Scouts attacked him. Williams quickly saw that the leader was well ahead of the other six enemy machines and he made a swift turn and placed his Camel behind the Albatros leader and in front of the six behind him who dared not fire because of the risk of hitting their own leader. Williams fired about 150 rounds into the enemy leader's machine, aiming around the cockpit; it went down in a slow spin and crashed at Coucou. Its end was confirmed by all the other Camel pilots. As soon as his opponent went down Williams quickly nipped back under Frew's formation at full throttle. None of the other Albatros pilots fought, nor did the Camels. When the Camel pilots returned to the mess Frew went over to Williams, threw his arms around him, and exclaimed: 'Now we have a Voss amongst us!' And Thomas Frederic has been 'Voss' Williams to all the WW1 pilots of 45 Squadron ever since; when he writes to me from time to time his letters are still signed 'Voss'. The nickname was a tribute to the speed of Williams' reflexes and keen shooting and a compliment to the noted fighter who was the outstanding Jewish pilot of the German Air Service.

On 5 November Firth led a six-machine north offensive patrol. Williams had to return with his engine vibrating badly. Ten minutes later he took off again and while trying to find Firth's formation was attacked by 11 enemy scouts east of Houthulst. According to the record he escaped by spinning down from 12,000 to 2,000 feet and again to 200 feet when he managed to escape and cross the lines unscathed. Some spin!

During the period from 12 October to 5 November 1917 we suffered four killed, three in action and one accidentally; two wounded and POW, and one wounded. All the killed were newcomers, the old story of lack of *experientia docet*. They had survived one month, 12 days, three days and one day, respectively. The last never saw action. He took a Camel for a practice flight on the afternoon of the day after he arrived and crashed when taking off. After tea he took up another Camel and 15 minutes after take-off he dived from 3,000 feet with his engine full on. Before he hit the ground the tailplane and wings fell off. With the Camel so completely wrecked it was impossible to find any clue to explain the crash. Pearson had come to us with a total of 47 hours of flying, of which five and a half were on Camels, and this was about average for that period. He was in Frew's 'B' Flight. Apart from Clarke and Smith, who flew on ground strafing, all the others were lost on patrols led by Firth, who seemed to have a run of bad luck at that time.

On the evening of Pearson's death, a Church Army hut was opened for all the NCOs and men at St Marie Cappel, with writing tables, writing paper, newspapers and magazines for their use every evening when off duty. It was the first amenity they had had at the airfield and was long overdue, but our men were not to have long to enjoy it.

On 5 November Clarke was awarded the fourth MC to be won by our squadron's pilots and on the same day Frew received a Bar to his. Clarke had five victories; his award recognised also his gallantry on his last, low-strafing patrol. Smith had an equally gallant record, but by the misfortune of being taken POW, received nothing. Which just shows that it always pays to land on the right side.

Watts, a Canadian from Winnipeg, came to us with rather less than current flying experience, having flown only a total of about 33 hours but with six and a half of these on Camels. During one of his earliest flights he lost control on the ground and rammed the squadron office, partly demolishing both it and his Camel. Vaucour could not say much, because when he had first arrived at St Marie Cappel one of his feet had slipped off the rudder-bar during take-off and jammed in a cross-bracing, causing the Camel to swerve at high speed and crash into three others lined up at the end of the airfield. Watts went around for a time with his head swathed in bandages, lucky to have only slight injuries.

Part Three

ITALY

Chapter XIII

A CHANGE OF FRONT

The Austro-German offensive of 1917, culminating in the twelfth Battle of the Isonzo, forced the Italian retreat from Caporetto. At first it looked like complete disaster, which called forth British and French reinforcements from the Western Front. Nos. 28, 45 and 66 Squadrons of the RFC, all equipped with Camels, were selected to proceed to Italy, with Nos. 34 and 42 RE8 Squadrons, together with kite balloons and all associated elements, making up an RFC Brigade commanded by Webb-Bowen to support the Army under Lord Cavan. But the Italians held the Austro-German advance at the River Piave, which had not been foreseen before the reinforcements were detailed; all went.

Our squadron was struck off strength of 11th Wing on 16 November 1917 when we flew 16 serviceable Camels from St Marie Cappel to No. 2 Aircraft Depot at Candas and were taken on the strength of HQ, RFC. Van Ryneveld came to see us off. He had returned to France as a lieutenant-colonel to command the 11th Wing in relief of Scott, looking still thin and weak but with the old familiar wry smile crossing his face when he said farewell. His quaint final words were: 'I hope you'll all come back with the Order of the Rising Cock.'

We flew by way of Armentières, Béthune, Arras and Doullens, with as much of our personal gear as we could tie on our Camels, for the quantity we were permitted to send by transport was strictly limited. As soon as we landed our Camels were dismantled and prepared for packing.

We deeply regretted not being allowed to fly all the way to Italy. Two trains were requisitioned for our needs and our packing-case Camels were loaded on waggons. Small, antiquated carriages provided accommodation for officers and senior NCOs, horse waggons '*40 hommes, 8 chevaux*' for the men. Our transport and stores were loaded on trucks and the transport drivers and mechanics travelled in their own tenders and lorries. We installed camp cookers in one horse waggon, which we turned into a travelling field kitchen by rigging temporary chimneys through the open doors. We placed the workshop lorry on a convenient truck behind the waggons for the men, wired their waggons and the officers' compartments and lit them from our own electric plant. We had fixed ourselves up as
174

comfortably as possible and were all ready to travel when the Battle of Cambrai broke out on 20 November, right in front of where we lay.

Reinforcements of men, munitions and material occupied the railways to capacity and our loaded trucks stood silent in a siding, waiting for a locomotive. We understood that a French locomotive was waiting just the other side of Amiens to couple up to carry us to the Italian frontier, but that from Fienvillers (the nearest rail point to Candas airfield) to Amiens we were dependent on British locomotives for our traction and that every one was in use.

Cambrai took precedence over Caporetto. Day after day we waited, billeted in Fienvillers village. Low clouds and mist made the battle operations difficult and we heard news of the gallant flying work being done in the duddest of weather all along the fighting front. We volunteered to unpack and take action in the fighting, but we were already struck off the strength in France and were told we simply had to wait. It did not make sense to us.

To give us practical occupation we were sent to Berck-sur-Mer for a rapid refresher course at an RFC school of aerial gunnery located there. We spent a pleasant enough off-season few days by the sea with little to do. We found a young French boy waif and stray walking on the beach. He attached himself to us while we remained at Berck-sur-Mer. He said his name was Paul Henri and that he had left his home to tramp along with a column of marching men with whom he lived and fed and to whom he became a mascot. He went into the trenches with them. One night a terrible artillery bombardment began to crumble the trenches about them. He was frightened and ran away and did not cease to put distance between the war front and himself until he reached the sea. Having been thrice buried in trenches by heavy shelling I could understand the effect on a young boy. I believe he was a 'shell-shock' case. He was ragged and hungry, clad in garments too big for him, and we did what we could for him until we returned to Candas. He had no inclination to go inland with us. He wanted to stay by the sea.

The first train, which I commanded, left Fienvillers on 12 December 1917. Our journey down the valley of the Rhône and along the Riviera occupied six moderately pleasant days. Halts at stated intervals enabled the train's occupants to get out to stretch their legs and perform natural functions for which no provision existed on the train. The kitchen waggon staff had hot food ready to dispense during these halts. Our dogs always welcomed a halt, jumping down and rushing about joyfully. At one, near a tiny hamlet in the lower Rhône, the Alsatian we had named Crash jumped down and trotted away towards the village. She turned a deaf ear to our whistles and calls of Crash, and the last we saw of our oldest pet was a slight trail of dust marking her passage round a distant bend in the roadway. We were very sorry to lose her, but sympathised completely with her attitude to journeying in French military trains; or had, perchance, she recognised her original home? Had she, like Paul Henri, followed a column of marching *poilus*?

Our carriage had an end stairway to a small roof platform and we spent quite a lot of time up there during the journey along the lower Rhône and the Riviera because it gave us a magnificent view of the delightful scenery.

We stopped at Ventimiglia for a considerable time and were interested in our first sight of Italian uniforms. The headgear of the Bersaglieri greatly appealed to some of our more youthful pilots, who insisted on trying on the highly polished patent leather head-dress with feathers curving horizontally round a wide brim. In exchange the Italian owners of those hats wore some of ours. At San Remo we were presented with books and fruit. One dear old lady came to ask us if we could tell her how her nephew was, the one who was in France with the Middlesex Regiment. She was quite disappointed, and even slightly incredulous, that we did not know him. The railway track was lined with boys, old men, women and girls, who waved to us in the Italian manner, with arm outstretched, palm upward and the fingers bending backward and forward as if in invitation. They waved flags and threw oranges and apples through the carriage windows.

Our greatest reception, however, was at Savona. We arrived about ten at night. An Italian corporal-interpreter came to the carriages seeking the train commandant. I had turned in for the night with a slight chill, perhaps from earlier riding on the roof. The corporal bore an invitation to a welcome which was prepared for us in the waiting-room of the station. The colonel commandant was there and wished to extend to us the greetings of our Italian allies. I begged to be excused on the plea of sickness. Some of our pilots in the next compartment were playing bridge and I asked them to deputise for me and attend the function at the station. The interpreter conducted them along the platform.

Presently one of my sergeants came forward to report a waggon running a hot axle. The railway officials were very dubious about its condition to continue the journey. They wanted the train commandant to go along and make a decision. I wound a silk RFC scarf about my neck, donned a fur-collared greatcoat, tucked the legs of my striped pyjama trousers into a pair of socks, and pulled on a pair of shoes. I passed the crowd that thronged about the waiting-room door unobserved, saw the waggon, gave instructions to have it detached, detailed a sergeant to remain with it, wrote out a special pass for him and gave him money to meet his needs.

The interpreter saw me on my way back and pounced on me with delight. My protests were useless and I was thrust into the waiting-room dressed as I was, announced as the commandant of the train. The room was set with long tables and chairs. The floor was carpeted. All available lights were lit and additional lamps had been brought in. The tables were laid as if for a banquet. Down the sides of the room were tables piled high with fruit and flowers, and little red, white and green Italian flags. Ladies were in attendance at these tables. I felt supremely self-conscious of my sleep-tousled hair and the striped pyjama legs that showed below my greatcoat and fell over my socks like grotesque plus-fours.

At the centre of the head table stood the colonel. He broke off in the middle of a speech to welcome me as one who had risen from a sick-bed to honour the loyalty of the English and Italian nations allied against a common foe. A murmur of gratification passed about the room. I sank into a chair beside the four pilots of the squadron. A soldier dashed up and charged the glass in front of me with a liqueur. I was proffered food. Amid general approval the colonel toasted England, the British Army, the Flying Service, Us. I asked Paddy O'Neill, who, having been educated at Bruges, spoke excellent French, to make an appropriate reply for me.

Glasses were re-filled and emptied.

The station-master dashed in and asked permission to dispatch our train from the station.

'*Cinque minute!*' replied the colonel.

Another speech followed. For three days and nights the colonel had welcomed trains (so we were told), had expressed to their officers the pride with which Italy saw her brave allies come to her assistance in her hour of need. His was an onerous task, for glasses had to be charged, emptied and recharged with every train's arrival. The station-master reappeared. He said he had six trains waiting outside in the tunnels to approach the station and he must really send ours on at once.

'*Cinque minute!*' replied the colonel with upraised hand.

In sheer desperation the station-master began to move our train. By the time the interpreter rushed in to tell the colonel what was afoot our carriages had disappeared inside the farther tunnel. The colonel, with dignity, commanded the station-master to come before him, commanded that our train be brought back until our very carriages were set in line with the red carpet that ran out across the stone platform from the waiting-room. This done we took our leave of the gallant and kindly colonel. As we passed down the side table towards the door the ladies handed to us fruit and flowers and little national flags. It was very touching. Soon our arms were full; and with our faces just showing above the golden oranges from which stuck out the brave little red, white and green flags, we crossed the platform to our carriage amid a throng of cheering Italians, and the harassed station-master dispatched our train immediately.

We arrived at Padua and were met by Lieutenant-Colonel Disney of HQ Staff, RFC, Italy. Our train was unloaded and our tenders trailed our Camels to the Caproni airfield at San Pelagio outside the old city, there to be assembled. We were in the VII Brigade, RFC, working with the XIV Army Corps.

On 23 December we tested our Camels to ensure that they were satisfactory before flying northward to our war airfield. Bad weather set in and we were ordered not to fly up the line until it cleared. On Christmas Eve we had a celebration dinner in Storioni's Restaurant in Padua and on Christmas Day because the weather was still dud went by road to install ourselves in billets at Fossalunga village near our airfield at Istrana. That day Barker, of 28 Squadron, flew across to one of the Austrian airfields and shot up the officers' mess, doing considerable damage.

On the following morning the Austrians came over for revenge. We were in our billets about two miles from our airfield which lay eight miles behind the trench-lines that flanked the south bank of the Piave River. Istrana was the airfield nearest to the lines, which may have been why the Austrians chose it for retaliation. It was not the home of 28 Squadron. We were dressing when we heard a sudden terrific rattle of machine-guns. We jumped to the windows and saw a cloud of planes wheeling round the airfield at about 200 feet. Bombs were dropping and exploding and machine-guns rattling from the air and ground. We dashed out to our tenders, sprang aboard and made full speed for the airfield. Italian fighting pilots were streaking off the ground in all directions in their single-seater Hanriots and climbing to defend their airfield. Their mechanics gallantly started the engines amid bombs and bullets that fell around the sheds from

11 two-seater raiders who were escorted by a host of fighters. Then hell let loose upon the Austrians. The air was thick with darting Hanriots. Hun after Hun came down as they flew back towards their lines; field-guns opened fire upon them; machine-guns and rifles shot at them from the ground; a patrol of British Camels saw them from a distance and pounced upon the remnants which had almost reached to safety. It was a débâcle, like that in the running fight of the ships of the Spanish Armada. Eight of the 11 two-seaters were shot down and their scout escort was powerless to avert the disaster that overtook them. Some of the crews who were captured were found to be befuddled. They had been having a Christmas celebration, from which they had not recovered when they set out to avenge the packet that Barker had handed out to them the previous day.

A second Austrian attempt to penetrate the defences at midday was met on the lines and driven back with losses.

We deeply regretted that our Camels were at San Pelagio and that we had not been able to participate in the rumpus of the Austrians' Boxing Day Revenge Party. We discussed it as we drove in tenders to Padua to collect our Camels and in the afternoon flew over Castelfranco to land upon Istrana airfield as a unit on the strength of the 51st Wing, RFC, commanded by Lieutenant-Colonel Joubert de la Ferté.

Chapter XIV

WORK IN ITALY

The country over which we flew was bad. The surface was cut up into tiny fields bordered with hedges, willows and ditches. It stretched out flat towards the rounded hog's-back of the Montebelluna Hill, on the farther side of which lay the river-bed of the Piave, at that season a small stream flowing in the centre of a wide expanse of pebbles. When the snows melted and the rains came the river ran like a torrent and the broad bed was none too wide.

Above this pebbly background an Austrian contact patrol two-seater ranged their artillery to shell the southern slopes of the Montebelluna, which were hidden from their ground observers. This Albatros two-seater was painted a chequer-board of black and white and whenever he was attacked he dived low above the pebbles where he was almost indistinguishable from his groundscape. Time after time in response to telephone messages the squadron chased him. Time after time he escaped; and it was many months before 'Connie', as that plane was code-named, went down before the squadron's guns.

We flew a practice formation on 27 December and then two days of bad weather set in during which no flying could be done. Low mist hung just above the ground. The weather at that time of year was very treacherous. Sudden fogs sprang up, not deep, but rising from just above the ground to some 200 feet, making location of the airfield difficult, while the nature of the surrounding countryside made a forced landing almost impossible to accomplish safely. The treacherous nature of the weather on the Venetian Plain was doubtless due in great measure to the fickle temperature resulting from shifts of wind, varying from the moist, mild air from the Adriatic to the bitter cold katabatic winds spilling downward from the nearer mountains, which, in clear weather, appeared very close, sharply defined against the snow-capped summits of the more distant Alps.

The squadron drew first blood on the last day of 1917 and the honour fell to the pilots of my flight. We left the airfield at 0845 on an offensive patrol, four strong, climbed to 8,000 feet and crossed the lines, when an exhaust valve broke in my engine and I had to turn back, after firing a signal light for Moody, as deputy leader, to take over.

During the patrol Moody saw three Albatros Scouts above his formation and flew in such a way that they were enticed to attack. As soon as they came down he went for the leader head on, forced him underneath, swung on to his tail and followed him down from 11,000 feet to 5,000, firing about 400 rounds at him from about 20 yards. The Albatros went down completely out of control, which Brownell confirmed. Brownie had singled out another opponent and went down after him from 11,000 feet, firing continuously at him until he crashed nose first into the ground. Dawes fired about 350 rounds at the third Albatros at close range and last saw it going down slowly out of control.

All three pilots said their opponents showed no inclination to fight, but dived away as soon as they were attacked. The strange point about this scrap is that all three Camel pilots used a vast amount of ammunition, which indicates that their opponents were using evasive tactics during their descent.

Moody and Brownell had almost run out of ammunition and both flew back to Istrana and had their ammunition boxes refilled. After leaving they saw an enemy plane manoeuvring to attack a French kite balloon which was being pulled down fast. They waited until the machine dived at the balloon and then attacked it. Moody opened fire at about five yards' range and saw smoke coming from the machine; Brownell then dived at it and continued firing until it burst into flames and crashed.

Next day, 1 January 1918, a GHQ reconnaissance to Vittorio was ordered. The reconnaissance was to be made by an RE8 of 34 Squadron, also based at Istrana, piloted by George Banting with Wedgwood Benn, the MP, as observer. I led my flight to escort the lone RE8. The trip took us about 25 miles over the lines and I saw a single enemy aircraft flying above and following us all the way as if to see what we did. At about the limit of our reconnaissance distance I saw four yellow and green camouflaged DIII Albatros Scouts climbing up from below. I wanted to go down and attack them, but could not leave the RE8 because of the enemy above. This was the great disadvantage of such escorts; they limited freedom of manoeuvre by the necessity to keep within reasonable distance of the escorted machine. So I held my place, just above and behind the RE8 until the four scouts were within measurable striking distance below the RE8, then ruddered down on top of them. The one I pounced on made no attempt to evade my fire, but, instead, pooped up at me as I came down. I fired about 100 rounds and saw it turn over while I was firing and closing to about 15 yards. Benn and the other pilots all saw it falling out of control from about 11,000 feet. The three other DIIIs sheered off and went down. I climbed back into place behind and above the RE8, rejoining the rest of my Camels, so that the reconnaissance could proceed with full escort. The enemy made no further attempt to interfere, but I looked up and saw the solitary vulture still hanging in the sky overhead – it did not come down. The pictures taken by Benn, including those of five enemy airfields, were excellent.

Next day Firth, myself, and Montgomery were simultaneously awarded the fifth, sixth, and seventh MCs of the squadron. It and the succeeding few days were quiet, with bad weather. I saw only one enemy plane on the three flights I made and it was Connie, which Brownell and I chased and lost sight of over the pebbles of the Piave.

On 6 January 1918 the King of Italy visited the airfield to inspect the Italian squadrons. A message was sent across to us that His Majesty would honour our squadron with an unofficial visit. Vaucour was away, visiting 14th Wing HQ, to which we had been transferred on the previous day, and in his absence I had the honour to receive the King and present the next most senior officers. The King took a deep interest in our Camels, for we had two guns to the one on the Hanriot biplanes the Italian squadrons had at Istrana. He climbed on to the wing of one Camel to inspect the guns and controls. Vittorio Emanuele III, being very short, found it difficult to step on to the wing and I assisted him up. By their expression his aides appeared horrified that I should have touched his tunic and breeches, but the King did not seem to mind. He spoke English fluently and was charming to converse with. He struck me as having much at heart the trials of his front line soldiers who were defending Italy in the snowy heights of the mountainous fighting line. He told me he had just been there, and exclaimed: 'God! It was cold!'

Our mess was in a pleasant villa in Fossalunga village, but its kitchen was inadequate for our numbers. So our cooks dug a shallow trench in the garden at the back of the house and lit a fire in it when cooking was necessary. After dinner that evening the embers were glowing very brightly. I went out by the French windows to tell the cooks to douse their fire, the light from which might attract enemy night raiders. Brownie came with me. I stood beside the firelit trench. The senior cook called to one of his assistants to throw over a can of water. The 3/AM lifted a two-gallon can and threw. It landed on the fire. Instantly there was an explosion at my feet. He had picked up a can of petrol in mistake for water, petrol they evidently kept, against orders, to help get fires going quickly. As the great gust of flame belched upward from the ground I jumped backward with my hands across my face, and when the flaming light had died away I realised I could not see. Someone led me into the mess and I sat down. The burn was hurting horribly, but not half so much as the realisation that my work with 45 Squadron was done. In support of Banting and Wedgwood Benn I had fought my last fight.

Into my mind came the memory of a visit I had made with three others nearly two years before to a fund-raising Red Cross bazaar in the Isle of Bute. There a fey Highland woman was telling fortunes for the funds at half a crown a person. She told me she did not know where it was, somewhere she had never been, but she saw me surrounded by white things that looked like cotton wool and there was a great noise and a mighty wind. I was still in the infantry then and she had no visible clue to flying, which her description fitted. Next she said: 'Something will come from your feet and you will never see fighting again.' If I had previously thought of her words I had pictured perhaps bullets or shells fired from the ground. I had never imagined this.

It seemed a long time before a doctor came and dressed my face with picric-acid solution. He examined my eyes, which were tight-shut with the burnt stubs of my eyelashes. Half the hair was burnt from my head and my moustache and eyebrows were gone. Vaucour held an inquiry into the accident. The man who did it was given seven days' Field Punishment No. 1 for wilfully disobeying General Routine and Squadron Standing Orders, which prohibited the use of petrol for heating and cooking, or storing it near any stove, brazier, fireplace or lamp.

Several days passed before the doctor decided that I would not lose the sight of my right eye.

I was now useless to the squadron as a pilot, but I still commanded my flight while awaiting orders. During the short period I continued with the squadron there was quite a lot of fighting. Combat Reports Nos. 117 and 120 contain accounts of adventures on another reconnaissance and their aftermath brought me into use. These reports read as follows:

'... in the vicinity of Vittorio it (the formation) was suddenly attacked by 10 enemy scouts which dived at the three Camels on either side of the RE8, and a general mixed-up encounter took place in which the Camels were seriously handicapped through having to stay close to and protect the reconnaissance machine. 2/Lt E. McN. Hand, who was slightly higher than the rest, was attacked most persistently by two of the enemy machines. He got several good bursts into one at close range, and after stalling it went down completely out of control. The other one had by this time got several bursts into him, but he went for it nose on, both firing hard till they almost collided, and turning round he saw it turning over and over, then falling completely out of control. His machine was seriously damaged having half the tail plane shot away, one gun cowling and centre section all badly shot about, but managed to land his machine in vicinity of Villorba. 2/Lt T. F. Williams dived on one of the E.A. as it was attacking the RE8, and after firing about 80/100 rounds into it at about 50/60 feet range the machine went down in a dive well past the vertical, and when last seen by the observer of the RE8 was close to the ground still in the dive and certainly crashed. Capt. J. C. B. Firth, who up to this time had been engaged in guarding the RE8, now saw one of the E.A. sitting on a Camel's tail, and immediately dived down firing as hard as he could. He was successful in shooting the E.A. off, and when it was last seen was going down completely out of control. The RE8 had by this time turned on a particularly aggressive E.A. and was seen to be more than holding its own when the remainder of the Camels, three in number, closed in again and escorted it safely back to the lines. Owing to the nature of the duty the pilots could not follow the E.A. down to finish them off, nor did they see them crash, but the observer in the RE8 saw the Camels shoot down 3 E.A. completely out of control. The enemy machines were well handled, the pilots most aggressive and put up a good fight.'

In this engagement Hand was forced to land on our side of the lines, Ross was shot down and later reported dead, while Thompson was missing and believed shot down. But, although slightly wounded, Thompson had managed to fight his way clear of the enemy planes, and finally landed far to the south. When news came through that he had landed I took the squadron car and in company with Hocking, the squadron equipment officer, went off to arrange whatever might be necessary for both Thompson and his Camel. We had a most pleasant run through the heart of old northern Italy and found Thompson the smiling hero of all the people in the little town of Mirandilla. The official account of his adventure read as follows:

'When attacked by the E.A. over Vittorio I singled out one of the E.A. painted all red and for about 3 minutes a most exciting encounter at short range took place. Shortly after it started I was struck by a bullet in the throat, which bled freely all the time. Although the E.A. was much faster than the Camel, I could manoeuvre much quicker, and soon got on his tail and fired a good burst into him. The E.A. then dived down to about 1,000 feet and I followed firing bursts all the time, till I heard the sound of bullets coming from behind. On turning round I observed 2 other E.A. on my tail, so by doing a quick right-hand climbing turn I reversed the order, and getting behind one, fired about 30 rounds into the pilot at about 20 feet range. The machine immediately dived straight into the ground about the outskirts of Vittorio. I was then attacked by 5 or 6 E.A. and escaped by side-slipping to within about 10 feet from the ground, and started "hedge-hopping", steering into the sun as I had lost all sense of direction. The E.A. followed at about the same height, and soon a bullet struck my thumb and smashed the rev. counter, the propeller was also struck and the engine was vibrating badly; but by continual zigzagging, as my ammunition was all finished, and by throttling back my engine and letting them fly past me, I managed after about 15 minutes flying to reach the sea, where the E.A. turned off. I then climbed to about 8,000 till I came to a river (the Po), and as my petrol was almost finished, I flew inland looking for a suitable place to land, and on selecting a field landed safely at Massafanalesia near Mirandilla without further damage to the machine. I was most hospitably received by the Italians and taken to hospital. The farmhouse where I landed was christened Thompsonia Aeroplani amidst great *éclat*.'

Before I left the squadron Frew won his DSO in another thrilling fight. It can hardly be better described than in the Combat Report dated 15 January 1918:

'Whilst on a Central Patrol, Capt. Frew observed one 2-seater and an escort of four scouts being heavily engaged by anti-aircraft guns on our side of the lines. He immediately led his formation around behind them to intercept them coming back. By careful manoeuvring and by taking advantage of the sun, he was able to select the most opportune time and place to attack. When the moment arrived he dived from 12,000 feet at the 2-seater (one scout was above the 2-seater) and after firing only four shots at point blank range at the 2-seater, it went down in flames and crashed at Rai. s. Vazzola. Capt. Frew then attacked two scouts with only one gun; it was impossible to rectify the stoppage in the other, but after a hotly contested combat he shot both down, one in flames and one crashed. He then noticed E.A. aggressively attacking a Camel, nose on. Capt. Frew dived on the E.A. and shot it down out of control.

'Capt. Frew then collected his formation and seeing only one E.A. high up and a long way off started for the lines. Immediately hostile AA opened up a heavy and accurate fire on the Camels, which were now about five miles from the lines, and at about 3,000 feet high. Capt. Frew's machine was struck by a direct hit and severely damaged, the rear main plane connecting rod being severed, allowing the plane to tilt up, the centre section was damaged and one wheel shot off. He immediately shut off his engine and glided towards the lines, the AA gunners putting up a heavy barrage in front of him, which he could only glide through owing to the weak state of his machine. On nearing the Piave the case seemed hopeless as the machine was close to the ground. Capt. Frew, however, as a last resort momentarily switched on his engine, thus giving him the necessary impetus to skim over the river and land behind the Italian Front Line at Salitto, without further damage to his machine. The Italian Officers who had gathered round informed him that they had observed the whole combat and had seen four enemy aircraft go down, two being in flames.'

Frew's total score of victories was 26, five of these on 1½-Strutters. The analysis shows eight crashed, six shot down in flames, 10 out of control and two driven down; his observers accounted for the two crashed and one in flames on 1½-Strutters.

I was still useless to the squadron because the doctor told me I would not be able to fly for at least two months owing to the danger of cold attacking my eyes, unprotected by lashes, and also the skin, which was badly burned. It was not possible to arrange my transfer to England quickly, so, to enable the squadron to strike me off strength and apply for a pilot to replace me, I consented to enter hospital for a couple of days.

Thereafter I spent about 10 days acting in liaison with the British AA gunners on the Montebelluna Hill, observing the movements of enemy planes and reporting any peculiarities I observed to the squadron. During this time I had several amusing experiences at the battery with Lieutenant Seddon, son of one of the Prime Ministers of New Zealand, who commanded it. The battery was on the reverse slope of the hill and our old friend Connie knew this very well. He used to come along the river-bed and pop up above the hill just high enough to make his observations, but too low to permit our guns to fire at him because of the rise of the hill between. We could see him from the farmhouse that served as AA mess and billet, but could not shoot at him, while all the time he registered the Austrian field guns on our position and they plastered us with shrapnel and howitzer high explosive. It must have been a most amusing game for Connie, but he played it once too often and was shot down by our Camels in the end.

These things happened in a war infinitely more happy than the Western Front in France where everything was much more adult and earnest. For instance, the British troops in the front-line trenches in Italy occasioned the promulgation of a divisional order which said that 'troops must not hang their washing out to dry upon the barbed wire entanglements'.

Again it was popularly rumoured (although I never personally confirmed it) that after the retreat from Caporetto to the Piave many Italians were left within the Austrian area of advance. Many of their houses carried telephones and the authorities refused to cut the lines when the trenches settled down upon opposite sides of the Piave River because subscribers on the enemy-held side had paid their subscriptions up to date and were entitled to their telephone service!

It was with regret that I said goodbye to 45 Squadron in the mess at Fossalunga on the evening of 28 January 1918 before setting out for Padua Station to entrain for Home Establishment.

I had said goodbye earlier to my flight sergeant and the men of my flight and thanked them for all they had done. My head was still partly bandaged, but was healing, the yellow stains of picric acid making it look worse than it really was.

To Frew and Firth, my fellow flight commanders and their flights, I bade farewell and, to my own flight, Lieutenants Moody, Brownell, Dawes, Hand, Howell, and Drummond, I bade good luck and until we meet again. Four of these have since gone upon the long, last flight; Howell drowned off Corfu in 1919 when pioneer flying to Australia; Drummond died in England after bravely enduring for many years the terrible handicap for a tall man of two feet severed at the ankles, the consequence of a crash in a Camel. I last saw him, cheerful as ever, at the International Light Aeroplane Meeting at Lympne in 1923; he was a Drummond of Drummond's Bank. Moody, killed in a 1930 air collision near Tangmere airfield in Sussex. Hand, who died in Toronto at a later date. In 1968 Brownell still lives near Perth, Australia, and Dawes in Montreal, Canada.

To Vaucour I bade farewell in private, for he occupied a special ante-
room of his own in the mess. I recognised in him a man of brave spirit, of
keenness and ambition, and in many ways of kindness and consideration,
and when I said farewell to him I little thought that he would meet in a
few short months one of the most tragic deaths that a warrior of the skies
could meet.

To the recording officer, Higgins, I wished good luck and then I was in
the tender and away, glad to be gone since it had to be, for I never could
abide farewells.

During my stint with 45 Squadron I had flown 163 sorties: 87 on
1½-Strutters and two-seater Nieuports and 76 on Camels.

I travelled home in company with another officer I had never met
before. The provost marshal at Milan allowed us a 24-hour stop-over
there and we enjoyed a theatre with a dual presentation of *Columbine* and
Cavalleria rusticana; ever since, the intermezzo of Mascagni's two-act opera
has carried me back to Milan whenever I have heard its plaintive cadences.
Next morning we spent some time admiring the cathedral. At the provost
marshal's office in Paris, Major the Hon. Maurice Brett considerately gave
us a pass for a couple of days there, and we had different theatrical fare at
the Folies-Bergère and the Bal Tabarin, the droll vulgarities of which on
the many times I have seen them, both then and since, have always made
me laugh. We scouted Paris, visiting Notre Dame, the Bois de Boulogne,
Montmartre and Montparnasse, strolled some of the boulevards, and from
our newly acquired city map went to see the Bastille (clearly marked on it)
only to find it was nothing but a station on the Metro. Paris seemed rather
a joke then, but afterward, when I knew it better, I grew to love the city.

Part Four

INSTRUCTOR

Chapter XV

AMBAGES

I reported in London and was granted one month's leave. The time passed all too quickly and on 8 March 1918 I left Scotland to report to No. 13 Group, Midland Area, RFC, Birmingham. There I was posted to No. 67 Training Squadron, commanded by Major Tedder at Shawbury airfield, near Shrewsbury. I flew a Camel there and while aerobating over the airfield saw Tedder standing by himself, watching, pipe in mouth, a non-committal expression on his poker face. The number of flight commanders already at 67 Squadron left no vacancies, however, and two days later I reported to No. 34 Training Squadron commanded by Major Mansell at Tern Hill airfield, near Market Drayton, which occupied the airfield in company with No. 43 TS. Later, Mansell was succeeded by Summers.

During the next few days I put in some practice flying on Camels. Then Captain Tweedie and later Captain Bottomley, the wing examining officers, gave me some instruction in Mono Avros in the art of teaching others to fly. Four days after I arrived at Tern Hill the two squadrons were ordered to move. The excellent airfield, with its splendid hangarage, was required to house Handley Page bombing squadrons, which were unable to adapt themselves to less favoured conditions. I was asked by the commanding officer to fly to our new airfield at Stockbridge in Hampshire to make advance preparations for the move.

On 15 March I flew south in a Camel via Birmingham and Oxford, landing at Port Meadow airfield, near the Oxford-Woodstock road, to refuel my Camel and myself; then on again after lunch via Newbury and Winchester. When I landed on the raw airfield of Chattis Hill, a mile west of Stockbridge village, I was thoroughly disgusted. I had left a beautiful, grassy airfield with splendid hangars and had landed on a stretch of muddy bog on the Hampshire Downs, with a row of canvas hangars to house machines. There three training squadrons, Nos. 91, 92, and 93, were under orders to leave for Tangmere airfield, near Chichester, where their Spad and Dolphin single-seaters could find better landing facilities.

Only one bright spot shone in the otherwise dull prospect and that I found in the extreme kindliness of Lieutenant-Colonel Cairnes, the wing commander, at whose invitation I stayed at Wing HQ. The squadrons' mess was in the Grosvenor Arms, the village hotel, and those officers who could not be accommodated in the hotel were billeted in the village.

Stockbridge owes its name to the far-off days when the valley of the River Test was a morass; a crossing at that point was known as the bridge of stocks. Two miles higher up river, near Longbridge, are the remains of an ancient Roman dock, in which the barges that came north from Southampton Water were moored. The neighbourhood is rich in lore of olden times and when the mess and quarters were later moved to canvas on the airfield, our tents were pitched upon the barrows of Ancient Britons. Danebury Hill, which, wood-clad, looked down upon the landing-ground, was a Neolithic camp, ringed about and fortified, with a dew-pond on the summit, and a burial mound of tribal chiefs nearby. On the farther side, where lay the gallops used by Mr Withington in training steeplechasers, was the site of the once celebrated Stockbridge Racecourse, to which the beauty and gallantry not only of the county but of even far-off London used to throng. This racecourse, set in beautiful surroundings, might have become famous in these days of easy travel had it not been killed by the whim of an old lady who sternly set her Victorian mind against the horrors of horse-racing and gambling, and refused to allow a much-needed extension of the course to infringe upon her land. And so the Stockbridge Racecourse faded away until it has left naught but a faint impression of its circular course upon the downs. Farther south, near the Stockbridge-Salisbury highway, stood the stables of Mr Atty Persse, famous for many winners.

Needless to say, the training of the horses, which continued during our stay at Chattis Hill, was not assisted by the droning of our planes overhead, nor by the regular taking-off and landing of our instructional Avros going up and down. We were not really popular at Chattis Hill, especially since our landing-ground had interfered with part of Mr Persse's exercising space. However, we managed to adjust our divergent points of view to the amelioration of any nuisance to the minimum.

I stayed at Stockbridge for a couple of days arranging billets for officers and men, then returned to Tern Hill by train and brought another Camel south to the new airfield. On this trip Birmingham was obscured by fog, which extended to and enveloped Coventry, and for a few minutes over the heart of Birmingham I had to circle round to determine accurately my course for Oxford, which, after a few miles, carried me out of the fog area.

For a few days I ran my new flight at Chattis Hill, while we settled in under the most depressing conditions. Instead of living in quarters on the airfield we had to get up and down (literally) to and from the village. The airfield was a slough of mud, which made it difficult to move machines out of and into hangars and made propeller swinging to start engines very dangerous; there was no alternative way of starting. In addition, Nos. 34 and 43 Squadrons had left a mess at Tern Hill well equipped with ample credit funds and were told they had to leave everything behind. The mess in the Grosvenor Arms at Stockbridge was ill-equipped and possessed a debit balance. There was, then, some justification for the feeling among the members of the squadrons who had helped to build up the former mess, that they had been arbitrarily robbed with no chance of redress.

I took up one or two pupils, but was told not to try to carry out serious instructing until I had been to the Gosport Special School of Flying for a course in methods of instruction. I led some of the most advanced pupils, however, on cross-country formation flights on Camels.

Captain H. D. Davis, who was the Wing examining officer, and who afterward ran the Brooklands School of Flying and was connected with the Chelsea School of Aeronautics, asked me to fly over to tea with some friends of his. I had just landed from a formation flight and had told some of our fledglings one or two details about their formation habits, and I jumped into the rear cockpit of Davis' Avro just as I was. I tried to fasten the belt about me but found it much too big, and so discarded it. Davis flew over to a house on the other side of the Test and pointed out a meadow where he proposed to land alongside the garden. I nodded back to him. Next minute he put the nose down and gathered speed, before hoicking her upward. I expected an ordinary loop and did not bother overmuch about not being belted in. But on the top of the loop Duncan shoved the stick forward so that we glided upside down. Just as I began to fall out I clutched the seat support-runners. As though on parallel bars my body left the seat and I hung, clinging desperately, upside down, with my head and shoulders inside the cockpit and the rest of my body out. The weight became unbearable until I knew I could not hold on another second and then the plane came round in a dive to right way up and spun me, like an acrobat, into my seat again with a sprained wrist to remind me of my inversion. We landed and our hostess, a dear old lady, came up. When Davis introduced me, the lady said: 'Really, I don't know how you manage to stay inside the machine when Captain Davis does all those wonderful things.'

Nursing my swollen hand I felt myself in entire agreement with our hostess, and I replied: 'As a matter of fact, I very nearly didn't.' And I rather think the old lady thought I was being mildly sarcastic.

Davis was a very fine Avro pilot and loved stunting. To distinguish his machine as Wing examiner's from the others he had 'H.D.D.' painted in large white letters on the brown top wing, and we always pulled his leg and said it was because everyone would know who it was every time he turned her upside down. But he was genuinely sorry that he had unwittingly given me such a bad time through not telling me that he intended to fly inverted. For my part it was the first and last tea-party I flew to. The daughter of the house was quite an attractive girl, except that she had a cast in one eye; and I always feel embarrassed by such a defect because I never know which eye to look at and I find I cannot look at both as I usually do.

Next day I flew to Gosport to the Special School of Flying, commanded, and originated, by Lieutenant-Colonel Smith-Barry. Using the Mono-Avro 504 trainers his RFC/RAF school was the first in the world to reduce flying instruction to an exact science, so different from the mediocre way I had been 'taught' at CFS. Now the instructor occupied the front cockpit; his pupil sat in the rear one, in which he would later fly solo. Every movement of each control was analysed in flight individually and then in co-ordination and the correct and incorrect ways to execute all manoeuvres were dissected to the minutest variation in the functions of each control, with engine both on and off. Not only that, but a complete grammar book of flying instruction was drawn up and printed so that all pilots passed out by the Gosport School taught every pupil by the same method. It was the first flying school to teach instructors. Before its inception every flying school, and almost every flying instructor, had devised a different way of teaching pupils how to fly. Some sympathetic individuals were good, many were indifferent, while some were frankly bad; and none had an analytical method. The Gosport School standardised the instructional method throughout the RFC and RAF (and after the war, the world); the unimaginative were given rules and precedents, while the inarticulate were given words. The result was wonderful. Pupils were trained with greater certainty by instructors who were educated to a real standard in their work.

The man who created this system was a genius. Smith-Barry believed in short hours and concentrated work. At his school instruction began at 10 a.m. and ceased at noon; recommenced at 2 p.m. and finished for the day at

4. Instructors were permitted, and encouraged, to fly for their own pleasure between 9 and 10 a.m. and between 4 and 5 p.m. Smith-Barry held the view that if instructors worked really hard for four hours a day it was as much as they could do efficiently. He believed that extending instructional flying beyond four hours divided into two sessions would result in lack of concentration, loss of enthusiasm, and a fall in proficiency. His personality was strong and heterodox and few senior officers cared to question either his methods or his ideas, the more so since he gained excellent results. His actions were always direct, unequivocal.

At that time the Air Ministry was hard pressed in its volume of work and not infrequently very junior officers and even NCOs were instructed by senior officers to convey by telephone orders of a definite nature to officers of field rank who commanded important posts in the country. It is told of Smith-Barry that he would brook no such interference in his conduct of the Gosport School. One day his telephone bell rang. He picked up the receiver.

'Hello! Yes, Smith-Barry speaking. . . . Who are you? . . . The Air Ministry. . . . What's that? . . . You want me to. . . ? . . . . Who did you say you were? . . . The Air Ministry? Yes, I know that, but what's your own name? . . . Ah! Brown. And what's your rank? . . . Corporal. Well, funny notion your mother had when she christened you "Air Ministry" Brown.'

Colonel Smith-Barry replaced the telephone receiver and carried on with his work, unperturbed by the interruption.

On one occasion Captain 'Billy' Williams, one of the greatest exponents of Avro flying that Gosport ever possessed, took up an Avro to practise completely stalled landings. At 500 feet he stalled until the engine and propeller ceased revolving, then glided slowly down at a steep angle, rather like the descent of an autogiro, holding his machine in balance by sheer skill in piloting. In attempting to land from the stalled glide he misjudged the final movement of the elevator and fell heavily the last few feet, crashing the undercarriage. Smith-Barry stood on the tarmac and, without a word, watched Williams jump out of the wrecked Avro and order out another. The second Avro, too, stalled heavily near the ground, and crashed. Still the colonel watched, unspeaking. Williams, determined to succeed, went up on a third machine, and this time achieved his purpose, making an almost stationary landing right in front of his own hangar with his engine stopped. The colonel stepped forward.

'Good show, Williams,' he said, 'but it's a good thing for you that you didn't stop trying at number two.'

And this illustrates the character of the Gosport CO. He did not count the cost of successful achievement, for he believed that the result fully justified the cost. But failure he would not brook at any price, and so long as Williams continued his effort until it was crowned with success the colonel would not interfere. But woe betide anyone who gave in and knuckled under to his failures.

Another Smith-Barry story relates to the time when well-earned promotion took him from his beloved Gosport School to command a Group in the north. There he laid down the same principles of working hours and exhorted all in his command to concentrate thoroughly during flying hours. The area commander objected to this method. He wanted flying to continue from dawn till dusk; he wanted flying hours to grow to paper snowballs of enormous hours spent in the air so that his area would outrival all other areas in the returns of flying done.

Brigadier-General Smith-Barry refused to alter his ideas, and, since reconciliation appeared impossible, he ordered out a Sopwith 1½-Strutter, put some kit in the back cockpit, and flew off south to Gosport, where he arrived to find his successor seated in his office.

'Who are you?' he questioned.

'I'm the new CO of Gosport School, sir,' came the proud answer.

'Well, I'm Smith-Barry, and I've returned. You can go.'

This, then, was the man who built the system of flying training which spread throughout the world to become the universal method of instructional flying. Some modifications have crept in to meet the needs of later days and later machines, but the method is still basically that of the Gosport Special School of Flying. Perhaps it was his personal heterodoxy that prevented him from receiving adequate military honours and reward for his achievement. If so, in this respect, he is not alone.

Under its efficient and popular CO a band of extremely fine pilots taught the budding instructors of the RFC and RAF to teach others to fly efficiently. Of these none were better than Captain Williams and Lieutenant Deighton, under whose tuition I took the Gosport course in six days. This was much less than the normal time, but my course was interrupted by the outbreak of the German attack under Ludendorff which caused the British retreat towards Amiens. For three days I flew with Deighton and learned the principles underlying an art which I had acquired entirely without theory. I memorised the 'patter' (the wording of the instructor's directions) and the rotation in which the lessons were given; the analysis of straight flying, of gentle turns with engine and without, of steep turns with engine on, of steep turns with engine off, of landing in small fields easily by the use of sideslips. It was fascinating, so simple and direct, so easy that one wondered why the method had not been evolved even before the war.

Then came the news of the great German attack. Machines had to be rushed to France. Telephones buzzed. I was detailed to start off for Hounslow at dawn flying a Le Rhône-engined Camel which had been used as an instructor's hack. It was put into the aeroplane repair shops and given a quick check up. It had no guns. These were to be mounted at Hounslow. In company with two other pilots I had an early breakfast in the dark mess of Fort Grange and took the air just after dawn, landing at the London airfield, where Major Bishop's new squadron was readying to go overseas, within an hour. Our Camels were taken over by the armament section and quickly fitted with machine-guns. Gun synchronising gears were not available, however, and we were held up for two days awaiting them. Finally only one part was missing, the auxiliary oil reservoir on the instrument board; it was unobtainable and one was improvised by the Hounslow armament section out of a round size-fifty Gold Flake cigarette tin.

We tested our guns at the gun butts, ran up the engines, and cleared the machines to be ready to leave on the following morning. I was detailed to lead two less-experienced pilots, Colquhoun and Stoddart, who were also flying Camels to France.

At 9 a.m. on 1 April 1918, the day the RAF came into being, we left Hounslow in a rainstorm and flew to Lympne airfield, then the final dispatch station for aircraft proceeding to France by air. There were papers to be filled in and signed at Lympne, equipment to be checked, and it was late afternoon when we left, with instructions to proceed to No. 1 Aircraft Depot, St Omer. The wildest rumours were flying round at Lympne. It was said that the Germans had completely broken through; Bailleul and Hazebrouck had both fallen; St Omer and Amiens were both threatened. We were warned to be careful when landing at St Omer because bomb-holes might have torn up the airfield. It was rumoured that No. 1 Aircraft Depot was already on the move from St Omer and was to recross the Channel to Lympne, which was now scheduled as the new No. 1 Aircraft Depot should the Huns' advance continue. The air was electrical. No one knew the real truth. One fact alone emerged: That we were hard-pressed in France. Captain Carleton, who had been one of the early 1½-Strutter pilots I had known in 45 Squadron, and was now officer in charge of dispatch at Lympne, made things as easy for us as possible and expedited our departure. We lunched in the old mess in Lympne Castle and took off towards the Channel at 3.45 p.m.

The Camel I flew was not the one I had brought from Gosport, but a later one, also with Le Rhône engine, which ran sweetly. This was my first aerial crossing of the English Channel and I was thrilled at the thought of it and of the reason why I was making it. I had seen enough of war to know the call of urgency behind this hurried rush of converted instructional planes from England to France. For we had not been alone at Lympne. All types of aircraft were there, old, new, and second-hand. There was need of numbers to stem the tide of Hun attack, and so long as a plane could drop a bomb or fire a gun it was wanted over there. Reinforcements in men and material were essential. And, since the way of the air was the swiftest way of all, the guns and bombs of the aeroplanes could be thrown into the breach while yet the supporting infantry were marching eastward towards the battle-line, or entraining for Folkestone and Southampton to reach the boats.

I climbed to 7,000 feet and we crossed the Channel swiftly, the panorama of the coastlines shining in the April sunlight. Away to the left lay Nieuport and Ostend: Hunland, over which I had flown so often in the planes of 45 Squadron; it looked so peaceful that it was hard to imagine the crash of eight-inch Archie shells bursting round one's cockpit. In that wonderful passage through the clean air, I foretasted in imagination the flight of post-war transport planes that would follow in the train of the fighters then mounting upward to the skies. To the left not a ship moved. There the face of the waters was still. But to the right, where the Channel widened beyond Dungeness, the convoys moved about their guarded business.

We crossed the French coastline between Boulogne and Calais and passed above the wide, open fields of France, until I saw before us the little town of St Omer, with the airfield on its outskirts. We circled down, landed and taxied in, after a 45-minute flight. The depot, in a state of great excitement, was in readiness for immediate evacuation. Where they were to go they did not know, but they were to be prepared to move at less than 24 hours' notice. No one knew what we were to do, or what was to be done with our Camels. While inquiries were being made we had a rough and ready cup of tea. Then instructions came through that we were to proceed to No. 2 Aircraft Depot, which had moved back to Hesdin. We located it on our maps and pushed off at about 6 p.m., flying south.

The number of planes tied down in the open made Hesdin airfield prominent from above. Not only the landing-field, but the adjacent meadow and plough land were dotted with planes of all descriptions arranged in what appeared to be the utmost disorder. There was no grouping of types, and there were wide irregular spaces between the planes. We glided down to land 30 minutes after leaving St Omer and saw the reason for the disarray of parked planes, for the landing-field was pitted with bomb-holes, and we had to S-turn in and out among them to find an alighting spot on which we could land safely. We taxied in and handed over our Camels. The officer in command had no instructions regarding us and rang up RAF HQ to find out what we were to do. He was requested to say where we had come from and the duty on which we had been employed in England. My two companions, newly out to France, were told to report to Camel squadrons there, I was hoping to be posted to a scout squadron also, but wondering what I should do about my kit left at Gosport, when HQ rang through to ask how long I had been back in England, how long I had served with 45 Squadron, and what unit I had flown out from. When told I had been back two months after serving 10 in 45 Squadron and that I was undergoing a course at Gosport, the reply was final: 'Captain Macmillan is to return to England tonight.'

A tender took me to Boulogne. The town was a seething mass of officers reporting back from recalled leave or drafted out to units. I had never seen it so full; every hotel was packed. There was no boat going out that night. After hunting around I found a corner in which to sleep in Mrs D'Arcy Hilliard's Home for Soldiers. A double row of stretchers had been placed upon the attic floor, with an Army blanket to each one. I was very fortunate to secure one of the last vacant stretchers. On my right was a colonel and on my left a brigadier-general. During the night Hun planes came over and dropped bombs. Machine-guns opened fire. Ground guns went off. Pieces of shrapnel and bullets rained down on the thick red pantiles that with their rafters were only a few feet above our heads. Through a thick glass skylight we saw the beams of a searchlight playing about the sky. The din woke us, but no one troubled to rise. There was nothing we could do, and we were all hardened to the racket. A few muttered imprecations against the disturbers of the peace, and here and there a quiet conversation, were all the attention the temporary inhabitants of the attic gave the raiders.

Next day I boarded the first boat, which was returning to Folkestone almost empty, and entrained there for London, where I reported before going on to Gosport, to find that Wright, of 45 Squadron, had come there to take the Gosport Course. On the following day he and I flew in an Avro to Upavon to visit some other 45 Squadron pilots. On our return I went up with Billy Williams for a test of my knowledge of the interrupted course. Next day I flew to Chattis Hill and on my return made forced-landing tests with Williams. He put the Avro into many different attitudes, then suddenly switched off the engine without warning; from each and every attitude I had to forced land anywhere without power, in a field or on the airfield, which ever I could reach; it seldom was the airfield. This practice was to stand me in good stead when, during the succeeding years, I flew far and wide with the unreliable engines of the time. On the morning of 5 April I ran through the whole course with Williams in 20 minutes and was passed out as a qualified instructor.

I shall always remember one stunt as peculiar to Williams, that past-master in the art of Avro flying. He first climbed to some 800 feet and shut off his engine, stalled until the propeller ceased revolving, then glided slowly with the propeller stationary. I always think there is something very fascinating about such an unmotored glide, but with Williams that was just a prelude. With a graceful, gull-like sweep he passed east behind the sheds, circled and came down, still turning, in the space between his own and the next hangar, completed the circle on the glide and finished, pointing directly towards his own hangar doorway with one wheel in gentle contact with the ground. He made the final levelling from the turn with that one wheel already on the ground, a levelling which took him straight towards the shed. As his decelerating run carried him up the sloping tarmac, if any of his mechanics ran to touch his wing-tips to assist him, he shouted and waved them back, so that the finish of his engineless descent and landing trundled the Avro gently inside the hangar, to come to a standstill somewhere near the oil-drip tray marking its usual place. I do not think I have ever met anyone who was quite the equal of Captain Billy Williams in flying judgment of this nature.

Chapter XVI

CHATTIS HILL

I began the preliminary training of raw pupils in my flight at Chattis Hill on 12 April 1918, with Lieutenant W. Jones as assistant instructor. At first the work was interesting, and a study of the pupils who came under my observation was remunerative in giving me an ever-expanding knowledge of human nature. Some took to the air like ducks to water, naturally, as if it were the normal thing to do; others were nervously self-conscious, with doubts about their ability to fly, with fears of insensitive hands and feet, or with knowledge of slow mental processes; some were overconfident; some hopelessly unsuited physically to control an aeroplane's flight; a few were afraid, some frankly so (which could be tactfully overcome by an instructor), while others tried to gloss over their funk (which made things worse). They came from all quarters of the globe; Canadians, Americans (some with central or eastern European names), Cockneys, Australians, Scots, South Africans. It could not be said that the product of one country was outstandingly better than that of another, but the Canadians as a whole were of a very high standard, with fine physique, and most of them had received preliminary flight training in Canada, which helped them tremendously.

For days I flew nothing but Avros, until I was heartily tired of going up and down, up and down with pupils, making certain of the sound ones and working up the duds to better their conception of flight control.

One of my elementary pupils was rather a nervous type. He never could judge his height from the ground when landing, despite a lengthened time of coaching, that eventually ran to about 20 hours of dual instruction. Time and again I had to correct to prevent a crash when he tried to land 20 feet above or 20 feet below the airfield's surface. We had no medical officer resident at Chattis Hill then (Doc Loveless, whose parents lived in Stockbridge, came later) and I was unable to have his eyesight or binocular vision checked. I was loth to scrub him because of the time and money already spent on his training; but, finally, I decided it was either that or risk sending him up solo to find out for himself just what a mutt he was. I chose the second course, although I felt sure he would bend the Avro, perhaps break it badly, perhaps even injure himself, although I hoped to be spared the last possibility.

I told him it was his last chance to make good as a pilot; if he failed to pull off his landings, he must be turned down. When he pulled his ill-fitting issue flying helmet over his head, nothing more than a leathern bag with an oblong opening in front (the eyes were protected by goggles), I thought how much like a rabbit he looked. His bunny-shaped nose and lips seemed to twitch before he took off for his first solo. His take-off wasn't too bad, just a little uncertain with the elevator and rudder. He flew around in the Avro 504, then came down to make his first solo landing. I watched, with my heart beating slightly faster than usual. I did not want him to hurt himself because I was not with him. I was supremely conscious that I was responsible for sending him up alone. A report from me to the station CO would have ended his flying and ensured his survival.

Good! He's not going to land at hangar top height. At least he won't stall. Oh God! He's coming too low. Flare out, Rabbit, flatten out before you hit the ground. Don't dive into your hole. Damn! He's done it again. Hit nose in, without any attempt to level out. Undercarriage and propeller broken, cowling and upper wings dented, engine perhaps damaged. The thoughts raced through my brain. He hadn't been worth sending up alone. I ought to have turned him down.

The Avro's tail was high in the air. Rabbit climbed down from his cockpit, unhurt, and almost ran to me.

'I've got it, sir. I've got it. I know where I went wrong. Let me have another try, sir. I can do it now.'

I thought of the wasted time and money, the cost of the broken Avro. Mentally I balanced the relative values of wiping him off or risking his smashing another machine.

'All right, then, one more; but only one. Show me you know how.'

He took off, better this time, flew around for about five minutes, then came down and landed reasonably well, went up again and made another landing, then taxied in. He had had to crash to learn how not to do so, and having learned he recovered his confidence. He also apologised for breaking the first Avro. He duly received his wings, but I cannot believe that he ever became more than a very ordinary pilot. He was the nearest pupil I ever had to be classed as a failure; with his scraping through I could say that I never had to turn down a single pupil; all who came to me passed out as pilots. But some of them tried one's patience.

During this period I put all I knew into the work, concentrating on the individuality of the pupils who, I soon found, placed their confidence unreservedly in my hands. But it was tiring work. There was no joy in the actual flying. My Avro had become an aerial schoolroom with a class of one, and for the life of me I cannot see why the work of the air instructor cannot be made lighter by teaching in triple or even quadruple control aeroplanes, reserving the two-seater dual machine only for the final advanced work prior to the pupil's going solo. All the elementary principles of the control of an aeroplane could be explained quite as well to three pupils in the air as to just one, with a great saving in time and cost; ability to cut the pupils' controls adrift from his own would place the instructor in the position of becoming absolute master of his aircraft in the event of any pupil endangering the machine or its occupants.

Occasional amusing interludes occurred in the otherwise persistent monotony of our work. An American construction unit was attached to Chattis Hill to build permanent hangars. The boys were very keen on flying, so much so that their repeated requests for joyrides became a nuisance to our regular work. So, when one more came over and said: 'Say, Cap'n, can I have a ride in your gasoline kite?' I determined to end the procession of begging joyriders if I could. We went up to 1,000 feet and I did everything I could with the Avro; steep turns with sudden sideslips, loops with sideslips out on top from upside down, spins and dives and zooms, and finally a yawing, rolling, pitching flight that more than equalled the roughest Channel crossing. The effect more than exceeded expectations. My joyrider was very sick. But he was very game, for when we landed he said: 'Say, Cap'n, I sure felt sick an' I guess I'll never go up in another darned airplane, but golly! I'm darned glad I've done everything jest this once!' I had no further requests for joyrides. Early in May I flew to Farnborough to collect a new Camel for our station. A second Avro flew alongside with a spare pilot to bring my Avro back. Equally engined and loaded we flew along comfortably together. When some few miles from Farnborough airfield at 1,500 feet I put my nose down and throttled slightly so that I should reach the airfield and land first. Suddenly I felt the Avro rattle and dither and noticed that my revs had unaccountably increased. My nose was pointing downward in a glide, but the finger of the altimeter on my instrument board moved rapidly over the calibrations, indicating increasing height. I felt the Avro rising under me with the motion of a slowly ascending elevator. I looked round for the other Avro and for a moment could not see him. Then I saw him away below and well behind me. It seemed incredible that I could have outpaced him by so much and yet risen high above him.

And then my Avro flew out of the disturbed air and returned to her usual horizontal flight. The engine revolutions became normal. The dithering ceased. The altimeter needle stayed motionless 800 feet above my original cruising level. The other Avro behind me was 800 feet lower, having missed the aerial escalator on which I had ascended. It was my first encounter with a big thermal air current and I was vastly tickled by the perplexity of the pilot of the second Avro who, when he landed, said he thought I was a modern necromancer.

There were occasional trips on calm evenings which brought relief from the drudgery of the daily instructional flying. Flights to Southampton Water, where we enjoyed the open view of the Solent and the Isle of Wight; where the frightened gulls rose screaming from the mud-flats when the tide was out. Once, innocently, we were the perpetrators of a practical joke. A man, sailing a tiny boat, stood up to wave to us, with one foot on the gunwale and one hand holding the mast. In return for his salutation I wheeled and dived past him, then turned upward in a zoom. Unintentionally, the blast of air from our propeller caught his sail and almost blew him over. As we climbed we saw him clinging to the mast with both arms and legs, while his little craft rocked in the tornado of our slipstream. Even though my passenger and I felt sorry for him we could not forbear laughter.

Above the valley of the famous trout-river Test we flew back to Chattis Hill, over Romsey Abbey Church, squat when viewed from the ground, but magnificent from the air. It was the changed aspect of this Norman Abbey which first made me realise that most buildings are designed with a view to beauty of façade. Many of our churches and cathedrals, however, are infinitely more beautiful when viewed from above; whereas many of our beautiful country houses frequently present an untidy array of ill-matching roofs, both in line and colour. The advent of aircraft will in time change the outlook and architects will then be required to consider beauty of plan equally as important as that of elevation. The country squire of the future (if there are any) arriving home by air from his more frequent visits to London and the Continent, will not be content with unkempt gutters and tiles making an un-resolvable collection of triangles.

About mid-May the Sopwith Pup became finally obsolete as a Service type and senior instructors were allowed to have those which were available in the Group, and were granted permission to use them to fly on leave in lieu of travelling by train. The one allotted to me was a perfect little beauty. There never was, and never can be, a nicer aeroplane to fly than

the Sopwith Pup. Stable, sweet on controls, light in weight, and with an
engine (the 80 horsepower Le Rhône nine-cylinder rotary) which ran like
a sewing machine, she was the realisation of my mental picture of what
flying ought to be, for she positively glided through the air. I have heard
it said that the late Mr H. G. Hawker, one evening, in the factory of the
Sopwith Aviation Company, in a mood of inspiration, drew the original
lines of the Pup on the floor with a piece of chalk.

On a gentle evening in mid-May I cruised above the sweet countryside
of Hampshire. It was hard to realise that over there, away beyond the
stretching coast of England, the guns flashed and the dancing aeroplanes
tumbled as they fought their duels in the sky. Here, the faint perfume
of early summer scented the air and mingled with the tang of castor oil.
Occasionally a plover flapped aside in sudden fright at my approach.

The Isle of Wight lay green across the waters of the Solent. Her white
cliffs, sparkling in the westering sunshine, stood like upended snow-flakes
in diminuendo towards the Needles. The flat mainland by the Beaulieu   ·
River rose into the cliffs of Christchurch. I flew above the water towards
Bournemouth at about half the height of the cliffs. The setting was glorious,
the sense of flight superb. The only signs of war obtruding on the scene
were the couples on the cliffs, for all the men were clad in khaki. The spot
was a lovers' paradise, secure from prying eyes anywhere on land, but from
the cockpit of the Pup I saw that the cliff-face was very well inhabited.
Wheeling round high above the pier I climbed up over the cliff and with
the sun behind me chased the long shadows down the woody dells or the
New Forest on the homeward run. Ah! Those trips were as a breath of fresh
air to one imprisoned on an irksome task. But my sense of duty to the
youngsters who were training for the job in France made me work day in
and out at Chattis Hill on my uninspiring routine. Happily sometimes, for
diversion, we took our planes out at night, and climbing upward from the
darkened airfield, we looped and rolled. It is a priceless sensation to loop
the loop by moonlight. One feels for the very first time since one has grown
up that there is much truth in the nursery rhymes after all and that one's
childish joy in them was not ill-founded. When one sees the crescent moon
disappear beneath an aeroplane's nose, then re-appear above the top wing
and slide down the starry sky, one feels inclined to shout aloud:

High-diddle-diddle
The Cat and the Fiddle

The Pup jumped over the Moon...

Our tents, erected on the grassy slope to the west of the landing area, rose snowy white above the barrows of the early Britons. And if their ancient bones lay uneasy in their last resting-places, surely it was because such things happened over and above them as they never would have dreamed of in their wildest nightmares. Every day the buzzing Mono-Avros rose up overhead and anon the snowy canvases were mottled with the falling spots of oil. So the work proceeded; new men being tested; taught how to fly straight and level; how to execute gentle turns, steep turns, how to glide and how to land, how to stunt and fly blindfold in clouds, how to fly by compass, and the way of fighting in the air, how to fly to pinpoints on the ground and record them by photography. On the ground there were lectures on machine-guns, aeroplanes, engines, wireless and other subjects. There were the anxious moments when one's pupils made their first solo on the Avro and, later on, the still more anxious ones when they went up alone for the very first time on a Camel. We always chose a still evening for that somewhat perilous ascent and watched the tiro's effort with a catch in our breath, lest the boy should make a slip; for the Camel was unkind to those who made mistakes. We were not much older than our pupils, but we thought of them as boys, for our experience of warfare at the front had bred in us a seniority far beyond our difference in years.

Occasionally there were dances in the neighbourhood. Hospitality was extended to us and, in return, our station sometimes organised a dance. These functions were usually held in the village; but there were others in Andover, or Winchester, rather grander affairs. One almost had a fatal ending. The party, returning from a fancy-dress dance one glorious, summer morning at about 5 a.m., decided to wade in the River Test. This process over, they reached the airfield, and one hothead, still insufficiently cooled, decided to fly. He ordered out his little single-seater, a Bristol Scout. The flight-sergeant, realising the situation to a nicety, deftly disconnected the high tension lead as they wheeled the plane out of the hangar. The pilot climbed into the cockpit, clad in the silken costume of a Chinese, complete with a long pigtail. After several futile efforts to start the engine, the pilot exclaimed: 'I know what you've done. You don't want me to fly. Well, I'm jolly well going to fly. You've taken the ignition lead off.'

He climbed out, pushed the plug into position, and scrambled back into his cockpit.

'Now start up!' he commanded.

The engine buzzed into life. For a minute he ran her up, then waved away the chocks. Off, down the shadowed lane between the canvas hangars he careered, then rose upward into the sunlight, pigtail streaming in the air behind him. A crowd of the returned dancers watched him. The station CO, who had also been to the dance, had retired to his tent and was fast asleep. The flyer conceived the idea that it would be fun to dive at Major Nethersole's tent. He was very fond of the CO, and, in his way, this was just an expression of his affection. Down he swooped, just missing the isolated tent which was the sleeping quarters of the station commander. The Bristol rose upward and came down a second time. It roared a few feet above the tent and came perilously near the ground beyond. A third time he dived, still more steeply. His wheels all but grazed the apex of the tent and, a second later, his plane struck the grass 20 feet beyond. Crash! It crumpled into fragments and rolled into a ball of metal, wood and fabric intertwined with wire. It seemed impossible that anything could be alive within the tangle.

Solemnly, in the morning sunlight, the group of watching dancers joined hands in a circle round the wreckage, while the flight-sergeant and mechanics rushed over from the flight hangar. Dressed in all manner of garments – cowboys, Red Indians, sailors, Persians – they danced around with glee, singing to the tune of Ring-a-Rosie:

Poor old Gilroy's dead,
Poor old Gilroy's dead,
He's killed himself,
His bloody self,
Poor old Gilroy's dead.

Then, out from the wreck of the little scout rose the wreck of a silk-clad Chinese with un-Chinese-like features, pigtail torn from his wig scalp, garments ripped.

'You're all damn well wrong,' he said. 'I'm not dead!'

He ought to have been. Evidently Chinese levitation had saved him. Stunned by the crash, he had lain for a few minutes before he came to. When he arose he was completely sober. Realisation came to him and he was devoutly thankful that he had missed the CO's tent. He knew that he might have written that off also. He turned in. The colonel held an inquiry into the affair and dealt leniently with the culprit by banning him from flying any single-seater for a period of one month. But it was a true punishment, for the erring one told me he would have suffered anything rather than lose the joy of flying his single-seater for a whole month. He was a true sportsman, however, and took his wigging and his suspension from single-seaters in the correct manner, knowing he was very lucky. As for the CO, when he was told of it, he just laughed and pulled his cap a bit more over one eye. He had slept right through the whole affair and if it hadn't been for the inquiry into the crashed aircraft and the finding of the cause, I think nothing more would have been heard of the matter.

Nethersole was a wonderful character. When war broke out he dropped his career at Oxford and went out to France in the first month as a dispatch rider. After a few months he asked to be transferred to the RFC to learn to fly. His application was turned down without even being forwarded. When he realised that he could not achieve his wish to fly in that way he applied for leave to proceed to England for 'urgent business reasons'. This was granted. As soon as he set foot in England he went to a civilian flying school and took his ticket within a week. Armed with it he went to the HQ of the RFC in London and applied for a commission as pilot. He filled in the necessary papers and returned to France on the expiration of his eight days' leave. Not long after rejoining his unit his papers came through and he bade farewell to the officer who had refused his application for transfer with a twinkle in his eyes.

Later he commanded a squadron in France. He was a great believer in encouraging the offensive spirit among his pilots, and he adopted two methods in the overseas squadron. Not far from the airfield was a steep hill. Near the bottom of the hill he had a trench dug. On the higher side of the trench he had a sloping ramp constructed. His idea was to dash down the hill on a pedal cycle, rise up the ramp and take off, clear the trench like a ski-jumper, and land on the other side. The trench was filled with water to make a fall soft. At the third attempt he succeeded in landing on the farther side. No one was allowed to try until he, personally, tested the runway and had it modified until the trench could be cleared and the landing made. But thereafter he expected all his pilots to make the run. He considered it a splendid test of the nerve and 'guts' of new arrivals to his squadron and I believe it was not until a broken leg resulted from one run that the cycle-jumping test of the offensive spirit ended.

At other times he lined up his pilots to face each other at about 40 yards range and armed them with tent mallets, which they had to hurl at each other as hard as they could.

At Chattis Hill his offensive spirit developed into a raid against the Wireless School which had arrived there during the early summer. Its BE2e two-seaters flew up and down in ones and threes, trailing long wire aerials, and taking up a lot of room in the sky, which hampered our work of flying instruction. Their school HQ erected an enormous notice board giving details of their programme of routine instruction, from which any pupil could find exactly what he had to do each day. The notice board was very like a hoarding in a meadow near a railway line and became known among our flying training squadrons as the 'Owbridge Lung Tonic Board'.

One night when the moon was full we raided the Wireless School. We uprooted the 'Lung Tonic Advertisement', carried it half a mile away, and flung it into a wood with a rending crash of timber. Then we raided their camp, which had been erected alongside our own, and slacked off their tent ropes. One after another their tents fell and, sometimes, to waken the more deeply slumbering ones, we splashed clean washing water from their buckets over the canvas. Not long after the raid began, the camp of the Wireless School was razed to the ground. Only one of their number came out from the canvas which enveloped him and laughed, at which we promptly re-erected his tent.

The Wireless School adjutant heard someone moving outside his tent.

'Who's that?' he called out.

'The adjutant of 43 TDS,'[3] was the answer.

'What are you doing?'

'Letting down your tent, sir.'

'Well, don't!'

'I'm sorry, sir, it's too late,' replied our adjutant, and with a gentle push the tent collapsed.

Many of the members of the Wireless School crawled out from their fallen tents and went up to the marquee which served them as mess. We surrounded them and let that fall also. Not once were there any reprisals or any show of resistance. They were taken completely by surprise.

In the morning their camp looked a sorry sight. We offered to give them breakfast in our own mess marquee, still proudly standing, but they refused, and we saw them sit at tables in the open, eating heartily.

---

[3] Training Depot Squadron.

Their CO, Major Peck, lived out and when he came up to the airfield in the morning he, not surprisingly, could see no joke in what we had done. He held an immediate inquiry into the whole affair as reported by his own school's officers and passed the matter on immediately to the Group HQ, who in turn reported to Area HQ, and the rag became a grave disciplinary matter.

Brass Hats came down to Chattis Hill and inspected the camp and heard the tale from the Wireless School. They viewed the re-erected and somewhat damaged instructions board. They sent for Nethersole and asked for an explanation of the disgraceful conduct of his unit.

'I do not consider the conduct disgraceful, sir,' he replied. 'In fact, I have never at any time seen such complete success attend a raid of this nature. I command a fighting instructional unit, and it is part of my principle to foster the offensive spirit in my instructors so that they will pass it on to their pupils.

'I have asked to see a copy of the report sent in by the Wireless School so that I can prepare my reply, but my request has not been granted. I have heard that it is alleged, however, that the contents of lavatory buckets were thrown over their tents. That is absolutely untrue. Nothing but clean and fresh water was used and that only in small quantities.'

The Brass Hats listened gravely and the CO continued: 'There is no one to blame but me. I am responsible. I organised the raid, and led it, and I am proud to say it was the finest show of its kind I have ever known.'

Nethersole's point of view was novel. It struck the Brass Hats dumb. They decided that the matter would be considered further at HQ.

Our CO did not know whether he would be court-martialled and reduced in rank, or what fate would befall, but finally he was told that he must see that such affairs did not occur in future and it was left at that.

Not long afterward he was posted overseas to command a bombing squadron in France and on one occasion, to make certain of his target when leading a raid, he dropped his bombs from so low an altitude that he nearly blew his own machine to pieces. And the offensive spirit which aroused trouble in England brought him a DSO in France. I was told that after the war he sat for the first Indian Civil Service examination, came out top of the list, and became a judge in India.

Just about this time the development of the RAF produced changes in our organisation. We had already become a Training Depot Station. The Wing was abolished and we came directly under No. 8 Group with HQ in Southampton. Brigadier-General J. M. Steel assumed command of the Group. He was formerly a naval officer and had commanded a ship at the Battle of Jutland and he introduced some forms of naval procedure into our RAF methods. An officer of the watch was appointed at the airfield armed with telescope and notebook. An airfield bell rang out the watches. Organisation was the group commander's watchword. He determined to fly himself and got his Group SO2 to teach him. First on an Avro, then on a DH9, he flew and in the latter he piloted himself around the airfields in his command. Sometimes we saw his DH9 come up from the south toward Chattis Hill, and as it glided down to land on our airfield we could hear the voice of Major Grenfell shouting out instructions to the group commander. We admired them both, the group commander for his pluck in learning to fly, and the SO2 for his pluck in teaching him and then flying with him in the rear seat of the DH9 without dual control.

In this new organisation I was selected to become the commander of the new Fighting Flight Group at Chattis Hill, charged with the duty of passing all instructors' pupils through my flight group for a final course of advanced flying and fighting in the air.

Chapter XVII

THE ENDING OF THE WAR

In June 1918 I was sent to No. 1 School of Fighting at Turnberry in Ayrshire, primarily to note the lines on which the school was run before I started the Fighting Flight Group at 43 TDS. For a week we received lectures on machine-guns, with practical lessons and tests on the range. Then the flying side of the course began. While this part of the course was very useful to a young pilot who had never been overseas, there was not much to learn for one who had spent some months leading a flight in a fighting squadron in France. We flew in formations, practised fighting in Camels against Camels, DH9s and Bristol Fighters, and fired at ground targets from the air. There I first met James McCudden and Jack Woodhouse, who were two of the instructors, the former famous as a fighter pilot, the latter more known as a pre-war racing motor-cyclist and for the landing of spies behind the enemy lines in France.

But I think my most interesting experience there was my first flight in a monoplane, the Le Rhône-engined Bristol M1c. This was a very nice little aeroplane, even though its elevator and aileron controls were rather heavy. Its wings projected from the top rails of the fuselage; the pilot sat with his head above and just about the centre of the wings. It was a beautiful sensation to fly along on wings which appeared to grow right out of one's shoulders, with only the clear blue sky above. This monoplane was used in small numbers in the Middle East and in Mesopotamia, but never on the Western Front or in Italy. It was said to have been reported on adversely as difficult to land by Dunn, under whom I had been a pupil at Upavon, and therefore unsuitable for the small airfields in Europe. But Dunn was a very short man, so that his view from it would have been affected; I found no difficulty in landing it; although the wing partly obstructed view while bringing the tail down when landing, one could do this by feel of the aircraft.

It was with deep regret that I learned of the death of one of my former pupils while I was at Turnberry. Lieutenant Clarence Tanner was a blue-eyed Canadian from Regina, a fine, strong, clean fellow. He had done some time on Curtiss Jenny's at Camp Bordon in Canada before coming over and he was one of my most promising pupils at Chattis Hill. He was very good as a pilot and very keen and I recommended him to be an assistant flying instructor, which I thought would give him more flying time before being sent to fight overseas. Two days after I left for Turnberry he took off in the front seat of an Avro with a pupil behind, climbed to about 100 feet, then suddenly nose-dived into the ground. There was no explanation. The pupil in the back seat was stunned and could not tell us anything about it. Poor young Tanner was killed outright. We laid him to rest in the graveyard of the Parish Church at Andover, where so many flying men lie buried to remind the visitor of the war-training flying which took place on the plain beyond that little market town.

Some time afterward I had a letter from Tanner's father in Canada. The death of his son was a sad blow to him. In his letter he pathetically wrote that he felt, from all his son had written to him about me, that if I had only been at Chattis Hill on that date his son would not have been killed. Who knows? Lacking knowledge of the reason for the crash, I could formulate no opinion, but I have never believed that Tanner just stalled. Often the workings of the Power that appears to control the destiny of human lives are inscrutable to mortal man.

I was back at Chattis Hill by the end of June and took over the organisation of the new unit. I collected my first pupils and began to teach them fighting tactics in two-seater Avros. They were all pupils who had flown at least five hours' solo on Camels. Lieutenant A. C. McArthur, a soft-spoken New Zealander, with an expression that dissolved into a complete smile, was posted to assist me. Some people smile with their mouths, some with their eyes, but not both; but McArthur smiled with eyes, mouth, wrinkling nose, and creasing cheeks. He had that necessary attribute for the instructor, patience.

From that time on, until the morning of 11 November 1918, I worked from early morning until late at night teaching pupils all I knew. When they were first posted to me, I took them up in two-seaters to test their flying. Very occasionally I found it necessary to return one to his instructor for further elementary flying tuition, but mostly they were good enough, while some were very good. Thereafter followed two-seater lessons in how to fly an aeroplane for fighting purposes as against normal flight handling, with instruction on how to dive and flatten out when diving on ground targets, and how to allow for correct deflection when firing at another plane in the air. The use of a camera gun showed the pupil his errors and successes in the developed film and prints made from it. Then the pupil started on the Camels and first practised stunting until reasonably proficient, after which he was coached in fighting tactics and close-in fighting; formation flying, taking off and landing in formation, flying in high formations and low formations; flying in clouds and across country over clouds; and the art of contour chasing and diving to shoot up ground targets; these made up the programme, together with ground lectures which explained all manoeuvres and the reasons for them.

By means of models I demonstrated all the difficult and dangerous situations in which pupils might find themselves, and showed them how to recover from them without waste of time. I impressed upon them the need for quick thinking and rapid action. I gave them lectures on rigging and the duty that devolved upon every one of them to report all heavy landings even if by doing so the report exposed them to something which had not been seen by their instructors or the ground staff. I knew that heavy landings in a Camel strained the rigging of the central fuselage and the bracing of the centre section of the upper wing and that the control of the aircraft would be affected adversely until the rigging had been reset. I told them also to examine carefully the essential things in the aircraft which lie within the province of the pilot to take care of before every flight. There is no doubt that casualties both in men and machines were minimised during the weeks and months ahead. I had no human casualties at all in my instructional work and it was rare for a flying training station to say this when Camels were in use. It was arduous work, but I could not do otherwise than put my best into it, for I knew from my own bitter experience of inadequate tuition what a difference it would make to my pupils when they went overseas to fight.

Nearly 50 years afterwards, shortly before he died, I was talking with Sir Sydney Camm, the famous designer of Hawker fighters. He told me he believed that many Camel crashes were due to the struts between the fuselage and the upper centre section not having been pinned but merely fitted into sockets, which meant that they were held in position only by the bracing wires. If these wires were slack, he said, the centre section struts could move and end loads applied to the upper wing spars in flying manoeuvres could cause the spars to curve between the interplane struts and the centre section struts, perhaps even to a degree which might lift the upper socket off the centre section strut. This was enough to explain the then inexplicable fatal accidents not only to pupils but to the most skilful pilots. Immediately I thought of my rigid insistence at Chattis Hill that every heavy landing had to be reported and my instructions to my flight sergeant that between every flight the rigging had to be inspected at that part of the aircraft and also at the tailplane; and after a heavy-landing report, the inspection was to be rigorous. Looking back I do not doubt that this policy paid dividends in my never having had a pupil injured while in my charge at Chattis Hill, a record I take as much pride in as in any other in which I have played a part.

There were many difficulties, of machines, and engines, of mechanics, of other flights' and of senior officers' desires in matters of procedure. We were so busy working that we had little time for the additional paper work that coincided with the formation of the RAF. Doubtless there was more order about it and much method, but anything that involved the time of working instructors other than flying was, in those days, undesirable.

Sometimes the group commander flew up to Chattis Hill and inspected all the units from Headquarters to flights and aeroplane repair shops. The GOC was quick to drop on anyone who did not appear to be making the most of the material he possessed, and became somewhat unpopular with many amiable but easy-going individuals.

My unit was housed in two separate hangars well apart from the remainder of the station. We worked hard from dawn till dusk. Often the ack emmas worked half through the night to keep the aircraft in condition, for I would not have any plane used for pupils' flying that was not known to be absolutely perfect. I balanced up their hard work by getting a regular weekly leave-tender allotted to my unit and sent half of them into Winchester or Salisbury on Saturday and the other half on Sunday. I also got them freedom from parades and guard duties, on the very proper grounds that with any reduction in man-hours I could not turn out the number of pupils required, and since every pupil from all the other flights on the station had to pass though my fighting group flight these privileges were granted. These liberties were very popular in my flight, but were rather resented in the other flights and they caused some friction in the sergeants' mess.

Throughout this period I was helped by F. F. Bramwell and T. Leask in addition to McArthur who had helped me to build up the flight from the beginning and went overseas just before the Armistice. The other two were pupils who passed through my Fighting Group Flight and who were promoted to become instructors. Between the wars they were scattered across the world, to New Zealand, Kenya, and Assam.

Hughes was the best pupil I ever had. He was so good on Camels that once he was on the tail of another machine he could not be shaken off. He would stick there, just five yards behind, through loops, rolls, turns, or any other manoeuvre. I had great hopes that he would make yet another champion Canadian air fighter, and I recommended him strongly for immediate posting to a Camel squadron in France, where I was sure he would do splendidly. Instead, he was transferred to Dolphins, probably as a result of my report; because the Dolphin was gaining a bad reputation as a difficult machine to fly, Hughes may have been picked as a suitable pilot to fly them. And all his skill was thrown away, because he never reached the fighting front at all. He was still with a Dolphin squadron in England when the Armistice was signed, chafing his heart out at never getting a chance to fight, thanks to the bad offices of some paper merchant in the manning department who thought he knew better than the pupil's own instructor.

In 1918 we received Camels with wing spars made from kiln-dried spruce because the earlier fully seasoned timber had all been used and artificial seasoning had to be accepted to obtain the necessary supplies. This timber was short-grained and weaker, but the spars were still made to the same dimensions in order to preserve the designed wing section. Bill Jones, who had been my *ab initio* assistant instructor, was a lover of rough handling when flying and one day he yanked a Camel out of a dive and broke one lower wing front spar. It bowed upward, but the aileron control cable running through the former ribs in front of the spar took the load and Jones gingerly flew round and landed. When he found what had happened he took a delight in diving and pulling out roughly all subsequent Camels he flew and when he broke another lower front spar he landed and laughingly exclaimed: 'Red-hot !' Thereafter he was known as 'Red-hot Jones'. It was a silly, risky game, but he loved it and tried to break as many Camels as he could. After the war he continued in the RAF for several years and when attached to a Fleet Air Arm unit he flew a Parnall Plover ship-fighter at Leuchars and broke its upper centre section by rough handling. He laughed with glee and said he was the 'man who put the "P" in Plover', an aircraft which received no more than the original order for a dozen production aircraft. He finished his flying career as flying instructor to the Karachi Flying Club. He certainly proved the inherent weakness in Camel spars when made of kiln-dried timber.

There were incidents and accidents, forced landings and crashes, the last, fortunately, few at Chattis Hill. Two stand out. One was a boy, little more, an assistant instructor in one of the flights, who thought it was fun to spin down towards the deep gulley on the east side of the airfield and disappear from view behind the hangars, still spinning. He did this to enjoy the joke of making the waiting ambulance start up and rush across the airfield to the expected crash. In the meantime the pilot recovered, flattened out, and flew along the valley out of sight. Then he rose upward and coming over the airfield dived towards the ambulance. Although it was fooled several times the ambulance never failed to go out. We told the boy of his folly, but the thing became a mania with him, and one day the ambulance was not fooled. Some trick of the Camel that fooled so many expert pilots, some variation in her recovery or the pilot's manipulation of the controls, caused a slight retarding of the Camel in the spin, so that she crashed, and he was killed outright. It could have been slack centre section bracing allowing movement of the top wing on its centre section struts, for in a spin the span loading is not constant and the wing angles to the air flow vary throughout the span and this combination of irregularities might have warped the wings.

The other was a tragic accident. Some of the flight hangars formed, with the engine and aeroplane repair shops, tall borders forming an artificial gulley down which some of the planes took off. One of our pupils, an extremely nice fellow and a poet of no mean order, walked across the mouth of the gulley and was not seen by the pilot of a plane taking off. The poor fellow was hit on the back of the head by the axle tube of the undercarriage and the top of his skull was knocked off his head. He was killed instantly. The pilot felt his plane strike something, flew round and landed with a strained undercarriage. From outside my fighting group flight office I saw the accident about to happen and shouted to him, but it was too late, even if he heard me above the noise of the engine. I saw him crumple up like a falling sack of potatoes and I turned away from the sight, for I knew he must be dead. Bramwell ran across to him, but of course he was dead, his quite thick skull ripped off at the top, leaving his brain exposed.

During this time my brother Sandy was killed in France with the Seaforth Highlanders. I dreamt I saw how he died, as if I were watching from a few feet above the ground; and when he was dead we rose together to a height of about 200 feet and the ground became blurred as if seen through rain, instead of clear as it had been before he died. It seemed as if we were together for about half an hour, during which I saw the stretcher-bearers carry his body back; then the dream ended. I told McArthur in the morning that I had dreamt my brother was killed. He said there was nothing in dreams and that people often dreamt things that were contrary to fact; probably he said this out of kindness. But confirmation of my brother's death came only too soon and later his company commander told my mother how his platoon commander had died, and his words corroborated my dream.

It happened in the last final effort of the German Army and he with his platoon were on the extreme right of the British Army and alongside the French. The attack was beaten back, but after the bloody fighting was over a single bullet from a sniper hit him and he died almost at once. I badly wanted to go overseas after that, for I wanted to avenge him. I applied again and again for permission, but always I was refused. All I could do was to put into the hands and feet and brains of those boys who came to me for final training all that I knew to help them to go out to France to shoot and not be shot.

One detail which has always stuck in my memory of those days concerned a court martial assembled to mete out the justice of the Army court upon some youngster who had kicked over the traces. I have forgotten the name of the accused, that of the President of the Court, and all the others, save one. This one was that of the officer who prosecuted. Doubtless it was his duty (he was in the Judge Advocate General's department) to press his case with icy coldness in his voice, with judicial indifference to the human side of the little drama. He was too great a man, his mind too detached to perceive the tragedy of the boy caught in the machine of war and treated as a man. I could not stifle my feeling of pity as the prosecutor presented his all too logical case with words which seemed to fit the physical expression in his long, thin fingers. The personal side of the matter did not appear to affect him or enter into his thoughts and I do not suppose that any point of view other than his functional one obtruded on the remoteness of his intellectual mind. I wondered idly what other jobs he did in war besides the prosecution of erring war-babes.

Another court martial had a lighter note. I was the prisoner's friend. It was a case of absence without leave, a serious offence. On the day the body assembled, the case against the accused was in no doubt, neither did he attempt to deny it. Before passing sentence, the President asked if the prisoner's friend had anything to say. I rose and said that the accused had already been punished and that in English law a person could not be punished twice for the same offence. I was asked to give details. I told the court that when the delinquent had returned voluntarily, the station adjutant had confined him to his tent and placed an officer on guard over him and therefore he had already been punished by the station adjutant. The case was dismissed. I can understand the subtle enjoyment of a barrister who by some quirk of the law obtains the acquittal of an accused person even when he knows him to have been guilty of the crime alleged against him.

When Nethersole departed, his place was taken by a delightful Irish officer, Major Mulcahy-Morgan, who had flown to France with the original Expeditionary Force in August 1914, but had the misfortune to come down on the other side of the lines and be taken prisoner. He had escaped and returned to England, but the interlude had affected his promotion and had also left its mark in a nasty visible scar across his chin, which must have been badly gashed. He owned a sporting Daimler racing car, had an equable Irish humour, and knew how to wear a velvet glove while maintaining impeccable discipline. I never served under a nicer or more efficient commanding officer.

There, too, came Major H. J. 'Daddy' Payn, a smiling, brown-eyed pilot who was married and lived out in Stockbridge village. He had flown DH2s in France and was an excellent pilot and in off-time an enthusiastic amateur violinist who performed quite well on that instrument. After continuing in the RAF for a number of years of peace, he joined the staff of Vickers Aviation. He was a very pleasant assistant to Mulcahy-Morgan, always helpful, never irritable, the very antithesis to Nethersole, who was ebullient, a D'Artignan type who sallied forth in search of what he called a 'bivalve parlour', in other words an oyster bar, to eat a delicacy of which he was very fond.

An American doctor, Major Gallacher, came to Chattis Hill. The RAF Medical Branch was then experimenting with the assessment of flying aptitude by clinical methods. Colonel Flack, the President of the RAF Central Medical Board, was, I believe, the originator of the idea. I was invited to collaborate with Gallacher and we evolved a mutually acceptable method of working. I would assess the aptitudes of different pupils by flight tests and make out my report in writing. Gallacher, in his Station Medical Hut, would examine the pupils and write his report on their assumed flying aptitudes from a medical assessment. The two quite independent reports were then compared. It was remarkable how closely all our separately made reports agreed, one made purely from the MO's non-flying physio-psychological tests and mine made during actual instructional flight tests. These were part of the foundations of aviation medicine and the genesis of the subsequent aptitude tests and medical assessments applied to candidates at the RAF Aircrew Selection Centre.

We flew right up until the morning of the Armistice and then everything just stopped. A grizzling rain began soon after the news came through, making it impossible to fly up to London through the November fog that blanketed the ground between. We drove into Southampton in a tender. We were asked to leave the local music-hall because we wanted to hold a rival show at the back of the circle. Refused the joy of this self-expression, we formed a glee party round a lamp standard between the tramlines not far from the Bar or Gateway of the old city wall. Our amusement was harmless and brought some mirth to others in addition to ourselves. After dining in an hotel we heated some pennies on a shovel held over the lounge fire and threw them out of the window. Boys ran and picked them up, only to drop them quickly like 'hot pennies'.

Those days at Chattis Hill are pleasant to recall. We had some tough types there. One who made money at the mess bar betting that he would bite a piece of glass from out a heavy tumbler, and he did it despite the cuts from glass that caused his lips and gums to bleed.

On one occasion someone was posted overseas. A farewell luncheon was being celebrated in the officers' mess, after having started in the bar. The meal was over and speeches were being made, when our padre came in. Before the war he was a country village parson and he had never been overseas. His character and outlook were at variance with most of the men among whom he messed. When he had first arrived he had called for a station church parade. It had been held in the open air on the airfield, for we had no church. When it was first included in station orders I protested to the adjutant that it was an Anglican service and that non-conformists could not be compelled to attend. But on the first day no arrangements were made for them to fall out. I therefore took the question up again and on the next Sunday I was in command of all non-conformists (the Roman Catholics had been exempted because they went earlier to the nearest church of their denomination). After the parade ceremony was over I requested permission to fall out and march off the non-conformists and a very large number left the scene. The padre had been delighted with his first parade, but now he faced a much depleted audience. I should not have objected if the thing had been done properly, but the idea of compulsory attendance at a service not of one's choice naturally aroused the rebel that lies dormant in all human beings.

Now, in the mess, this parson in khaki urgently called the waiter.

'Quick, waiter, some soup, please.'

He turned to me just as someone jumped upon the table to say something about our departing member of the mess. The speaker emphasised his remarks by picking up a plate and letting it crash down upon the table; sometimes to call attention to some very special point he broke a plate upon the crown of the nearest person's head, amid lots of laughter. It was all innocent, although a bit rough-house, but the padre could not see that.

'This is terrible, terrible! And they call themselves officers and gentlemen!'

A piece of flying china dropped into his almost finished soup. He beckoned the waiter.

'Some meat, quick, and then a sweet, please.'

The meat before him, he proceeded to it with avidity. He looked at me with eyes which were full of an emotion I did not recognise. The din rose higher as the speaker was applauded by the clatter of knives and forks and the rattling of plates.

'This is Babel,' the parson exclaimed. 'Why cannot these men be Christians and enjoy themselves in a befitting manner?'

A man from the opposite side of the table leant forward and spoke in reply.

'It is no use, padre! You need not try to convert me, for, thank God, I am an atheist!'

The padre pushed his half-finished plate of food from before him and fled to the shelter of his tent.

We had others, who were interesting, among the non-flying personnel. The catering officer was Captain Roger Pocock, who then held the record for the world's longest cross-country ride on horseback, from Fort MacKenzie to Mexico City, during which he had lost a part of one foot. He was the founder of the Legion of Frontiersmen, an author, and a man of wide culture, yet who had formerly served in the Canadian Mounties. He was a brother of the Shakespearian actress Lena Ashwell, who in that war worked to entertain the troops in France; she married Dr (later Sir) Henry Simson, gynaecologist to Her Majesty Queen Elizabeth the Queen Mother and ushered Queen Elizabeth II and Princess Margaret into this world. I recall that their home in Brook Street, Mayfair, was the only place where I ever found rose petals floating in the toilet bowl, an action that somehow seemed to fit the gracious nature of Miss Lena Ashwell, Lady Simson.

Looking after the workshops, transport and other groundwork were C. Dougan 'Nobby' Clarke, first husband of Storm Jameson, the novelist; later Nobby was a private secretary to 'Manny' Shinwell; he was a Litt.D. and a moving spirit in P. E. N. Smallbone did not appear to have such unusual associations, and Handcock was in private life a prosperous Kentish gentleman farmer; Soanes was always smiling; Willis grimly looked after our engine overhauls, and Dowty our stores.

Coram, a pupil at Chattis Hill, was the son of the celebrated ventriloquist who gave performances with his doll under the title of 'Coram and Jerry'. The son was a nice fellow, but not a very promising pilot. He was among those who adopted the optional-in-wartime very light blue uniform, the second RAF pattern uniform which rumourists said was designed jointly by Admiral Mark Kerr of the Air Council and Miss Lily Elsie, the popular and beautiful actress. This light blue uniform followed the first drab khaki outfit that much resembled the field service dress worn by the officers of the RNAS fighter squadrons in France. Rank badges on the light blue cloth were denoted by gold lace. It proved a most impracticable dress for flyers, particularly for those who flew the oil-slinging rotary engines; their sky-blue dress soon became spotted with oil stains that could not be removed, but only made worse by attempts to do so, after which the super-smart outfit looked a pathetic parody of its former glory.

After the war, a musical in London had a male chorus supposed to belong to the army of a Ruritanian power. Its members were kitted out in that RAF sky-blue uniform (then superseded by the grey-blue pattern) with other buttons and much more gold lace; it looked excellent on the stage. Coram was a member of that chorus and when I met him by chance in London one day he asked me to come and see the show. I enjoyed it, but I have forgotten the names of both the musical and the theatre, yet recall my amusement at the appropriateness of the colour of the uniforms worn by the gentlemen of the chorus, many of whom had been in the RAF (and may have been wearing their own original uniform modified for the part). Coram took me round the wings behind the stage after the show ended to meet some of the former RAF boys and introduced me to Miss Joyce Barbour, who played lead, a charming and attractive blonde of whom Coram could not speak too highly as a lady. Never having been closely associated with the theatre I found this experience illuminating in presenting the difference between the two sides of the footlights, the plushy glitter and the dusty drabness.

All in all they were a wonderful lot to have lived with.

After the Armistice instructional flying ceased. No one knew what would happen. Volunteers were asked for the Russian Expeditionary Force and I applied, but to my disappointment was not selected.

We moved into our permanent mess which was ready for occupation. We had moved from tents to huts in October. The permanent hangars were almost complete, but were never occupied. The American construction unit, which had built the sheds and mess and WRAF's quarters, entrained for Liverpool within a week of the signing of the Armistice and thereafter no further work was done on anything.

Owing to the fragmentary method of demobilisation, which eliminated too many of our transport drivers while their services were still needed, volunteer drivers were called for. I volunteered and had much driving both in Crossley tenders and Leyland lorries, with trailers on the latter when required. One of our officers asked me to teach him how to drive so that he, too, could volunteer. Tuition was made more difficult because the gearbox had spur gear wheels (syncromesh then lay far in the future) which the driver had to make run at equal speed in order to engage the different gears. Changing down involved double de-clutching and to change up demanded an appropriate pause in neutral. Gear-changing then was an art. The shift lever was on the right-hand side of the driver, with the hand-brake lever outside that again, so it was difficult for an instructor sitting on the pupil driver's left to have any control over gear-changing or braking. I quickly discovered that my pupil had no knowledge of how the gears worked and that he could not effect changes without distressing noises from the much abused gearbox. He also had the novice's bad habit of wanting to look down at the quadrant gate when trying to change. To help him I stood on the running board (which motor vehicles then had) outside his seat and with my hand over his guided it to feel the gears into mesh, at the same time telling him what to do with clutch and accelerator. During one such run along a narrow road he muffed his gears, looked down at the gate, pulled the steering wheel unconsciously, went too far to the offside of the road and I found the seat of my whipcord breeches being rubbed by the thorns of the hedge. I quickly seized the wheel and steered my breeches off the thorns. But by this means I taught him to drive and he soon became quite expert after he had mastered the gate change and double de-clutching.

Seccombe, who came from Birmingham, also wanted to learn to drive, but as a pupil and not on the staff he was not eligible. However, he discovered a car for sale; a 6 hp two-seater, two-cylinder De Dion-Bouton of about 1906 vintage. It had a coiled external radiator wound about a bonnet shaped rather like an antique coal-scuttle inverted. One sat very upright in the seats and the small diameter steering wheel was almost horizontal on a nearly vertical column. Final drive to the rear axle was by chain. The gear shift lever was a long, massive piece of metal with a hand grip near the top end that raised an auxiliary rod the lower end of which, when the grip was released, entered notches cut in a straight through quadrant. To change gear one had to press the grip to release the lever, move the lever and let the spring-loaded auxiliary rod slip its end into the correct notch. There was a big difference in travel between the top of the lever and its movement over the quadrant and this demanded a delicacy of handling that a novice found far from simple to acquire. Outside the shift lever another massive lever operated the hand brake; this also had a hand grip to effect engagement with or release from the saw-tooth quadrant that held the brake on and which was mounted a little way above the lever's fulcrum.

Seccombe and I bought the little vehicle in partnership for £40, each with a half share. I began teaching him to drive it. At first all went well because he drove slowly and carefully and we jogged about the byways near the airfield. Then one day, growing bolder, he let her out to about 30 miles an hour down a gradient. She began to take charge and swing from one side of the road to the other and repeat the performance. The oscillations were quite unstable and I thought she might run right off the road and perhaps turn over, with ourselves quite unprotected in our very open and high chariot imitation of a horse-drawn vehicle. Keeping his eyes on the road, Seccombe steered with his left hand and I aided him with my right as he reached out for the brake lever. His groping hand grasped the end of a lever with a grip and he pulled hard back believing he was putting on the brake. Unfortunately it was the gear lever and it moved from the forward top gear position right through second and first and neutral and finished up at the rear end of the quadrant in reverse. There were terrible noises from the gearbox and transmission, but the car stopped in a series of lurches. We saw that the steel top of the gearbox was cracked across but I managed to drive back to the airfield slowly in first gear. We took the lid off the box and found some of the teeth chipped, but none stripped. We had the cracked top welded and the teeth smoothed so that the old car ran almost as well as before. Then Seccombe sold her for £50, so that we each made a slight profit on the deal; he was an astute business man. This was my first and last joint ownership of a motor vehicle.

Before he left us the padre came to me and asked for a flight. He felt he could not leave the RAF without having ever flown. But he asked me (and said he came to me because he felt I would do as he asked) not to stunt him, but to fly gently. I promised and did so and he was pleased to say he had flown. But how much he missed in life; yet he could not help it; one is as one is and too often so remains.

Christmas leave almost precipitated a riot because an overworked adjutant allotted the leave in alphabetical order, the simplest way to do it quickly. Some men were down for leave including Christmas Day, some including New Year's Day, and some missing both, dependent entirely on the first letter of their father's surname. Boys with two months' service were getting Christmas Day leave while veterans of the whole war were not.

My old flight sergeant came running up to the flight office completely out of breath, to tell me what was happening.

'It will be mutiny, sir,' he said. 'We cannot hold them.'

I saw the unfairness of the situation, the first I knew of it.

'Run back, Rye, and tell the sergeant-major that all leave arrangements are cancelled and that there will be a special parade in the big hangar at two o'clock. I'll go and fix it with the CO.'

I walked down to the Station HQ and explained what I had done and Mulcahy-Morgan asked me to settle the matter in my own way.

'You are quite right, Mac,' he said. 'I leave it to you.' Meanwhile, the sergeant-major's announcement pacified the dissatisfaction.

I took the two o'clock parade and told them all to stand easy.

'The sergeant-major has announced that all leave arrangements are cancelled,' I said. 'This parade has been called to make other arrangements. It is only fair that those who have been away from home longest or those who have served overseas should be considered first. I want all those who enlisted in 1914 to come forward.'

A respectable number came to the front.

'All these will have their choice of either Christmas Day or New Year's Day leave,' I said.

The orderly sergeant took their names.

I applied the same ruling to 1915 and 1916. Then, after that, to those who enlisted after 1916 but had served overseas. Then from the remainder

I asked all who had any special reasons which they considered should entitle them to preferential treatment to come forward.

A new leave roster was made out and all signs of mutiny were at an end. Some other RAF stations were not so fortunate, and a few actually witnessed scenes of real mutiny, the culmination of unduly harsh military repression upon the civilian population during their service in what was virtually a citizen army.

After returning from leave I was asked to apply for a post-war commission in the RAF, but decided not to do so. Nevertheless, I was posted to the first post-war engineering course for officers at Halton Camp, a course which was, I believe, supposed to have been created purely for officers who were remaining permanently in the Service (as all the others who attended did). During this period Chattis Hill became a repository for all the unwanted aeroplanes in the neighbourhood.

BE2cs, RE8s, and Armstrong Whitworth FK8s were flown to us for storage and we gave them all an airing with what fuel was left in their tanks. Many of our own little planes were 'reduced to produce', the bureaucratic jargon for smashing them up, but keeping certain specified parts. The sudden ending of hostilities left the country with a tidal mark of useless aeroplanes that were more expensive to maintain than to destroy.

I took my pet Sopwith Pup to Halton airfield, but we were not encouraged to fly there by the station commander, and I was told to take it back.

The course finished at the beginning of April. Shortly after, in the final war awards, I was gazetted recipient of the Air Force Cross.

We flew as much as we could. Once I flew to Oxford, accompanied by Leask in another Pup. When taking off the air was misty. We rose to a reasonable height and looped in unison and I looped again. Somehow, on his second loop Leask stalled, and before he could recover had hit the ground hard, smashing the Pup and breaking an ankle. I landed alongside and helped him out and the ambulance took him to hospital; I flew to Oxford again to visit him. His accident was pure bad luck, due to the mist giving him no horizon.

Bramwell went back to the Kenya he had come from but I saw him some years afterward. He had married, but his marriage had ended with the early death of his wife and this hurt him terribly but for the joy of his two children. He died, still a comparatively young man.

I tried to buy my own pet Pup, but could not agree a price with the official Disposal Board. They had no second-hand terms. Every Pup was priced at £250. I pointed out that mine had flown a great many hours. It made no difference to the bureaucratic mind. The answer was that I could have a brand new one for the same price, but if I wanted one that had flown as much as mine, well, that was my own choice, not theirs. I refused to buy on such uncommercial terms. I flew her last on 14 June 1919 and later learned that she had 'been reduced to produce', or, in other words, broken up. I left Chattis Hill the same day and the war and its ways had ended for me. It was a good time and a bad time rolled into one, a picnic and a term of penal servitude combined, but it was a great and glorious adventure, too. Looking back I cannot say I have much admiration for the higher strategy of that war, nor of those who made it and did not count the cost in casualties. The men who flew evolved the field strategy and tactics in the air and laid the foundation for the future. They were the salt of the earth. I raise my glass to them all.

INDEX

NOTES

NOTES